Teenagers, HIV, and AIDS

TEENAGERS, HIV, AND AIDS

Insights from Youths Living with the Virus

Edited by Maureen E. Lyon, Ph.D.
and Lawrence J. D'Angelo, M.D.

Sex, Love, and Psychology
Judy Kuriansky, Series Editor

PRAEGER

Westport, Connecticut
London

Library of Congress Cataloging-in-Publication Data

Teenagers, HIV, and AIDS : insights from youths living with the virus / edited by
Maureen E. Lyon and Lawrence J. D'Angelo.
     p. cm.— (Sex, love, and psychology, ISSN 1554–222X)
    Includes bibliographical references and index.
    ISBN 0–275–98892–9 (alk. paper)
    1. AIDS (Disease) in adolescence—Anecdotes. 2. HIV infections—Anecdotes.
3. Teenagers—Diseases—Anecdotes. I. Lyon, Maureen E. II. D'Angelo,
Lawrence J. III. Series.
  RJ387.A25T442 2006
  618.92'9792—dc22   2006021971

British Library Cataloguing in Publication Data is available.

Library of Congress Catalog Card Number: 2006021971
ISBN: 0–275–98892–9
ISSN: 1554–222X

First published in 2006

Praeger Publishers, 88 Post Road West, Westport, CT 06881
An imprint of Greenwood Publishing Group, Inc.
www.praeger.com

Printed in the United States of America

The paper used in this book complies with the
Permanent Paper Standard issued by the National
Information Standards Organization (Z39.48–1984).

10 9 8 7 6 5 4 3 2 1

This book is dedicated to all the adolescent patients with HIV infection who have entrusted their care to us. They have served as teachers to us all, distributing lessons in compassion with each interaction. We attempt to honor them by including their poems as introductions to each chapter, but the true honor is ours.

We include their families and friends in this dedication as well, and thank them for administering doses of unconditional love, which is the most powerful of all therapies.

We give thanks to our colleagues at the Burgess Clinic, the medical and psychosocial care providers involved in helping each of our patients. Through the exchange of knowledge and the demonstration of their great respect and caring, we have collectively grown in wisdom and have been able to provide the best possible care for these young patients. This level of excellence could not be achieved without their commitment to working as a team.

CONTENTS

PART II   MATTERS OF MIND

PART III   PROVIDING SUPPORT

FOREWORD

Afraid, anxious, and alone—that's how Heather described her predicament living with the deadly AIDS virus. The teen's poem is one of many such touching accounts interspersed throughout chapters in this book, which are rich in the latest crucial information about one of the most important and pressing problems in sexual health today. With shocking numbers of youth infected or at risk—more than 1 in 10 of nearly 5 million new infections recently reported worldwide are youth under age 14, and teens the most sexually active age group—all health professionals, parents, and policymakers need to be aware of the problems and solutions for adolescents living with the virus. Editors Lyon and D'Angelo have put together a volume that is must-reading for every professional in the field, as it is the only volume of its kind and one that is essential in light of this contemporary "new face of AIDS." Exceptionally qualified to know this field, Lyon and D'Angelo have chosen a perfect combination of colleagues to address a comprehensive array of topics relative to helping young people with the infection, giving a holistic picture that includes biological, psychological, and social perspectives. The chapters are exceptionally well documented, as well as being readable and compelling, as voices of teens come alive with their needs, feelings, and experiences.

For years I have heard such voices from teens about HIV/AIDS on my call-in radio show, as young people wondered about whether they could catch the deadly disease from holding hands with an infected teen, or by kissing someone, and asked about what they can do to protect themselves. I'll never forget the teen who recited, "A ticket, a tasket, a condom or a casket." Condoms of course matter, but the question of HIV/AIDS is so much more vast, as Lyon and D'Angelo show.

In this book, myths are busted, stigmas confronted, guidelines for disclosure and healthy behavior are outlined, the impact on families is highlighted, and treatments are described. The health situation for infected youth is desperate, as shown in this volume, from the stories of once-bar-hopping Stuart to Keisha, who was raped at age 11. This volume expertly addresses the need for up-to-date knowledge to help such teens. The chapters include erudite medical approaches—from understanding about genomes, retroviruses, and co-infections—to programs helping teens living with AIDS, such as TLC, which stands for "Teens Linked to Care," but also is mindful of another meaning of TLC—the necessity of offering "tender loving care."

The chapters point out good news about advances in treatments for infected teens, but alert us that teens face different issues than other age groups; we are left with hope to save youth from facing a devastating future. As one of the teens calling my radio show said, AIDS among youth has become a matter of AfrAIDS—as fear surrounds the illness. But Lyon and D'Angelo's book of up-to-date knowledge gives us hope to calm those fears. Through the information here, the lament of Heather, in her poem about being afraid, anxious, and alone, is transformed into inspiration, kindness, and acceptance that she yearns for—and that thousands of more teens exposed and at risk need to live a healthy life.

Dr. Judy Kuriansky, Series Editor

INTRODUCTION

It has been 25 years since we saw and cared for our first adolescent patient with HIV infection. He was a 19-year-old man who shuttled up and down the East Coast corridor between New York and Washington, D.C. D.C. was his home, but New York was the heart of his social life, which included the sex industry in and around Times Square. We had no idea what his illness was until a medical student pointed out a bluish nodule along this young man's waistline that turned out to be Kaposi's sarcoma. Three months later he was dead of this strange illness, which we were still calling GRIDS, gay-related immune deficiency.

It was another three years before we recorded our second case of HIV infection in a teenager. This time it was discovered as we investigated a recurrent pneumonia in a young woman who had had open heart surgery two years earlier to correct a long-standing defect in one of the chambers separating the right and left sides of her heart, an atrial septal defect. Again, there was a long delay in making the diagnosis because no one thought that a blood transfusion could result in the transmission of this still mysterious and overwhelming disease.

Since these early days, more than 40,000 cases of AIDS in individuals between the ages of 13 and 25 have been reported to the Centers for Disease Control and Prevention (CDC). Although this figure is worrisome, it becomes more ominous when we consider that it takes at least 8 to 12 years for most patients to go from HIV infection to a point where they meet the case definition as a case of AIDS. This means that a majority of individuals diagnosed with AIDS in their thirties and into their forties may have acquired their HIV infection as teenagers and young adults. Indeed, the CDC still estimates that as many as 50% of new HIV infections in the United States occur in individuals under the age of 25. The other fact that makes HIV infection in adolescents so unique is that 50% of new HIV infections in this age group occur in women, particularly in African American and Latina young women. This is a pattern reminiscent of HIV infection in other parts of the world.

If we consider what this epidemic looks like for us in 2006, at the Burgess Clinic at Children's National Medical Center in Washington, D.C., we have now cared for more than 400 adolescents with HIV infection at all stages of illness. We have been involved in watching too many of them get sick and die, particularly early on in the epidemic when we had little if any way to stop the inexorable course of the illness. Despite all the advances that have been made in diagnosing and treating HIV infection, challenges still remain, even at the most basic level. Twice in the past year, for instance, we have seen patients whose diagnosis of HIV infection was missed during previous hospitalizations months to years earlier for acute illnesses that could have been recognized as related to HIV infection. Similarly, we still are challenged by our patients who are nearing the end of their lives. And for the many who are living on with their illness, we are still trying to help them struggle with the stigma and discrimination associated with this infection. Finally, we face the challenge of guiding our patients through the process of getting the help they need from family, friends, and health professionals.

We have tried to capture much of this experience in this book, but we know that it is not enough to give everyone all they need to know about adolescents and HIV infection. What we most fervently hope, however, is that this book gives the reader a sense of the complexity of our patients' struggles and the great respect we have for their individual and collective courage. This is a respect that is shared by all health professionals who have been involved in caring for these patients in the many centers around the country that specialize in treating HIV-infected teenagers.

We hope that the futures of all HIV-infected individuals will be improved by this publication through an appreciation of the complexities of this disease and the struggles associated with its treatment.

Finally, a sincere word of appreciation to our co-workers here at Children's. They have supported our efforts and the health and well-being of our patients. That same appreciation and love extends to our families. They have shared us with our patients and with our work, always understanding the importance of what we were trying to do.

Maureen E. Lyon, Ph.D., A.B.P.P.
Lawrence J. D'Angelo, M.D., M.P.H.

Part I

UNDERSTANDING MEDICAL AND TREATMENT ISSUES

Chapter 1

HIV IN YOUTH: HOW ARE THEY DIFFERENT?

Audrey Smith Rogers, Ph.D., M.P.H.

Undaunting Courage

By Michael and Shaina

What will they think, what will they say,
will they stand by our side or make us have a price to pay
AIDS is a word people dare not to speak
But reality to us causes the heart to continually weep
People don't understand the pain
which will cause our spirit to continually drain
There are ignorant people in the world
Some can and others can't be unfurled
We give them a choice
And if they accept, we rejoice
If they fear for their life or what others would say
Then losing me is a price they will have to pay
For life to them may mean money cars and gold
Life to us means treasures untold
So, I might again find myself standing alone,
But spiritually enriched we have grown
What will they think, what will they say,
It matters none to us because we thank god for each and every day

It is commonly accepted that somewhere deep in an African forest as many as 50 years ago, someone got infected with a virus that jumped species as viruses tend to do. Such events are not uncommon and have been occurring for millennia. People get inadvertently cut while butchering infected animals for food.[1] What made this jump unusual was not how particularly virulent the virus ended up being; it seems fairly certain that where people have lived at the edges of very fertile forests with abundant wildlife, rapidly fatal infections have historically flared and devastated whole villages without trace or notice. What made this species jump different was its timing. This infection was a slow killer. Many people had no idea they were infected, although some may have had a transient viral syndrome of muscle aches and fever that rapidly cleared, like any virus infection. People felt well and thought nothing of it. And it happened at a time of economic expansion, social upheaval, and enhanced transcontinental mobility in Africa. Further, economic deprivation drove many male heads of households to relocate for employment, bringing large numbers of men together far from their wives and children. The infection moved from the forests to the cities and from the cities of Africa to the cities of the world. Now in the next century, this infection caused by HIV is firmly established in populations around the world and has not spared the United States where it has ended up disproportionately affecting racial and ethnic minority communities, particularly their young people. It has been estimated that 11.8 million young people ages 15 to 24 are living with HIV/AIDS worldwide[2] and, more disturbing, each day another 6,000 young people are added to their ranks, translating to 250 new infections every hour.[3] American youth have not been spared. There are an estimated 40,000 new HIV infections every year,[4] with one-quarter of them occurring in youth under the age of 25.

The HIV epidemic in American youth is quite different from that in adult populations, and these differences are found primarily in three areas: *transmission group, clinical course,* and *service needs.* It is important to trace the history of the HIV subepidemics in American youth to be able to understand the important and distinctive manifestations of HIV infection in young people. There have been three predominant transmission waves: blood, perinatal, and sexual. Small numbers of teens have been infected through injection drug use, but this has never been a major route of infection in young people.

HIV TRANSMISSION: THROUGH THE RECEPTION OF BLOOD OR BLOOD PRODUCTS

Many children and young adults were infected through the reception of blood products to treat conditions such as hemophilia in which missing clotting factors have to be regularly replenished from donor supplies. When AIDS cases were first reported in the early 1980s, the cause of AIDS was unknown, and few appreciated that the nation's blood supply could be vulnerable. In the time it took from the earliest case reporting to the identification of the virus and the development of a screening test in 1984 to exclude infected blood from donation pools, thousands of children and young people with blood disorders were infected. Many of these youth had underlying chronic disability, received large amounts of virus, and became ill rapidly with HIV infection in a time when no treatments existed. It has been more than 20 years since the blood supply has been effectively screened and, although it may take years for someone with HIV infection to develop AIDS, the numbers of young people developing AIDS from this transmission route have dramatically declined.

HIV TRANSMISSION: MOTHER TO CHILD TRANSFER

The primary introduction and rapid spread of HIV infection in North American gay populations, in whom the first AIDS cases were reported, were documented nearly 30 years ago.[5] Almost immediately after these first cases were reported, eerily similar cases were being seen in newborn babies who were developing unusual infections, sickening quickly, and dying. Soon the overlapping injection drug use link was determined: sex partners moved the virus out to drug partners who moved the virus out to other sex or drug partners. Women who were in this mix were having babies, and one of every four of these babies became infected. HIV became established in every major American city. Tens of thousands of infected babies were born before a major study in 1994 was able to show that if the HIV-infected mother was treated with a single antiretroviral drug, the infection rate could be reduced from 25% to 8%.[6] This intervention was quickly made available with immediate and dramatic results. The transmission rate has been reduced even further since 1994, as combinations of antiretroviral drugs are used and the amount of HIV (viral load) in the mother's system, a major factor in infecting the baby, is kept low during pregnancy and childbirth. Effective treatments were also developed for the infected babies and many began to survive.

These babies predominantly infected in the 1980s and early 1990s are now, in this first decade of the new millennium, adolescents and young adults. Often, their survival has not been without a cost. Many have experienced delays in puberty with their physical, social, and sexual development being far behind their peers,[7,8] although some have not.[9,10] More have high levels of psychological distress,[11] including depression and anxiety, and have suffered multiple losses of family members.[12] Some may have specific cognitive deficits compared to their uninfected brothers and sisters.[13,14] These are adolescents who have been isolated from their peers, held to keeping family secrets, and have undergone repeated hospitalizations. Many have bounced around foster care systems without the sustained care of a loving family. This experience is unlike anything HIV-infected adults encounter.

At the same time, it is also not unusual for clinics to identify HIV-infected older children with no HIV risk of their own who have been presumably infected at birth and have done very well despite receiving no specialized care.

Some perinatally infected children never developed the signal diseases that caused physicians to test them for HIV infection. It is becoming increasingly clear that certain genetic endowments may be protective against HIV disease progression[15,16] although this has not been fully investigated for children infected from birth. In addition, the family histories for older HIV-infected children new to care and doing well are often difficult to sort out. A mother may have died from a drug overdose, accident, or homicide with her HIV status never known. There can be incest and sexual abuse; such deep family secrets may never be learned. The stories that are learned are painful to hear.

Nicole*

Nicole is never the first to speak and slow to smile but when she does smile, her face can light up the room. And when she speaks, too, her comments are insightful and intelligent. Nicole and her sister were born to a chronically depressed single mother who had a series of boyfriends. Nicole remembers always taking care of her mother and younger sister. She says that her childhood was spent living in an abandoned house where, for four years, she, her sister, and mother had no lights and no running water. She and her sister tried to think of it as camping and spent their time pretending they were a normal family. When she was seven years old, her mother's boyfriend started to molest both her and her sister. This continued until Nicole was 16 years old and became very ill with an abscess on her neck for which she was hospitalized twice. During her second time in the hospital, she was tested for HIV. When the doctor who told her stood at the foot of her bed and, in a matter-of-fact tone, said she was HIV-positive, Nicole said she just smiled because she knew that HIV infection meant no more molesting. She called it her "ticket to freedom."

HIV TRANSMISSION: SEXUAL TRANSFER BETWEEN PARTNERS

With HIV infection cases owing to blood and perinatal transmission diminishing in the United States, it is clear that the sexual transmission of HIV is fueling the caseload in teens and young adults; 79% of all HIV/AIDS cases diagnosed in 2003 were through sexual transmission.[17] The particular forces that have produced and sustained the HIV epidemic in racial and ethnic minority communities in the United States appear to be linked to the interplay of three forces: lack of socioeconomic development, institutional ineffectiveness, and little political will. These have combined to produce inadequate education and preventive programs, scarce health care services, culturally mediated gender- and age-based vulnerability to HIV infection, paralyzing stigma, and punishing blame. When society's institutions fail, youth are always

---

* The details of cases have been changed to protect the identity of individuals.

the most profoundly affected. It is society that supports the families who must prepare young people to be responsible, productive, and functional adults.[18, 19] Traditional foundations have been eroded over the last 40 years and no consensus community ethic has yet emerged.[20] Society has divided into bitter factions with a pronounced shortage of wisdom and common sense. Left on their own, youth have developed their own media-based, high-energy culture, appealing to their predilection to reject authority. This is another area where youth differ radically from adults. Young people are in the process of clarifying their values and establishing a moral code. These two critical developments cannot be accomplished in a vacuum; both depend on the involvement and care of elders.

SEXUAL TRANSMISSION IN YOUNG WOMEN

In the United States, HIV transmission in teenage girls is predominantly sexual. In 2001, one-third of reported AIDS cases and reported HIV infections in 13- to 19-year-old females were due to known sexual transmission. Another three-fifths were categorized as "no identified risk" (NIR). Cases are categorized as NIR when the young person is unsure how infection occurred but denies personal injecting drug use or blood reception.[21] Most of these NIR infections occur in young women who are unaware of any high-risk behaviors in their sexual partners. This pattern has held for the last decade. Further, the HIV epidemic in the United States is disproportionately borne by racial and ethnic minorities: two of every three AIDS cases in females ages 13 to 19 years were African American and almost one in every five were Latina in 2001.[22]

There are many reasons for the surge in HIV infections among young American women. Many young women start to have sex where they live, many in areas where HIV is firmly established.[23] Although they may know of people in the neighborhood who have died from AIDS, they do not necessarily perceive themselves to be at risk, and social institutions have not provided them with the knowledge and skills that might help them think otherwise. Furthermore, many of the decisions end up not being theirs at all. One study showed that 9% of first vaginal penetrative sex in young women was involuntary and approximately one-quarter of the sexual intercourse events, although voluntary, were unwanted.[24]

Keisha

Keisha was the third of the four children her parents had together. She recalls a childhood with her parents being high on drugs and otherwise absent, with her older sister high as well and tricking on the streets and her older brother dealing. She and a younger sister were often left on their own. When Keisha was 11 years old in 1990, she was returning home alone from a visit with her grandmother, when she was dragged in an alley, had a gun put to her head, and was raped by two young men. A little over a year later, an enlarged lymph node was noticed during a physical examination; she was tested and found to be HIV-positive. She had had no other sex but the rape.

Her parents continued to abuse drugs. Family members gave them money to help feed the family and pay the rent, but it went to drugs. When she was 13, Keisha came home from school to find her little sister alone and crying from hunger. In the house, there were only a single potato and a jar of mustard. She left the house, went to the drug-dealing corner, and sold herself to get money for food. For the next three years, her prostitution fed her sister and herself and went toward the rent. She dropped out of school. She cries at the memory of what she had to do for money.

In time, she found her way into the health care system. For months, she was seeing two psychiatrists a week. She dealt with the circumstances of her life by emotionally shutting down and disassociating from feelings other than anger. In time, she gained some insight. She started to take antiretroviral drugs. Social services found her a place of her own. She was 18 years old. She got her GED and a job. Her older sister, strung out and prostituting, had two children by then. She left the older one with Keisha and went to another state with her 10-month-old baby. Two weeks later, Keisha got a phone call from a stranger saying her sister had abandoned the baby and if Keisha did not come for the baby, he would be turned over to foster care. Keisha bought a bus ticket, went to the other state, and retrieved the baby. That was eight years ago. She continues to raise the boys, now 12 and 8, despite occasional bouts herself with major illnesses.

Many adolescent girls date older men. The girls get a sense of importance with such attention, particularly when their self-esteem may be low because of poor school performance or lack of family support. Older partners also provide monetary resources that same-age partners cannot match, a factor that may be of considerable importance to disadvantaged youth. Unfortunately, older partners can also introduce a power imbalance into the relationship that often introduces the young woman to older alcohol- and drug-using social networks, and expose her to unwanted pregnancy and sexually transmitted infections (STIs).[25] Age difference between adolescent girls and their older sexual partners has been significantly associated with unprotected sexual activity.[25–27] In one study, only half the young women reported using effective contraception consistently despite its availability[28]; consequently, pregnancy rates in the HIV-infected young women were documented to be twice the national rate.[29] Young women contract multiple recurrent STIs that markedly predispose them to HIV transmission if a partner happens to be HIV-infected. Compared to older adults, adolescents (age 10–19 years) and young adults (age 20–24 years) are at higher risk for acquiring STIs for a number of reasons: they may be more likely to have multiple (sequential or concurrent) sexual partners instead of a single long-term relationship and they may select partners at higher risk.[30] In one study, 43% of HIV-positive adolescents had had more than eight sexual partners before age 19 years.[31] Young women share issues of power imbalance from gender inequality with older women, but their situation is further complicated by their age difference, their lack of resources, their inexperience, and their often poorly developed judgment.

SEXUAL TRANSMISSION IN YOUNG MEN

Although the blood transmission cases dominated the AIDS case statistics for young men in the United States, sexual transmission AIDS cases in male youth ages 13 to 19 years outnumbered all other transmission routes as early as 1995.[32] In 2001, half the reported AIDS cases and reported HIV infections in young men were due to known sexual transmission.[22] For both, an additional 44% were categorized as NIR. Same-sex activity accounts for 91% of this sexual transmission category. AIDS in young men in the United States, like AIDS in young women, is disproportionately borne by racial and ethnic minorities: 40% of the AIDS cases in males ages 13 to 19 years old were African American and 22% were Latino in 2001.[22]

In the United States, AIDS cases in young men have always outnumbered those in young women. But HIV case data in the 13- to 19-year-old old age group seems to indicate a shift in numbers, with more cases being reported in females. Frontline workers do not believe this apparent shift, thinking the difference in numbers is due more to unequal diagnosis and reporting than to real differences in the dynamics of the epidemic. Young women who have become sexually active usually have more contact with the health care system, accessing obstetrical and contraceptive care, and thus may be more likely to be screened for HIV infection than sexually active young men. In fact, one study indicated that young women appear to access HIV-testing outside of health care more frequently than young men as well.[33] This view is supported by an HIV-seroprevalence study of 3,492 young men, ages 15 to 22 years, engaging in same-sex behavior at high-risk venues in seven American cities where HIV infection rates ranged between 2.2% and 12.1%; notably 82% were unaware of their infection status before testing.[34] Being unaware is a function of the individual's perception of risk. Not only do young men adhere to the general perception of youth that nothing will happen to them, they often adopt the current belief system of the gay culture in the West that HIV infection is now no more significant than another chronic disease for which treatment is available.

The particularly frustrating fact is that many of these young men do not want to be engaged in, or known to, any institutional system despite having special and compelling prevention needs. The antigay discrimination of society in general and the social stigma within their own ethnic culture in particular produce a disabling fear of disclosure.[35, 36] This can translate into anonymous social and sexual networking that intensifies the absence of personal responsibility. Older partners are not uncommon and, similar to the relationship dynamics in young women, they bring a sense of importance to young men whose self-esteem may be low and whose family support is lacking. There can be a power imbalance in the encounter or in the sexual relationship that prevents the youth from reducing personal risk.

Stuart

Stuart is a soft-spoken young African American man who carefully weighs his words when he speaks. He is now 25 years old and has known he is HIV-positive since 2000 when he was offered an HIV test while he was waiting for a friend to get treated for a sexually transmitted infection. He says he wasn't surprised by the positive result, but the news devastated him nonetheless. Stuart looks back on a good childhood, the only son of his parents who are still together. He realized his gay identity in high school and although he became sexually active, he did not have receptive anal intercourse until his senior year when he met his first partner in a bar. When he finished high school, he went on to college for a few semesters but dropped out and worked in restaurants. During this time, he had about 16 different partners and sometimes used protection and sometimes did not. Why sometimes and not others? "I was the one receiving and my partner was older and I let him take the lead. If he said we use condoms, we did; otherwise, we didn't." Stuart says he knew about protection, but it just did not seem to be important in the press of the moment. Still it was a nagging thought that he had been at risk, and that is why the positive test when he was 20 years old did not surprise him. Through all this, Stuart's family and friends have stood by him. He credits them with helping him cope. Helping him, too, is a strong faith based on an apparently deep spirituality. When he went to the clinic for HIV care, the staff asked him to join the Community Advisory Board, which he did. Reaching out to others has become a mission for him. Stuart thinks if he had been able to interact with someone like himself, a black, gay, HIV-positive young man, things could have been different for him.

The kind of counseling that Stuart believes could have saved him is in short supply. Many school bureaucracies and school boards that are responsible for prevention programs for youth in general believe firmly that providing comprehensive sexual health information actually promotes sexual behavior and erodes traditional values.[37] The prevention needs of gay youth are often ignored altogether. Adult gay organizations involved in prevention efforts and that may be best positioned to provide effective counsel and education are often reluctant to risk working with youth, leaving these youth unsupported by institutions and adults who understand their life issues. This is another area where youth differ fundamentally from adults: they do not control the distribution of resources to meet their needs.

African American adolescents are more likely to report more frequent sex, recent STIs, and drug use during sex if there has been a history of adjudication.[38] Young men may exhibit a full range of risk and deviance entering prison, but the process itself hardens them and introduces them to same-sex activity with weaker or manipulative partners. HIV prevalence rates are high in prison because of the overwhelming proportion of drug-using inmates, and thus prison itself has become the great engine fueling the HIV epidemic in urban minority communities as these young men are released and move into community sexual networks.[39-41]

THE CLINICAL COURSE OF HIV INFECTION IN YOUTH

How young people do with HIV infection depends on the mode of HIV transmission; their general health, nutrition, and socioeconomic conditions; and the other infectious diseases prevalent in their community, all within the context of the individual's genetic make-up. All these factors interact to determine if and when a young person gets engaged into health care and how able they are to benefit from it.

Even with adequate nutrition and engagement in health care, however, HIV infection may affect metabolic and endocrine function and alter hormonal systems involved in the control of growth and pubertal development. A growth lag appears early in babies[42, 43] and persists throughout later childhood, with HIV-positive boys and girls presenting shorter and weighing less than their uninfected peers. Antiretroviral treatment with protease inhibitors can give only modest improvement for these features.[7] A preliminary study in perinatally infected children[8] demonstrated delays in the age at which sexual maturation initiated compared to data on the general adolescent population. This was the same picture seen in HIV-infected boys with hemophilia.[44] There is considerable normal variation in sexual maturation patterns, however, so although the process may be delayed, it may not be considered abnormal in most cases, and there is no evidence to indicate that it fails to progress altogether. For example, there are reports of perinatally infected young women becoming pregnant and successfully carrying babies to term.[10]

Despite some perinatally infected youth doing exceptionally well, maintaining viral control with little or no therapy, the majority finds itself barely keeping pace with the development of newer treatments. Each time a new therapy is started, the viral pool mutates to escape the selective pressure imposed by it, and the remaining available therapeutic options become more limited. Some young people move from one debilitating illness to the next during this period, whereas others remain relatively illness-free, although both are losing ground and have few drugs that remain effective for them.

Sylvie

Sylvie was given up by her birth mother for adoption in 1984. Soon after, she developed a series of infections and strange symptoms from which she never quite fully recovered. She was tested for HIV infection when the screening test became available and she was found to be infected. Her adoptive mother saw to it that she received good care and had access to every antiretroviral drug as it became available. The mutual goal that they set in her childhood and worked toward was seeing Sylvie graduate from high school. She did achieve that goal two years ago, but in the process has developed resistance to every available antiretroviral drug. She currently is not taking any drugs against HIV; none are effective. Sylvie is back to taking an antibiotic to protect against some of the opportunistic infections that can occur when the immune system becomes exhausted.

The clinical course can be quite different for young people who become HIV-infected as teens. Information collected in large cohort studies of HIV-infected adult men shows that age at infection is an important predictor of the duration of the time to an AIDS diagnosis: the younger the age, the longer the period.[45–48] Less than one in five of HIV-infected adolescents in a major national study recruited through clinical sites developed AIDS over two to three years, and for 85% of those who did, their AIDS diagnoses were based on CD4$^+$ T-cell count criterion alone, not AIDS-defining comorbidities.[31] There seems to be evidence that HIV-infected youth have a greater immunologic reserve than adults based on studies of the number, proliferation rates, and markers for various immune cell subsets.[49,50] Even so, there is also a study that shows that HIV infection causes profound perturbations in the CD8+ T-cell compartment even though the youth were relatively early in the course of their HIV infection.[51] How this capacity to expand or regenerate immune cells relates to the functional capacity of the immune cells is not firmly established. This is an area of intense interest that may be unique to youth. If young people, newly infected with this reserve, can be treated with immune modulators that could recalibrate viral set-points or enhance immune control directly, then the potential to convert HIV disease into a subacute chronic infection may be achieved.

Young people infected as teens do become ill.

Keisha has developed end-stage renal disease that has placed her on hemodialysis three times per week. While she has periods in which the dialysis is effective, she has also suffered bouts when it has failed to prevent serious fluid build-up. She was hospitalized last year with pericarditis and experienced cardiopulmonary arrest with successful resuscitation. Recovery has been slow and hard, but she has made progress because of prescription drugs that have prevented a recurrence of the heart condition. But just last month, she was dropped from the Medicaid rolls and cannot afford the medicines without that coverage. She is borrowing money from relatives to purchase the pills and taking half the dose to stretch the medicine.

THE SPECTRUM OF REQUIRED SERVICES FOR AMERICAN YOUTH

It is clear from the social dynamics of the different transmission groups that no one set of services will be adequate to address the needs of HIV-infected youth in the United States.

Teens who are HIV-infected from birth and identified early because of their need for treatment will be familiar with the health care system and may exhibit the issues and dependencies of other children with chronic diseases. What they will not have in common, however, is a whole set of other issues: the death of parents, foster care system stress, and for the most part coming of age with the same neighborhood pressures that damaged their parents.

The young people, infected since infancy, will inevitably need to assume responsibility for their own health care, a task that can be complicated all too frequently by the failure of the family to disclose the true nature of their infection. Families have many reasons for keeping an HIV diagnosis secret. They may feel shame, be in denial, or need protection. Health care providers need to provide special support to families and guardians during the disclosure process, for without a careful and sensitive understanding of his infection and its implications, a teen will not be able to move forward to the intense anticipatory counseling he will need related to the initiation of sexual activity. Providing the full spectrum of adolescent health care needs is often best accomplished by helping the adolescent make the transition from the pediatric health care of her childhood to youth-friendly and focused health care services where these emerging needs can be better addressed. The shift from pediatric-based care will not only refocus the teen to learning adult skills but broaden the vision to set goals beyond those set in childhood.

Sylvie said she was lost after she graduated from high school. Her single focus and only goal had been that achievement; she had made no plans beyond that. She felt at loose ends, and with her medical prognosis worsening, became despondent. This, too, is another area in which youth differ dramatically from adults. Developmentally, youth who are Sylvie's age are making life decisions and career choices while adults are beyond these tasks. Within the constraints of her medical condition, Sylvie needs to explore her options and be empowered to make choices that can make her life meaningful.

Occasionally, an HIV infected preteen can move effortlessly into adolescent health care, but many more bring profound emotional problems with them.

When Nicole, who was infected through sexual abuse, was discharged from one hospital, it was to be readmitted to another for more treatment. She did not want to go, so her mother refused. This prompted an investigation by the County Social Services who assessed the home situation and her mother's status, and placed both Nicole and her sister in foster homes. They stayed there until Nicole was 19 and her sister was 18 years old. Today Nicole is 23 years old and has a job; she and her sister live together with her sister's little boy whom Nicole adores. She says as she looks back she realizes that she had shut down emotionally and never thought about her past molestation or her HIV status. She lived in the moment. But last year, she decided to tell her mother she had HIV, although she knew her mother already knew because relatives had told her. Nicole said she wanted her mother, who had so often failed her, to respond to her, as a mother should. It did not happen. Being rebuffed in this first small attempt to get a show of her mother's love threw Nicole into depression. She managed to find a group providing victim's services and has been attending sessions. Through the support of the program, Nicole was able to remember the abuse events and cried for the first time since she was a young child. She feels she is moving to an emotionally healthier place. She and her sister are both taking HIV medications and support each other. The man who molested her has died from AIDS. Her mother, who refuses to be tested herself, has now moved in with Nicole and her sister. Nicole speaks out about HIV. She feels she has more in common with the young people who were infected as babies than with youth who get infected as teens. She was, after all, nearly a baby herself when she was infected.

Adolescents as a group need sensitive and developmentally appropriate anticipatory guidance as they make the transition into the self-sufficiency and responsibilities of adulthood. But teens with HIV infection frequently need considerably more support. Some need grief counseling; others need victim support services. Many HIV-infected youth despair of ever finding someone who could love them and want to be with them. Some need financial assistance to afford medicines that are too expensive for far more financially well-off adults. All need help in adopting the demanding prescription drug-taking behaviors that will keep them healthy. While the need for many of these services is not unique to HIV youth, the content and process must be.

For youth infected as teens, the greatest barrier is their identification and linkage to care. Most young people do not think that they are personally at risk for the infection and therefore do not need to seek HIV screening services. Others like Stuart may have concerns but do not act on them. Complicating the situation for youth is that their attitude is so frequently shared by the health care providers from whom they receive services. Young people who have accepted screening report that the biggest contributing factor to their obtaining an HIV test was the recommendation of their physician or nurse to get one[52]; therefore the importance of the health care provider bringing up the topic of HIV testing cannot be overemphasized. Stuart tested when he was encouraged.

Epidemiologic mapping of morbidities, such as HIV seroprevalence estimates, sexually transmitted infection rates, and drug use information in adolescents,[53] can be used effectively to place screening and outreach services where young people congregate. Such services must include mechanisms for the linkage of newly identified HIV-positive youth to care. Attention to building this capacity to link the youth identified as HIV positive through screening to the health care team is a critical but frequently ignored component of an effective public health screening campaign.[54] Linkage is important at both the personal and the community level. Youth's denial is made quite easy by the asymptomatic nature of early HIV infection, but denial inhibits their seeking further care. They get neither the health assessment they personally need nor help in reducing behaviors in the community that put others at risk. Helping HIV-infected young people understand their role in accepting personal responsibility for stopping ongoing transmission is critical to stopping the cycle of infection at the community level.

Tailoring outreach and health services is complicated by gender identity issues in young men and young women. Some youth are openly gay or bisexual, some remain closeted and secretive, some are transgendered with difficult issues, and others are still questioning. Youth with these different characteristics relate to each other with difficulty, if at all. Service providers must appreciate these differences and be competent in responding to them.[55] These self-identity issues are described in the context of the prevailing American culture, but there are also powerful cultural forces for racial and ethnic minorities that shape gender identity differently. For these groups, gender identity may not be defined by same-sex activity per se, but rather by the role one assumes in that activity. Therefore young men performing insertive sex would thus gender identify as heterosexual and any outreach or services characterized as gay would be shunned.

Adolescent health services must be comprehensive and holistic to be effective.[56] A single-minded and exclusive focus on the biomedical aspects of the teen's HIV infection will doom the encounter to failure. Some adolescents will bring deep and urgent psychosocial problems to health care providers, and the early interactions around these problems are crucial for establishing the trust that it is the *sine qua non* of adolescent health care. The extent to which the provider can be flexible and shift from the medical agenda to the psychosocial one presented by the adolescent will determine the degree to which trust can be achieved and maintained. Thus, it is quite important that the health center have a wide range of services on site. Young people will not always have the resources or judgment to follow through on instructions to go elsewhere to complete an evaluation or obtain treatment.

Holistic care does not simply mean providing comprehensive services but rather also addressing the spirit and soul of the young person. Frequently, young people with HIV infection struggle with the meaning of the experience in which they find themselves but find verbalization difficult. When the press of urgent problems has been resolved, providers should consider sensitive questioning of how these bigger issues may be affecting the young person. Nothing clarifies quite like a serious illness, and when people have had this experience, they often need help in processing it. Young people can be surprisingly insightful and deep. Researchers have found altruism to be one of the important factors in young people joining and staying in a long-term study of HIV infection[57] and spiritual hope to be a protective factor against incident pregnancy in HIV-infected young women.[58]

Young people, unlike adults, have specific barriers to obtaining health care services. These include accessibility, availability, and cost as structural barriers; and privacy, confidentiality, and the role of parents as process barriers. The structural barriers are commonplace in American society, but the process barriers are unique to youth. Privacy and confidentiality are vitally important to youth who are developing a sense of self and autonomy apart from family structures. For HIV-infected youth, these may be even more crucial characteristics of health care, as they may not have disclosed their infection to their family, partners, or friends. The health care team providing services to the adolescent needs to achieve a balance between supporting the important developmental task of autonomy and encouraging the youth to involve parents for the wisdom and experience they could contribute to the youth's decision making. This parental involvement may be resisted by young people who fear parental reaction to the decisions they are making about their sexuality. The reasons for resistance need to be carefully explored with the young person to facilitate self-examination. At the same time, the health care team needs to understand that engaging parents may not always be in the best interests of those youth whose HIV infection may make them physically or economically vulnerable if parents are antagonistic.

SUMMARY

HIV-infected youth differ from adults on three basic levels: the many paths to HIV infection, the clinical course once infected, and the wide array of services that good, comprehensive care requires in light of the many social problems they endure. AIDS has brought health care delivery and public health programs to crisis level in many American cities. Adolescents are at their healthiest point in life and typically for that reason have been frequently neglected in routine health care programs. But we neglect the care of HIV-infected youth at great cost, for their numbers are growing and their ignorance of their HIV infection inevitably leads to its spread.

REFERENCES

1. AVERT. The origins of AIDS and HIV and the first cases of AIDS. http://www.avert.org/origins.htm.

2. Joint United Nations Programme on HIV/AIDS. 2002. Report on the global HIV/AIDS epidemic. Jul; Chapter 3: AIDS and young people.

3. 2004 Report on the Global AIDS Epidemic. UNAIDS Fourth Global Report, July 2004. http://www.unaids.org/bangkok2004/report.html.

4. HIV/AIDS among Youth. May 2005. Centers for Disease Control and Prevention.

5. Shilts, R. 1987. *And the Band Played On.* New York: St. Martin's Press.

6. Connor, E. M., R. S. Sperling, R. Gelber, P. Kiselev, G. Scott, M. J. O'Sullivan, R. VanDyke, M. Bey, W. Shearer, R. L. Jacobson, et al. 1994. Reduction of maternal-infant transmission of human immunodeficiency virus type 1 with zidovudine treatment. Pediatric AIDS Clinical Trials Group Protocol 076 Study Group. *N Engl J Med* 331 (18):1173–80.

7. Buchacz, K., J. S. Cervia, J. C. Lindsey, M. D. Hughes, G. R. Seage, 3rd, W. M. Dankner, J. M. Oleske, and J. Moye. 2001. Impact of protease inhibitor-containing combination antiretroviral therapies on height and weight growth in HIV-infected children. *Pediatrics* 108 (4):E72.

8. Buchacz, K., A. D. Rogol, J. C. Lindsey, C. M. Wilson, M. D. Hughes, G. R. Seage, 3rd, J. M. Oleske, and A. S. Rogers. 2003. Delayed onset of pubertal development in children and adolescents with perinatally acquired HIV infection. *J Acquir Immune Defic Syndr* 33 (1):56–65.

9. de Martino, M., P. A. Tovo, L. Galli, C. Gabiano, F. Chiarelli, M. Zappa, G. C. Gattinara, D. Bassetti, V. Giacomet, E. Chiappini, M. Duse, S. Garetto, and D. Caselli. 2001. Puberty in perinatal HIV-1 infection: A multicentre longitudinal study of 212 children. *Aids* 15 (12):1527–34.

10. Pregnancy in perinatally HIV-infected adolescents and young adults—Puerto Rico, 2002. 2003. *MMWR Morb Mortal Wkly Rep* 52 (8):149–51.

11. Forehand, R., R. Steele, L. Armistead, E. Morse, P. Simon, and L. Clark. 1998. The Family Health Project: psychosocial adjustment of children whose mothers are HIV infected. *J Consult Clin Psychol* 66 (3):513–20.

12. Levenson, R. L., and C. A. Mellins. 1992. Pediatric HIV disease: What psychologists need to know. *Professional Psychology: Research and Practice* 23:410–15.

13. Havens, J. F., and C. A. Mellins. 1996. Mental health issues in HIV-affected women and children. *International Review of Psychiatry* 8:217–25.

14. Mellins, C. A., and A. A. Ehrhardt. 1994. Families affected by pediatric acquired immunodeficiency syndrome: sources of stress and coping. *J Dev Behav Pediatr* 15 (3 Suppl):S54–60.

15. Kaslow, R. A., M. Carrington, R. Apple, L. Park, A. Munoz, A. J. Saah, J. J. Goedert, C. Winkler, S. J. O'Brien, C. Rinaldo, R. Detels, W. Blattner, J. Phair, H. Erlich, and D. L. Mann. 1996. Influence of combinations of human major histocompatibility complex genes on the course of HIV-1 infection. *Nat Med* 2 (4):405–11.

16. Tang, J., C. M. Wilson, S. Meleth, A. Myracle, E. Lobashevsky, M. J. Mulligan, S. D. Douglas, B. Korber, S. H. Vermund, and R. A. Kaslow. 2002. Host genetic profiles

predict virological and immunological control of HIV-1 infection in adolescents. *Aids* 16 (17):2275–84.

17.   Centers for Disease Control and Prevention. 2003. *HIV/AIDS Surveillance Report* (Vol. 15). Atlanta: US Department of Health and Human Services, Centers for Disease Control and Prevention:2004–6.

18.   Chalk, R., and D. A. Phillips, eds. 1996. National Research Council and Institute of Medicine. *Youth Development and Neighborhood Influences: Challenges and Opportunities.* Washington DC: National Academy Press.

19.   Eccles, J., and J. A. Gootman, eds. 2002. National Research Council and Institute of Medicine. *Community Programs to Promote Youth Development.* Washington DC: National Academy Press.

20.   National Research Council. 1993. *Losing Generations: Adolescents in High-Risk Setting. Panel on High Risk Youth, National Research Council.* Washington DC: National Academy Press.

21.   Centers for Disease Control and Prevention. 2001. *HIV/AIDS Surveillance Report* 3 (2):22.

22.   Centers for Disease Control and Prevention. 2001. *HIV/AIDS Surveillance Report* 13(2):16–7.

23.   Ford, K., W. Sohn, and J. Lepkowski. 2002. American adolescents: sexual mixing patterns, bridge partners, and concurrency. *Sex Transm Dis* 29 (1):13–19.

24.   Abma, J., A. Driscoll, and K. Moore. 1998. Young women's degree of control over first intercourse: An exploratory analysis. *Fam Plann Perspect* 30 (1):12–18.

25.   Sturdevant, M. S., M. Belzer, G. Weissman, L. B. Friedman, M. Sarr, and L. R. Muenz. 2001. The relationship of unsafe sexual behavior and the characteristics of sexual partners of HIV infected and HIV uninfected adolescent females. *J Adolesc Health* 29 (3 Suppl):64–71.

26.   Miller, K. S., L. F. Clark, and J. S. Moore. 1997. Sexual initiation with older male partners and subsequent HIV risk behavior among female adolescents. *Fam Plann Perspect* 29 (5):212–14.

27.   DiClemente, R. J., G. M. Wingood, R. A. Crosby, C. Sionean, B. K. Cobb, K. Harrington, S. L. Davies, E. W. Hook, 3rd, and M. K. Oh. 2002. Sexual risk behaviors associated with having older sex partners: A study of black adolescent females. *Sex Transm Dis* 29 (1):20–24.

28.   Belzer, M., A. S. Rogers, M. Camarca, D. Fuchs, L. Peralta, D. Tucker, and S. J. Durako. 2001. Contraceptive choices in HIV infected and HIV at-risk adolescent females. *J Adolesc Health* 29 (3 Suppl):93–100.

29.   Levin, L., L. Henry-Reid, D. A. Murphy, L. Peralta, M. Sarr, Y. Ma, and A. S. Rogers. 2001. Incident pregnancy rates in HIV infected and HIV uninfected at-risk adolescents. *J Adolesc Health* 29 (3 Suppl):101–108.

30.   Centers for Disease Control and Prevention. 2002. *Sexually Transmitted Disease Surveillance.* Atlanta: US Department of Health and Human Services, September 2002.

31.   Wilson, C. M., J. Houser, C. Partlow, B. J. Rudy, D. C. Futterman, and L. B. Friedman. 2001. The REACH (Reaching for Excellence in Adolescent Care and Health) project: Study design, methods, and population profile. *J Adolesc Health* 29 (3 Suppl):8–18.

32.   Centers for Disease Control and Prevention. 1995. *HIV/AIDS Surveillance Report* 7(2):14.

33.   Murphy, D. A., R. Mitchell, S. H. Vermund, and D. Futterman. 2002. Factors associated with HIV testing among HIV-positive and HIV-negative high-risk

adolescents: The REACH Study. Reaching for Excellence in Adolescent Care and Health. *Pediatrics* 110 (3):e36.

34. Valleroy, L. A., D. A. MacKellar, J. M. Karon, D. H. Rosen, W. McFarland, D. A. Shehan, S. R. Stoyanoff, M. LaLota, D. D. Celentano, B. A. Koblin, H. Thiede, M. H. Katz, L. V. Torian, and R. S. Janssen. 2000. HIV prevalence and associated risks in young men who have sex with men. Young Men's Survey Study Group. *JAMA* 284 (2):198–204.

35. HIV/STD risks in young men who have sex with men who do not disclose their sexual orientation—six U.S. cities, 1994–2000. 2003. *MMWR Morb Mortal Wkly Rep* 52 (5):81 86.

36. Unrecognized HIV infection, risk behaviors, and perceptions of risk among young black men who have sex with men—six U.S. cities, 1994–1998. 2002. *MMWR Morb Mortal Wkly Rep* 51 (33):733–6.

37. American Family Association. http://www.afa.net/

38. Crosby, R. A., R. J. DiClemente, G. M. Wingood, E. Rose, and D. Levine. 2003. Adjudication history and African American adolescents' risk for acquiring sexually transmitted diseases: an exploratory analysis. *Sex Transm Dis* 30 (8):634–38.

39. Hammett, T. M., M. P. Harmon, and W. Rhodes. 2002. The burden of infectious disease among inmates of and releasees from US correctional facilities, 1997. *Am J Public Health* 92 (11):1789–94.

40. Braithwaite, R. L., and K. R. Arriola. 2003. Male prisoners and HIV prevention: A call for action ignored. *Am J Public Health* 93 (5):759–63.

41. Krebs, C. P., and M. Simmons. 2002. Intraprison HIV transmission: An assessment of whether it occurs, how it occurs, and who is at risk. *AIDS Educ Prev* 14 (5 Suppl B):53–64.

42. McKinney, R. E., Jr., and J. W. Robertson. 1993. Effect of human immunodeficiency virus infection on the growth of young children. Duke Pediatric AIDS Clinical Trials Unit. *J Pediatr* 123 (4):579–82.

43. Moye, J., Jr., K. C. Rich, L. A. Kalish, A. R. Sheon, C. Diaz, E. R. Cooper, J. Pitt, and E. Handelsman. 1996. Natural history of somatic growth in infants born to women infected by human immunodeficiency virus. Women and Infants Transmission Study Group. *J Pediatr* 128 (1):58–69.

44. Mahoney, F. M., S. M. Donfield, C. Howard, F. Kaufman, and J. M. Gertner. 1999. HIV-associated immune dysfunction and delayed pubertal development in a cohort of young hemophiliacs. Hemophilia Growth and Development Study. *J Acquir Immune Defic Syndr* 21 (4):333–37.

45. Carre, N., C. Deveau, F. Belanger, F. Boufassa, A. Persoz, C. Jadand, C. Rouzioux, J. F. Delfraissy, and D. Bucquet. 1994. Effect of age and exposure group on the onset of AIDS in heterosexual and homosexual HIV-infected patients. SEROCO Study Group. *Aids* 8 (6):797–802.

46. Rosenberg, P. S., J. J. Goedert, and R. J. Biggar. 1994. Effect of age at seroconversion on the natural AIDS incubation distribution. Multicenter Hemophilia Cohort Study and the International Registry of Seroconverters. *Aids* 8 (6):803–10.

47. Goedert, J. J., C. M. Kessler, L. M. Aledort, R. J. Biggar, W. A. Andes, G. C. White, 2nd, J. E. Drummond, K. Vaidya, D. L. Mann, M. E. Eyster, et al. 1989. A prospective study of human immunodeficiency virus type 1 infection and the development of AIDS in subjects with hemophilia. *N Engl J Med* 321 (17):1141–48.

48. Munoz, A., and J. Xu. 1996. Models for the incubation of AIDS and variations according to age and period. *Stat Med* 15 (21–22):2459–73.

49. Starr, S. E., M. Sarr, D. E. Campbell, C. M. Wilson, and S. D. Douglas. 2002. Increased proliferation within T lymphocyte subsets of HIV-infected adolescents. *AIDS Res Hum Retroviruses* 18 (17):1301–10.

50. Pham, T., M. Belzer, J. A. Church, C. Kitchen, C. M. Wilson, S. D. Douglas, Y. Geng, M. Silva, R. M. Mitchell, and P. Krogstad. 2003. Assessment of thymic activity in human immunodeficiency virus-negative and -positive adolescents by real-time PCR quantitation of T-cell receptor rearrangement excision circles. *Clin Diagn Lab Immunol* 10 (2):323–28.

51. Pahwa, S., V. Chitnis, R. M. Mitchell, S. Fernandez, A. Chandrasekharan, C. M. Wilson, and S. D. Douglas. 2003. CD4+ and CD8+ T cell receptor repertoire perturbations with normal levels of T cell receptor excision circles in HIV-infected, therapy-naive adolescents. *AIDS Res Hum Retroviruses* 19 (6):487–95.

52. Samet, J. H., M. R. Winter, L. Grant, and R. Hingson. 1997. Factors associated with HIV testing among sexually active adolescents: A Massachusetts survey. *Pediatrics* 100 (3 Pt 1):371–77.

53. Michaud, J. M., J. Ellen, S. M. Johnson, and A. Rompalo. 2003. Responding to a community outbreak of syphilis by targeting sex partner meeting location: An example of a risk-space intervention. *Sex Transm Dis* 30 (7):533–38.

54. Chabon, B., and D. Futterman. 1999. Adolescents and HIV. *AIDS Clinical Care* 11 (2):9–11, 15–16.

55. Ryan, C., and D. Futterman. 1998. *Lesbian and Gay Youth Care and Counseling: The Comprehensive Guide to Health and Mental Health Care.* New York: Columbia University Press.

56. Advocates for Youth. Care of HIV Positive Youth. http://www.advocatesforyouth. org/publications/iag/hivpositive.htm.

57. Stanford, P. D., D. A. Monte, F. M. Briggs, P. M. Flynn, M. Tanney, J. H. Ellenberg, K. L. Clingan, and A. S. Rogers. 2003. Recruitment and retention of adolescent participants in HIV research: findings from the REACH (Reaching for Excellence in Adolescent Care and Health) Project. *J Adolesc Health* 32 (3):192–203.

58. Levin, L., L. Henry-Reid, D. A. Murphy, L. Peralta, M. Sarr, Y. Ma, and A. S. Rogers. 2001. Incident pregnancy rates in HIV infected and HIV uninfected at-risk adolescents. *J Adolesc Health* 29 (3 Suppl):101–108.

Chapter 2

HIV INFECTION AND AIDS: THE BIOLOGY OF THE DISEASE IN ADOLESCENTS

Hans Spiegel, M.D. and Lawrence J. D'Angelo, M.D., M.P.H.

HIV

By Heather

Afraid, attitude, alone, anxiety, AIDS
Belief, comfort, death, excited, end this disease
Family, good days, hope, that's HIV
Inspiration, jokes, kindness, we live with it all
Love, madness, nurses, new friends, new hope
Opportunistic infections, protocols, quietness, rest, same disease
Sickness, telling others, please understand our virus
Wishes, x-rays, yelling for acceptance
Zip-it-ee-doo-da. That's AIDS

Although the virus we now know as the human immunodeficiency virus (HIV) most likely was transformed from an animal virus (a "zoonosis") to a virus that could infect humans in the 1930s, the recognition of the infection in the United States and the disease it caused is well marked in time. In mid-1981, a number of cases of a rare form of pneumonia, *Pneumocystis carinii* pneumonia (PCP) was recognized in men at first in Los Angeles and shortly afterward in New York City. These individuals were primarily men who had a history of sexual contacts with other men. The common factor underlying this pneumonia was that all of these men had developed a severe weakness of their immune system: they were "immunodeficient."

The next 18 months was a period of confusion and frustration as a variety of hypotheses was actively investigated around the globe in an effort to find what was causing this illness that rapidly expanded from a few cases to epidemic proportions. In early 1983, researchers in France and the United States almost simultaneously announced the discovery of a human retrovirus they believed was causing this illness. In France, it was called the "lymphadenopathy associated virus," or LAV. In the United States, it was called "human T-cell lymphotropic virus, type III," or HTLV III. It took a special subcommittee of the Committee on the Taxonomy of Viruses to settle the dispute and arrive at the name we now know: human immunodeficiency virus, or HIV.

While these scientific debates were ongoing, a social conflict arose among those who were most often infected by the virus and affected by the illness it caused: gay males and the epidemiologists whose responsibility it is to track such disease outbreaks. Because the virus was causing a number of conditions that had never been seen before in otherwise healthy persons, it was difficult to define who had the new illness, and who didn't. One thing appeared to be true for all those who were recognized to have the infection: it severely damaged the immune system, in particular the T lymphocytes, those white blood cells responsible for protecting the body from viruses. Eventually, *acquired immune deficiency syndrome (AIDS)* was decided on as a name for the condition. The signs and symptoms necessary to fulfill the "case definition" of AIDS have changed over the years, but have remained relatively stable since 1993. A case of AIDS is defined as an individual with HIV infection who either has developed additional infections more commonly seen after severe weakening of the immune system or whose immune system is damaged to the point that a certain population of protective T lymphocytes, the CD4 lymphocytes, is reduced to below 200 cells/mm^3 (normal range is 800–1,500 cells/mm^3).

One of the hardest concepts for people to grasp about AIDS is that it is the latter part of the spectrum of illness caused by the HIV. Most individuals, even those not treated with medications, take 8 to 12 years from the time of infection with HIV to reach the point that they can be classified as having AIDS. Now, with new therapies emerging almost monthly, this progression of the infection can be put off longer and longer, to the point where we can now help individuals infected with HIV to live full and productive lives if they receive and *take* appropriate treatment. This is a particularly important point for adolescents and young adults with HIV infection who potentially have longer to live with HIV infection than any other age group, with the exception of children.

THE VIRUS

HIV is a retrovirus. This family of viruses is so named because it reverses the usual flow of genetic information. The genetic material of HIV is ribonucleic acid (RNA). Human cells have deoxyribonucleic acid (DNA) as their main genetic material. Having RNA as primary genetic material is common to many viruses, but the intention of retroviruses is to produce DNA once they infect new cells. Therefore, when human cells are invaded by the virus, retroviruses use a special enzyme called *reverse transcriptase* to copy their RNA to DNA (in human cells, this process runs in the opposite direction). This DNA can then replicate itself to become human-like, double-stranded DNA, to migrate to its new host cells nucleus, and to become "integrated" into the host cell's core genetic material. Once it is part of the cell's genetic material, it is called a *provirus*. At this point, two things can happen: (1) the virus can go into a resting or "latent" phase, or (2) it can get busy immediately producing new viral RNA from the integrated DNA with the intention of forming new viral particles and continuing its attack of the host.

The HIV *genome*, or the totality of its genetic material, contains at least nine recognizable genes that produce at least 15 different proteins. These proteins are either part of the virus's structure (structural proteins), necessary for regulating the behavior of the virus in a cell (regulatory proteins), or essential for other viral functions such as viral assembly, viral release, and viral infection of new cells (accessory proteins).

It was once thought that HIV invaded only actively replicating cells. We now know that unlike other retroviruses, HIV has evolved so that it can replicate in nondividing cells. This gives it a tremendous advantage and allows it to infect a wide range of different cells in the body. It chooses the cells it will infect by the presence of certain proteins that can function as *receptors* for the virus on the surface of those cells. The main target of the virus is the CD4 molecule, but other cellular receptors such as CXCR4 or CCR-5 may function as *co-receptors* for the virus.[1] There is a theoretical possibility that blocking these receptors might protect cells from invasion by the virus. Indeed, individuals who are genetically deficient for these cell surface proteins are resistant to infection.

Another assumption that has been disproved is that there was a long quiescent period from the time of infection with HIV until the virus population changed gears into rapid replication and triggered illness in the host. What appears to be the actual case is that there is a dynamic balance between rapidly replicating virus and host immune cells that destroy virus infected cells. One of the concerning features of this virus is its capacity to infect the T-cell lymphocytes with CD4 receptors on their surface, which are the very cells that the immune system needs to defend the body effectively against HIV and other viral infections. The newest concept of this struggle is that the body either can or cannot keep up with the replicating virus. If it can, the illness is less likely to progress to AIDS. If it can't, the host becomes ill by virtue of fewer immune cells to defend itself against other infectious agents known as "opportunistic infections."

During the process of reproducing itself, HIV makes "mistakes," or mutations, in the process. This sort of misreading of the genetic code is often a fatal flaw for some viruses, but HIV uses it as an advantage: these mutations have the potential to become new variants of the virus, variants that cause more tissue destruction and/or more resistance to medications. These variants arising from the initial HIV type are referred to as *quasispecies*. This perpetual evolution of the virus also makes it a difficult target for a vaccine. The potential differences are just enough so that a traditional vaccine has diminished hope for success.

Although there are two main types of HIV, HIV-1 and HIV-2, at this time the type mainly responsible for the illness we call AIDS is type 1 (HIV-1). To make matters more complicated, there are three groups of HIV-1: M, O, and N. Group M causes 99% of the world's HIV/AIDS. Within Group M, there are at least 11 subtypes or *clades* recognized by a letter, A through K. Certain clades predominate in certain parts of the world. For instance, in the United States, clade B predominates; in Africa, clades A, D, C, and recombinant forms are the major subtypes of the virus; and in China, India, and Thailand, it is again type C, E, and recombinant forms. This is important in that some of the features of the epidemic may be linked to the subtype of the virus prevalent in a particular geographic area. For instance, types C and E may be more easily acquired by heterosexual transmission than subtype B.

ADOLESCENTS AND HIV: IS THERE ANYTHING SPECIAL ABOUT INFECTED TEENS?

The same virus that infects adults infects adolescents. Are adolescents any different in their response to the virus? Because the majority of the first adolescents infected with HIV were adolescents who had hemophilia or had other reasons to have received blood products, it was initially hard to tell if, in a broad cross section of teens, the virus would behave differently than it did in adults. Early studies looking at adolescent and adults with hemophilia did show that teens appeared to progress more slowly in their disease stage. As there were no drugs available to treat HIV, this was clearly a relative observation, and infected teens pursued the same inexorably downhill course as adults.

Later studies did show that there were differences in the immune systems of adolescents and adults that are important for the response to HIV. Even when infected with HIV, adolescents appear to retain a larger population of the early precursors of T lymphocytes than do adults. This is potentially good news. If medications can halt the progression of the virus, these early precursor cells can possibly give rise to a more complete "family" of T lymphocytes, which might have the capability of fighting off a broader range of infectious agents.

What are some of the factors that may help predict how the infection will or will not progress in adolescents? Over the past years, many prognostic factors have been identified that influence HIV disease progression in adults, and many of these have also been confirmed to be of importance for both children and adolescents. These include a variety of physical health factors involving the infected host, properties that are specific for the virus that has been transmitted to the host, and environmental factors.

Unfortunately, there are only few comparative studies of the relative influence of these factors in relation to the age of the patient at the time of infection. For instance, the immunologic differences noted previously between adolescents and adults with regard to the presence of higher levels of "naïve" CD8+ T-cell, while present, are of uncertain clinical meaning.[2] It is hoped that this will translate into a better capacity for an infected adolescent to mount a more substantive immune response with "cytotoxic" (killer) T-cells.

What else can influence the biology of this virus in adolescents? A major influence can be the presence of other infections, called co-infections. These may or may not be the types of infections noted when the immune system is compromised, known as opportunistic infections. For instance, early in the epidemic when patients with hemophilia made up most of the HIV-infected adolescents, co-infections with hepatitis B were quite common. Studies of this co-infection did not show acceleration of HIV infection, but there was very clear evidence of more serious liver disease in these patients.[3] Likewise, co-infection with hepatitis C, particularly the genetic variant of this infection known as type 1, actually does lower the CD4 T-cell count, advance the likelihood of progression to AIDS, and put the individual at risk of more severe liver disease. No effect has been seen on the progression of HIV infection when co-infections occur with any of the herpes viruses (herpes simplex virus, cytomegalovirus, human herpes virus type 6, and human herpes virus type 8).[4] On the other hand, when an individual is co-infected, the presence of HIV infection can make these infections more severe.

Although less of a problem in this country, co-infections with tuberculosis can lead to the clinical decline of an HIV infected adolescent as it can for an adult. The mortality of patients with HIV-1 and HIV-2 infection who acquired tuberculosis infection (incident tuberculosis [TB]) is significantly increased. The overall mortality rate after a diagnosis of TB in one study was 43.5/100 person-years, and the overall median survival time for both HIV-1- and HIV-2-positive patients was less than 9 months.[5]

What other factors might influence the biological interaction of the infected adolescent and the virus? A major consideration may be the nutritional status of the teen.

Effects of malnutrition on the cellular and humoral immune response are well known and can lead to decreases in CD4+ and CD8+ T-lymphocyte numbers, diminished response to proteins injected under the skin to test immunity (delayed cutaneous hypersensitivity), lower antibody concentrations after immunization, and reduction of the ability to kill bacteria. Among the adolescents participating in the Reaching for Excellence in Adolescent Care and Health network (REACH) study, almost half the participants with absolute CD4+ T-cell counts above 500/mm³ had significantly lower intake of iron, vitamin C, and vitamin E, when compared with HIV-uninfected youth.[6] Supplementation of daily multivitamin intake has been found to reduce HIV disease progression among men and women in several observational studies and randomized trials.[7] In a European cohort of adults with HIV infection, followed for more than 10 years (Aquitaine Cohort/ France) weight loss greater than 10% increased the risk of HIV disease progression to AIDS threefold. The cross-sectional measure of body mass index (BMI) was shown to be a useful predictor for HIV disease progression. For patients with BMI under 16 kg/m², the relative risk for disease progression to AIDS was increased almost fivefold.[8,9] Differences in survival have also been shown when serum albumin, an important blood protein closely related to an individual's nutritional state, was used as indirect nutritional status parameter for separation and categorization of adult patients with HIV infection.[10] HIV infection can lead to poor absorption of lipids, which then affects the concentration of fat-soluble vitamins such as A and E. HIV infection increases the energy and protein requirements of an infected individual and leads to increased utilization of antioxidant vitamins such as beta-carotene and vitamins C and E. Deficiencies of micronutrients, in particular zinc and selenium, in patients with HIV infection have been associated with more rapid disease progression and increased mortality.[11,12]

Host factors such as the presence of co-infections and underlying nutritional status are important, but of equal importance are intrinsic features of the virus. Because most of the HIV infections that proceed to AIDS are HIV-1 infections, we focus our attention on this strain of the virus. Early on in the personal infection history of an individual with clade B HIV-1, strains of the virus that infect host CD4 T-cells and macrophages ("M-tropic"; use of the CCR5 co-receptor) predominate. As time passes and the disease progresses, patients can show a change in the characteristics of the virus so that it switches to a "phenotype" that has greater affinity for T-lymphocyte laboratory cell lines ("T-tropic"; use of CXCR4 co-receptor). In the infected individual, this change is accompanied by an increase in the virulence of the virus and its replication rate.[1] These dual changes result in a rapid loss of T-cells. Moreover, these changes are coupled with the increased rate of production of mutant strains of the virus, as discussed previously, including strains of the virus that are resistant to drugs used to combat the infection. Mutations of some of these genes that carry the information for the co-receptor proteins have also been identified as host factors that can lead to slower HIV disease progression.[13–16]

The final modifying factor in determining how an infected host and HIV will interact is the signature proteins adherent to the surface of the body's lymphocytes. One set of these proteins belong to a family of molecules referred to as *histocompatability antigens* or *human lymphocyte antigen* (HLA). Dependent on the type of HLA, this can result in weaker or stronger cellular immune responses to HIV-infected cells. More rapid progression to AIDS has been observed when similar HLA surface proteins are inherited from an infected individual's mother. In perinatally infected infants, this actually compromises the child's capacity to control HIV replication and has resulted in a shortened time to AIDS diagnosis or death.[17-19]

These and other identified genetic host factors have led to a cadre of youth who have survived for many years without significant evidence of progression of their disease. They are referred to as long-term non-progressors.

As with other chronic illnesses, we are only at the beginning of understanding the complexity of biological and genetic factors of the virus and the host and how these factors might interact with environmental, social, and psychological variables to determine disease progression and ultimately prognosis. In the rest of this book, we explore and try to understand these factors.

REFERENCES

1. Berger, E. A., P. M. Murphy, and J. M. Farber. 1999. Chemokine receptors as HIV-1 coreceptors: Roles in viral entry, tropism, and disease. *Annu Rev Immunol* 17:657–700.

2. Douglas, S. D., B. Rudy, L. Muenz, S. E. Starr, D. E. Campbell, C. Wilson, C. Holland, P. Crowley-Nowick, and S. H. Vermund. 2000. T-lymphocyte subsets in HIV-infected and high-risk HIV-uninfected adolescents: Retention of naive T lymphocytes in HIV-infected adolescents. The Adolescent Medicine HIV/AIDS Research Network. *Arch Pediatr Adolesc Med* 154 (4):375–80.

3. Konopnicki, D., A. Mocroft, S. de Wit, F. Antunes, B. Ledergerber, C. Katlama, K. Zilmer, S. Vella, O. Kirk, and J. D. Lundgren. 2005. Hepatitis B and HIV: Prevalence, AIDS progression, response to highly active antiretroviral therapy and increased mortality in the EuroSIDA cohort. *Aids* 19 (6):593–601.

4. Suligoi, B., M. Dorrucci, I. Uccella, M. Andreoni, and G. Rezza. 2003. Effect of multiple herpesvirus infections on the progression of HIV disease in a cohort of HIV sero-converters. *J Med Virol* 69 (2):182–87.

5. van der Sande, M. A., M. F. Schim van der Loeff, R. C. Bennett, M. Dowling, A. A. Aveika, T. O. Togun, S. Sabally, D. Jeffries, R. A. Adegbola, R. Sarge-Njie, A. Jaye, T. Corrah, S. McConkey, and H. C. Whittle. 2004. Incidence of tuberculosis and survival after its diagnosis in patients infected with HIV-1 and HIV-2. *Aids* 18 (14):1933–41.

6. Kruzich, L. A., G. S. Marquis, A. L. Carriquiry, C. M. Wilson, and C. B. Stephensen. 2004. US youths in the early stages of HIV disease have low intakes of some micronutrients important for optimal immune function. *J Am Diet Assoc* 104 (7):1095–1101.

7. Fawzi, W. 2003. Micronutrients and human immunodeficiency virus type 1 disease progression among adults and children. *Clin Infect Dis* 37 Suppl 2:S112–16.

8. Malvy, E., R. Thiebaut, C. Marimoutou, and F. Dabis. 2001. Weight loss and body mass index as predictors of HIV disease progression to AIDS in adults. Aquitaine cohort, France, 1985–1997. *J Am Coll Nutr* 20 (6):609–15.

9. van der Sande, M. A., M. F. Schim van der Loeff, A. A. Aveika, S. Sabally, T. Togun, R. Sarge-Njie, A. S. Alabi, A. Jaye, T. Corrah, and H. C. Whittle. 2004. Body mass index at time of HIV diagnosis: A strong and independent predictor of survival. *J Acquir Immune Defic Syndr* 37(2):1288–94.

10. Guenter, P., N. Muurahainen, G. Simons, A. Kosok, G. R. Cohan, R. Rudenstein, and J L. Turner. 1993. Relationships among nutritional status, disease progression, and survival in HIV infection. *J Acquir Immune Defic Syndr* 6 (10):1130–38.

11. Campa, A., G. Shor-Posner, F. Indacochea, G. Zhang, H. Lai, D. Asthana, G.B. Scott, and M. K. Baum. 1999. Mortality risk in selenium-deficient HIV-positive children. *J Acquir Immune Defic Syndr Hum Retrovirol* 20 (5):508–13.

12. Lai, H., S. Lai, G. Shor-Posner, F. Ma, E. Trapido, and M. K. Baum. 2001. Plasma zinc, copper, copper:zinc ratio, and survival in a cohort of HIV-1-infected homosexual men. *J Acquir Immune Defic Syndr* 27 (1):56–62.

13. Ioannidis, J. P., D. G. Contopoulos-Ioannidis, P. S. Rosenberg, J. J. Goedert, A. De Rossi, T. Espanol, L. Frenkel, M. J. Mayaux, M. L. Newell, S. G. Pahwa, C. Rousseau, G. Scarlatti, S. Sei, L. Sen, and T. R. O'Brien. 2003. Effects of CCR5-delta32 and CCR2–64I alleles on disease progression of perinatally HIV-1-infected children: An international meta-analysis. *Aids* 17 (11):1631–38.

14. Singh, K. K., C. F. Barroga, M. D. Hughes, J. Chen, C. Raskino, R. E. McKinney, and S. A. Spector. 2003. Genetic influence of CCR5, CCR2, and SDF1 variants on human immunodeficiency virus 1 (HIV-1)-related disease progression and neurological impairment, in children with symptomatic HIV-1 infection. *J Infect Dis* 188 (10):1461–72.

15. Tresoldi, E., M. L. Romiti, M. Boniotto, S. Crovella, F. Salvatori, E. Palomba, A. Pastore, C. Cancrini, M. de Martino, A. Plebani, G. Castelli, P. Rossi, P. A. Tovo, A. Amoroso, and G. Scarlatti. 2002. Prognostic value of the stromal cell-derived factor 1 3'A mutation in pediatric human immunodeficiency virus type 1 infection. *J Infect Dis* 185 (5):696–700.

16. Iversen, A. K., C. B. Christiansen, J. Attermann, J. Eugen-Olsen, S. Schulman, E. Berntorp, J. Ingerslev, L. Fugger, E. Scheibel, L. Tengborn, J. Gerstoft, E. Dickmeiss, A. Svejgaard, and P. Skinhoj. 2003. Limited protective effect of the CCR5Delta32/ CCR5Delta32 genotype on human immunodeficiency virus infection incidence in a cohort of patients with hemophilia and selection for genotypic X4 virus. *J Infect Dis* 187 (2):215–25.

17. Kuhn, L., E. J. Abrams, P. Palumbo, M. Bulterys, R. Aga, L. Louie, and T. Hodge. 2004. Maternal versus paternal inheritance of HLA class I alleles among HIV-infected children: Consequences for clinical disease progression. *Aids* 18 (9):1281–89.

18. Feeney, M. E., Y. Tang, K. A. Roosevelt, A. J. Leslie, K. McIntosh, N. Karthas, B.D. Walker, and P. J. Goulder. 2004. Immune escape precedes breakthrough human immunodeficiency virus type 1 viremia and broadening of the cytotoxic T-lymphocyte response in an HLA-B27-positive long-term-nonprogressing child. *J Virol* 78 (16):8927–30.

19. Kiepiela, P., A. J. Leslie, I. Honeyborne, D. Ramduth, C. Thobakgale, S. Chetty, P. Rathnavalu, C. Moore, K. J. Pfafferott, L. Hilton, P. Zimbwa, S. Moore, T. Allen, C. Brander, M. M. Addo, M. Altfeld, I. James, S. Mallal, M. Bunce, L. D. Barber, J. Szinger, C. Day, P. Klenerman, J. Mullins, B. Korber, H. M. Coovadia, B. D. Walker, and P. J. Goulder. 2004. Dominant influence of HLA-B in mediating the potential co-evolution of HIV and HLA. *Nature* 432 (7018):769–75.

Chapter 3

CARING FOR HIV-INFECTED TEENS

Lawrence J. D'Angelo, M.D., M.P.H.

When the Wind Blows

By Raquel Ramirez, age 17

Every time the wind blows
I know that it's just the souls of lost ones
Saying "Hello."
It is not a hard blow
It is a gentle blow.
It's not supposed to frighten you.
It's trying to tell you everything is all right
And that Heaven is a very beautiful place to go.
Everyone that you've loved and lost is up there
watching you and me.
They come down from Heaven disguised
as lady bugs, butterflies, and even
bumble bees.
They are waiting for the day that you
    will join them
But don't worry
You don't have to rush.
They be there waiting for eternity.
So just remember
Every time the wind blows
you know
That it is just the soul of lost ones
saying "Hello."

For most teenagers, getting routine health care is a challenge. Adolescents as a group see health care providers less frequently and less regularly than any other age group of patients. That is, they receive any kind of health care, including emergency care, less often and get scheduled, routine, and continuous health care even less frequently. Part of this lack of health care is just a consequence of being a teenager: they don't seek out adults for many things, and seeking out health care falls into that same category of advice/dependence. Part of the fault lies with the health care system: the needs of adolescents are rarely planned for by health care providers, and their training in caring for teenagers is spotty at best. And part of the fault lies with a society that renders teens the most poorly insured group in our population. It is just plain difficult for a teenager to get good health care!

It's not that teenagers don't have some idea what they would like in health care and who should be delivering that care. A study by Dr. Ken Ginsberg, an attending physician at the Children's Hospital of Philadelphia, established that teens want clean, confidential, and competent health care.[1] This is not unlike what we suppose most adults would like. The trouble is that finding the kind of care to match what they are looking for is not easy. They come into adolescence having been cared for by their pediatrician or by a family practitioner. In most states, they can't receive any kind of routine care, even from their regular provider, without parental permission. And although in most states they can get "confidential" care for sexually transmitted diseases, drug problems, pregnancy, and psychological problems, the teen may feel uncomfortable sharing personal experiences, particularly those involving sex, drugs, or other risk-taking behaviors with a previously trusted adult who may have known them and their family for many years.

WHAT TYPE OF CARE SHOULD ALL ADOLESCENTS RECEIVE?

First and foremost, medical care available to adolescents should be *regular* and *continuous*. Although the national medical organizations that have made recommendations on adolescent health care (American Academy of Pediatrics, American Medical Association, American Academy of Family Physicians, Health Resources and Services Administration, and the United States Preventive Services Task Force) don't necessarily agree on what these two terms mean. They do agree that a general assessment of the health of teenagers is important and that it should follow a reasonable schedule.[2] They also agree that this assessment must focus on the risk behaviors or health conditions that may lead to long-term health problems for teens. This means regular review of nutrition and eating problems, physical activity and exercise, dental health, skin conditions and protection, sexual behaviors, tobacco use, alcohol and other substance use, mood and thoughts of self injury or suicide, school performance and problems, physical and/or sexual threats or abuse, driving and recreational safety, and hearing and visual problems. And all of this in the annual 30-minute (or less) visit to a health care provider!

Continuous means that the same care provider(s) should provide services to teens over time. For many adolescents, the person or practice who did this when they were a child is likely to continue to provide this care into adolescence. This could be in a pediatrician's office, a family practice office, or in a neighborhood or regional outpatient clinic or office. For some teens, this environment poses a dilemma. The adolescent may not feel comfortable with a provider or setting that is associated with childhood. When you are 14, it is no longer "cool" to be sitting in a waiting room and getting a truck run over your foot by the 5-year-old sitting on the chair next to you. Likewise, the provider or office may not be geared to care for adolescents. Many clinic or office settings do not appreciate or understand confidentiality issues in teens[3,4] and may feel uncomfortable in dealing with sexuality or other risk behaviors.[5] Even if providers are willing to provide care, many are poorly trained in adolescent health issues and do not have the necessary skills to do so.[6]

Another dilemma for adolescents is that although national organizations have made these recommendations for the care of teenagers and young adults, they haven't necessarily filtered down to frontline primary care providers. Most of the recommended services are counseling services, and the current system of health care focuses instead on the *physical examination* model. Therefore many adolescents may get their heart listened to, but most likely will have few if any of these important health areas covered even if they do get to see a health care provider on some kind of a regular basis.[7] Compounding this fact is that any adolescent who needs any kind of additional health, social, or psychological service most likely will have to go elsewhere other than the health care provider's office, for that care. This means others visits to other places that may be miles away. It is a wonder that adolescents get any kind of care at all.

EVALUATING TEENS AT RISK FOR HIV INFECTION: WHO, WHERE, AND HOW?

What makes all this so important in the context of HIV infection is that this somewhat chaotic nonsystem of health care is still the entry point for most "at-risk" or HIV-infected teens for formal evaluation of their risk of HIV infection and care of this problem once it is identified. It is one of the major reasons that teens who are HIV-infected may not know it: no one thought or was able to test them. Whatever other care adolescents get, sexually active or drug-using teens need regular assessment for sexually transmitted infections and HIV.[8]

Years ago, this testing in and of itself was a problem. First, the adolescent had to get to a place where testing was available. Arguably the best place was the primary care provider's office, but many primary care providers didn't and still don't assess adolescents for HIV risk. This meant finding a testing site, which could be difficult or easy, depending on where the teen lived. Second, even knowledgeable adolescents might not feel comfortable seeking testing from a provider they had known since childhood or, by contrast, from someone they didn't know at all. Third, the testing process was cumbersome. Most states mandated in-depth counseling and a signed *informed consent* document that intimidated providers and patients alike. Patients who went through the process had to have a blood specimen obtained and would likely then have to return days to weeks later to get their results.

Recently all this has changed. The Centers for Disease Control and Prevention (CDC), capitalizing on the widespread availability of *rapid tests* (20 minutes from obtaining the sample to results), has recommended a streamlined procedure for HIV testing.[8] The emphasis is now on making testing widely available and a routine part of *all* health care visits, particularly "routine" and pregnancy-related care visits. Many of these tests use saliva not blood, further simplifying the process of obtaining specimens. A testing procedure this rapid more or less eliminates the problem of people not returning for results, but it does put increased pressure on those doing the testing to ensure they can counsel patients with a positive test and link them into care. There is still lingering anxiety on the part of some adolescent health experts that teenagers might be poorly served by any kind of testing schema used by programs or sites that haven't carefully planned the linkage to care providers. Despite these concerns, testing is now more readily available and may soon be a routine test for evaluating adolescents and adults on a regular basis. It is likely that given the simplicity of the test, it will begin to be used in nontraditional settings, which will make it available to the many teens who never come into contact with the health care system. If a *screening* test is positive, it is still necessary to *confirm* the rapid enzyme-linked immunosorbent assay (ELISA) with a more specific test, the Western blot. Although the screening test can at times be misleading, for the most part it is highly accurate. Confirming the test does give you additional time to plan for a smooth transition to care.

The *how* (via rapid testing) and *where* (virtually anywhere) of testing may be the easiest parts of the preceding question. The *who* has actually been a question that has been debated in the past, the other benefit of the easy-to-administer and virtually risk-free oral test is that it allows us to broaden our range of testing subjects. Therefore the answer becomes, "virtually anyone with any level of risk." That leads us to the next question, "Who has 'any level of risk'?" For those who we are screening for infection, the assumption is that they are being screened because of behaviors they have participated in during their adolescence. What behaviors put adolescents at risk? The answer to this is any behavior that puts them in contact with potentially infectious body fluids. This includes blood, semen, vaginal fluids, and breast milk.

So an adolescent could be considered at risk for HIV infection if he or she has received a blood transfusion from someone potentially infected, shared needles during injection drug use with someone who could be infected, was accidentally stuck with a needle that had been in contact with body fluids of someone at risk (or known to be HIV-positive), or exchanged semen or vaginal secretions through oral, anal, or vaginal sexual contact.

Many adolescents fall into one of these categories, particularly the last one. There are no definitive surveys of all types of sexual or injection drug use behaviors in teens, but the CDC's "Youth Risk Behavior Survey" is the best approximation of such a record of risk behaviors.[9] In a broad sample of U.S. youth, we know that 50% are "sexually active" by age 17 years, 14% have had more than four or more lifetime partners, and 2.3% claim to have ever injected drugs. Of those who have had sexual intercourse, only 58% used a condom at the time of their last sexual encounter, a behavior widely believed to offer a substantive degree of protection against HIV infection.[10] This would imply that the majority of adolescents would qualify for HIV-testing on the basis of "risk behaviors."

What has become clear over time is that not all risk behaviors are equal. Although not necessarily precise, estimates of the risk of infection by behavior type have been attempted by a number of authors (Table 3.1).[11,12]

Table 3.1
Estimated per-Act Risk for Acquisition of HIV, by Exposure Route*

Exposure Route	Risk per 10,000 Exposures to an Infected Source
Blood Transfusion	9,000
Needle-sharing injection-drug use	67
Receptive anal intercourse	50
Percutaneous needle stick	30
Receptive penile-vaginal intercourse	10
Insertive anal intercourse	6.5
Insertive penile-vaginal intercourse	5
Receptive oral intercourse	1
Insertive oral intercourse	0.5

*Estimates or risk for transmission from sexual exposures assume no condom use.

Source: Smith, D. K., L. A. Grohskopf, R. J. Black, J. D. Auerbach, F. Veronese, K. A. Struble, L. Cheever, M. Johnson, L. A. Paxton, I. M. Onorato, and A. E. Greenberg. 2005. Antiretroviral postexposure prophylaxis after sexual, injection-drug use, or other nonoccupational exposure to HIV in the United States: Recommendations from the U.S. Department of Health and Human Services. MMWR Recomm Rep 54 (RR-2):1–20.

Although the broad group of sexually active and drug-using adolescents deserve to be tested for HIV infection, this sort of analysis allows us to focus on certain adolescents who would need targeted interventions to ensure that they were initially and then regularly screened. These adolescents include young men who have sex with men, young men or women who use injection drugs or have sexual contact with injection drug users, or young men or women who have multiple sexual partners. There are subsets of youth who, for a variety of psychosocial reasons, may be more likely to be in one of these groups (homeless and runaway youth, transgender youth, youth involved in the sex industry, youth involved in drug trade, etc.), but this status classification can't change the fact that it is what you *do*, not who you *are*, that puts you at risk for HIV infection.

A final group not previously mentioned are youth who have been born to an HIV-infected mother. Although it is widely assumed that these teenagers would have been correctly classified as either HIV-infected or uninfected, our experience has shown that there are some youth who have what we call "missed perinatal transmission."[13] Therefore youth who have been born to HIV-infected parents may also need screening or rescreening.

AND WHEN THE TEST COMES BACK POSITIVE

Even in high-risk groups of adolescents, the majority of those screened will test negative for HIV infection. This testing process is a wonderful opportunity to counsel adolescents on risk reduction (condom use, partner selection, reducing the number of partners, needle exchange, etc.), many of which have proven efficacious in reducing the risk of infection. But there are cases when the screening test will be positive. In that case, the adolescent can be told factually that the screening test has been positive and that a confirmatory blood test is required. Patients should be offered the opportunity to bring a supportive individual with them to discuss the confirmatory results. If the testing site is not immediately linked to a care site, the testing site has the opportunity to refer the patient to a place where support at the time of confirmatory diagnosis can be provided (medical, social work, psychological). The majority of individuals either expect their diagnosis or at least are not surprised by it, but for some it will come as a true shock and support services should be in place to cope with possible acute grief reaction on the part of the patient.

All the challenges in getting appropriate health care that any adolescent faces are compounded when he or she receives a diagnosis of HIV infection. Few if any primary care providers will feel comfortable doing even the preliminary evaluation of an HIV-infected teenager. That need not be the case and a simple evaluation plan can be followed. Unfortunately, what will likely be missing in the traditional primary care setting will be the support services that are crucial to helping adolescents negotiate the rather complex care system that may confront them. This is one of the major factors arguing for adolescents who are HIV-infected getting their care in a specific HIV care center or at least through an HIV care specialist. The best settings appear to be programs that combine primary care, social and psychological support, and HIV expertise in one location and preferably in one clinical setting. Although 20 to 30 of these programs exist nationally, there are a larger number of HIV programs for adults and/or children that may easily adapt to meeting an adolescent's or multiple adolescents' needs. Local Ryan White Care programs are a good place to start to identify these resources in a community.

As soon as an individual definitively tests positive, a number of associated issues need to be dealt with by the patient and/or his or her provider. First, who should adolescents tell about their infection? Despite the official "climate of acceptance" that many would like to believe exists surrounding HIV/AIDS, there is still a strong current of intolerance in many families and many communities. This intolerance is often as likely to be directed toward the image of a particular behavioral lifestyle that a diagnosis of HIV infection evokes as it is against the infection itself. One of our patients related the following to us:

> I was sure I could tell my mom anything; I always had. So about a week after I came to the clinic and got my results, we were sitting around watching the news and a story came on about AIDS. This was a great time to tell her, or so I thought. I told her I had been to the clinic and that I had tested positive. I was stunned at what happened next; she looked at me and calmly said, "If that's true, you have to leave this house; I feel sorry for you that you are going to die, but I can't have someone like you living here knowing you are out having sex with men."

Other patients have told us that they have lost their jobs, that friends have stopped talking to them, or that they have been physically abused. The isolation this diagnosis can bring can be devastating, so we usually counsel our patients that they should tell someone and will often help them choose who that might be. Eventually, most patients do disclose to someone and the individual's mother is the most likely person to whom patients disclose.[14] Unfortunately, many HIV-infected patients do not disclose to their sexual partners, unless that individual is already HIV-infected as well. This creates an additional ethical burden for patients and for their care providers.

There are also a number of potential legal issues that possibly are relevant when an adolescent receives a diagnosis of HIV infection. Although in most states and jurisdictions adolescents can be tested for HIV either anonymously or confidentially, only 18 states stipulate that HIV is a condition for which adolescents can receive confidential *care*. In 17 states, providers may tell the parents of a minor patient who is HIV-infected.[15] Currently, 43 of the 50 states and one district require that HIV-infected individuals be reported by name to local health officials, as part of the mandated public health reporting system. CDC has announced that it will ultimately tie funding for surveillance to requiring "names reporting," rather than the heretofore widely used system of "unique identifiers." Confidentiality is guaranteed under all of these systems, but it often creates mistrust in adolescent patients when they are faced with the fact that their status is being shared "publicly."

Even before adolescents engage in clinical care, the hope is that they can begin building a trusting relationship with community advocates, case managers, or supportive members of their own infrastructure. We have successfully worked with school counselors, clergy, athletic coaches, and relatives to help structure a support system for patients. We have found that this is a crucial step in engaging patients in care and sometimes takes 6 to 12 months to successfully implement. Nonetheless, it is well worth the time and effort to ensure that patients feel supported as they begin what may be a difficult clinical odyssey.

THE ELEMENTS OF GOOD CARE

After I got my diagnosis, I went to a couple of different places to get care. In one place the patients were too old, in another the waiting room was filled with screaming kids. I was so upset; then my social worker told me that she had heard of this place called the Burgess Clinic. They were just plain cool, for real. Everyone seemed so comfortable with me. I think it is real important that teenagers have a place to go that understands them.

When an HIV-infected adolescent has developed a trusting relationship with clinical support staff and/or friends and family, we feel we can initiate a program of evaluation and treatment. Unless there is an acute clinical situation that demands more aggressive intervention, we prefer to start slowly in bringing a patient into the care process. Our first one to two visits usually focus on introducing patients to the clinical environment and meeting care providers and support staff. We will usually obtain a repeat confirmatory test in our laboratory for both our records and for the patient's peace of mind. This often sends a message that we want to be complete and want to always be accurate in our assumptions before recommending any kind of treatment. The laboratory testing we initially recommend is listed in Table 3.2.

Every patient gets a careful, complete physical examination. For male patients, this should include genitalia examination and rectal inspection, sexually transmitted disease (STD) screening, and digital examination. For female patients, this includes pelvic examination, STD screening, and specific testing for herpes papillomavirus (HPV) infection.

Obtaining CD4 cell counts and plasma HIV-1 RNA levels are the key to determining where, in the course of the infection, a specific patient is and what needs to be done. The former represents the state of the immune system of a

Table 3.2
Laboratory Tests Requested at Initial HIV Infection Evaluation Visit

Complete blood count (CBC)	Evaluates for anemia, white blood cell count, blood platelets
Blood urea nitrogen, Electolytes, Creatinine, Fasting blood sugar	Evaluates kidney function, blood sugar control
Bilirubin, Alkaline phosphatase, Aspartate aminotransferase	Evaluates liver function
Amylase, Lipase	Evaluates pancreatic status
Serologic tests (Syphilis, Hepatitis A, B, C, Toxoplasmosis, Cytomegalovirus)	Evaluates for prior or latent infections
Pap smear	Evaluates for prior human papillomavirus infection
PPD skin test	Evaluates for infection with tuberculosis bacteria
T-cell Subset	(CD4+ count)
RNA viral load	Measures amount of "free virus" (non-cell bound) in the infected host

Source: Adapted from Hammer, S. M. 2005. Clinical practice. Management of newly diagnosed HIV infection. *N Engl J Med* 353 (16):1702–10.

given patient. It is the way the patient's "disease stage" is determined (Table 3.3) and predicts the patient's susceptibility to opportunistic infections.

The latter test reflects the *viral burden* and the ability of the virus to replicate in spite of the host's immune response and/or medications. There is an increasing call to make resistance testing a regular part of the initial evaluation of patients. Depending on the test used, the genome of the patient's virus is compared to the genomes of viral isolates known to be resistant to certain medications to help identify medications that may be useful and to avoid drugs to which even newly infected patients may already be resistant.

For many patients, the next great decision becomes "when to treat." Since the availability of medications active against HIV, the philosophy as to when to initiate treatment has changed several times. When few medications were available, these medications were often reserved to treat symptomatic patients. As the number of medications increased, a philosophy of "hit hard, hit early" emerged. This approach called for maximal therapy early on with the intent of maintaining the immune system for as long a time as possible. Over time, the negative aspects of being on medications began to emerge. People who were otherwise asymptomatic suddenly felt ill, not because of their infection, but because of side effects of the drugs. Because of dosing schedules, some patients

Table 3.3
Staging of HIV Infection

Stage I:	CD4+ lymphocyte count >500 cells/mm³
	A. Asymptomatic
	B. Non-AIDS defining, but serious infections or health conditions*
	C. AIDS-defining "opportunistic" infections or health conditions**
Stage II:	CD4+ lymphocyte count >200 cells/mm³ but <500 cells/mm³
	A. Asymptomatic
	B. Non-AIDS defining but serious infections or health conditions*
	C. AIDS defining "opportunistic" infections or health conditions**
Stage III:	CD4+ lymphocyte count <200 cells/mm³
	A. Asymptomatic
	B. Non-AIDS defining but serious infections or health conditions*
	C. AIDS-defining "opportunistic" infections or health conditions**

* "B" conditions include, but are not limited to: bacillary angiomatosis, thrush, persistent vulvovaginitis, cervical dysplasia (moderate or severe), diarrhea > 1 month, oral hairy leukoplakia, herpes zoster (second episode or > 1 dermatome), idiopathic thrombocytopenia purpura (ITP), listerosis, pelvic inflammatory disease (especially with tuboovarian abscess), and peripheral neuropathy.

**AIDS-defining opportunistic infections or health conditions: *Candida* infection of esophagus, trachea, bronchi, or lungs; cervical cancer; coccidiomycosis (extrapulmonary); cryptococcosis (extrapulmonary); cytomegalovirus infection, herpes simplex > 1 month duration; histoplasmosis (extrapulmonary); dementia; wasting (weight loss > 10% of baseline); isoporosis; Kaposi's sarcoma; lymphoma; *Mycobacterium avium*; *Mycobacterium tuberculosis*; *Pneumocystis carinii* pneumonia; multifocal leukoencephalopathy; *Salmonella* bloodstream infections; toxoplasmosis.

Source: 1993 revised classification system for HIV infection and expanded surveillance case definition for AIDS among adolescents and adults. 1992. *MMWR Recomm Rep* 41 (RR-17):1–19.

were taking dozens of pills and had to maintain complicated schedules with regard to meals, with some pills needing to be taken with food and others needing to be taken on an empty stomach.

The current recommendations for initiating treatment are listed in Table 3.4.[16] These recommendations now seek to find a middle ground, which will maximize the benefit to patients, while lessening the impact of medication side effects. New medications and reformulation of older drugs now allow most patients to take medications at most twice daily. There are a number of possible therapeutic regimens in which patients need to take medications only once daily.

In addition to antiretroviral medications, many patients whose immune systems have been depressed by chronic or overwhelming HIV infection need to take other types of drugs that help their bodies fight off *opportunistic infections*, that is, infections that occur when the immune system is adversely impacted. The usual measure used to determine when such medications are necessary is once again the CD4 count: the lower the CD4 count, the more likely the occurrence of an opportunistic infection. Table 3.5 lists the infections often

Table 3.4
Current Antiretroviral Medications Useful in Treating HIV Infection

Nucleoside Reverse Transcriptase Inhibitors

Drug Category	Drug Name	Times Daily?
Nucleoside reverse transcription inhibitors (NRTIs)	Zidovudine (AZT)	Twice
	Lamivudine (3TC)	Once or twice
	Stavudine (D4T)	Twice
	Didanosine (DDI)	Once
	Abacavir	Once or twice
	Tenofovir	Once
Nonnucleoside reverse transcription inhibitors (NNRTIs)	Efavirenz	Once
	Nevarapine	Once
Protease inhibitors	Amprenivir	Twice
	Fosamprenivir	Once or twice
	Atazanavir	Once
	Indinavir	Three
	Lopinovir	Once or twice
	Nelfinavir	Twice
	Saquinavir	Twice
	Tipranavir	Twice
	Ritonovir*	Once or twice

*Medication used primary to raise concentrations of other medications.

Source: DHHS 2005 Guidelines for the use of antiretroviral agents in HIV-1-infected adults and adolescents. http://AIDSinfo.nih.gov.

seen in patients with AIDS and the medications suggested to help ward off these infections.[17]

Whether or not the patient is on medications, regular and consistent follow-up monitoring is essential in caring for HIV-infected adolescents. All patients, regardless of their stage of disease, should be seen at least every three months. At the outset of care, we prefer to see patients monthly or more often to help adolescents resolve some of the psychosocial aspects of "being positive." Patients with rapidly changing immune or viral parameters, patients who are symptomatic, and patients recently started on or patients having had a medication change should also be seen within a month. For those patients whose disease has progressed to profound immune suppression or who have experienced a complicated opportunistic infection, we prefer to see these patients weekly.

Even if medications are effective and have a low personal "burden," no regimen can be effective unless the patient takes the medications. Adherence to treatment regimens is the subject of an entire chapter of this book. Currently,

Table 3.5
"Opportunistic" Infections Seen in HIV-Infected Adolescents and Prophylactic Medications Used to Prevent Them

Infection or Health Condition	Indication	Medication
Pneumocystis carinii	CD4+ lymphocytes$<$200/mm^3	Trimethoprim/sulfamethoxazole, dapsone, or atovaquone
Mycobacterium tuberculosis	Positive skin test for TB	Isoniazid
Toxoplasma gondii	CD4+ lymphocytes$<$100/mm^3	Trimethoprim/sulfamethoxazole, dapsone, or atovaquone
Mycobacterium avium	CD4+ lymphocytes$<$100/mm^3	Azithromycin
Varicella	Exposure to someone with chickenpox and no history of prior infection	Varicella immune globulin
Pneumococcal pneumonia	All patients	Pneumococcal vaccine
Influenza	All patients	Influenza vaccine
Hepatitis B	No history of vaccine or prior infection	Hepatitis B vaccine
Hepatitis A	No history of vaccine or prior infection and "risk behaviors"	Hepatitis A vaccine

Source: Kaplan J. E., H. Masur, and K. K. Holmes. 2002. Guidelines for preventing opportunistic infections among HIV-infected persons. http://AIDSinfo.nih.gov.

high levels of adherence are predicted to be necessary to avoid the emergence of "resistant" virus. On the other hand, the drive to reduce side effects has led researchers to investige actually trying regimens that allow patients to omit doses on certain days. These "structured treatment interruptions" are currently being studied in teens and have recently become the source of a fair degree of controversy.

The overall health of HIV-infected adolescents is often better than the health of similarly infected adults. Adolescents retain more undifferentiated immune cells[18] and often have slower progression of illness.[19] The benefits of this for the individual patient are obvious, but the persistence of a growing number of infected persons creates increased risk of infection for heretofore uninfected teens who come into intimate contact with HIV-infected teens. This has led the CDC to initiate prevention programs that focus on infected individuals in an attempt to limit the spread of infection from this group. "Prevention for Positives"[8] seeks to change behaviors in those who can and do serve as the source of infection for others.

MEETING THE "OTHER NEEDS" OF INFECTED TEENS

Although the medical decisions involved in treating adolescents can range from simple and straightforward to complicated and vexing, the psychosocial needs of HIV-infected adolescents can be, and often are, overwhelming. The best systems of care for adolescents take this into account and offer support to help them cope with the myriad of things that can affect their access and use of health services. Depending on the program and its financial underpinnings, these support services can be delivered by peer advocates, case managers, social workers, and/or psychologists. These services can be simple: transportation to visits, meal vouchers, babysitting while seeing providers, and so forth. On the other hand, they can be significantly more complex: family counseling, sex abuse evaluation, adherence support groups, and others. Whatever the services offered, it is always best for these services to be offered at the clinical site itself.

AND WHEN IT'S TIME TO GO

As the care of patients with HIV/AIDS continues to improve, more and more adolescents and young adults will be living longer and longer. This already has and will continue to provide unique challenges to the patients and their care providers. The essence of this challenge is the same thing that challenges most patients who have, or providers who care for, patients with chronic illnesses as they age: where will they next get their care? To date this has not been well studied. Many programs where care for HIV-infected teens is provided have upper age ranges in the 18 to 24 bracket. As patients reach these required limits, they need to be "transitioned" to adult care providers in the community. This is often easier said than done. Many programs have deeply ingrained prejudices against teens. Many are used to dealing with adult patients who are capable of and willing to manage their own illnesses.

Transition to a different source of care is best undertaken in a deliberate but slow manner. We depend on our case managers and social workers to help the patient choose a site of care and to engage in seeking and connecting adolescents and young adults to care. This often means accompanying our patients and also inviting adult providers to see patients with us in our clinical setting. Regardless of the mechanism used, the key is gaining a large degree of trust for the new providers. This can be done, but will take a focused and a committed staff effort.

NOTES

In memory of all the friends I have known and lost who were also treated at NIH. Every time I walk up to the gazebo behind The Children's Inn, the wind blows. There is a plaque there to remember those children who have stayed at the Inn. The poem that opens this chapter was inspired by that plaque and the wind that will continue to blow.

"It's hard enough to find a doctor you want to see. And then I was diagnosed. There was nobody to turn to. The guy who told me was like, 'So you got this, so now you need to go somewhere; you can go to the Clinic. They know how to treat you guys'"

REFERENCES

1. Ginsburg, K. R., G. B. Slap, A. Cnaan, C. M. Forke, C. M. Balsley, and D. M. Rouselle. 1995. Adolescents' perceptions of factors affecting their decisions to seek health care. *JAMA* 273 (24):1913–18.

2. Elster, A. B. 1998. Comparison of recommendations for adolescent clinical preventive services developed by national organizations. *Arch Pediatr Adolesc Med* 152 (2):193–98.

3. Ford, C. A., S. G. Millstein, B. L. Halpern-Felsher, and C. E. Irwin, Jr. 1997. Influence of physician confidentiality assurances on adolescents' willingness to disclose information and seek future health care. A randomized controlled trial. *JAMA* 278 (12):1029–34.

4. Akinbami, L. J., H. Gandhi, and T. L. Cheng. 2003. Availability of adolescent health services and confidentiality in primary care practices. *Pediatrics* 111 (2):394–401.

5. Schuster, M. A., R. M. Bell, L. P. Petersen, and D. E. Kanouse. 1996. Communication between adolescents and physicians about sexual behavior and risk prevention. *Arch Pediatr Adolesc Med* 150 (9):906–13.

6. Halpern-Felsher, B. L., E. M. Ozer, S. G. Millstein, C. J. Wibbelsman, C. D. Fuster, A. B. Elster, and C. E. Irwin, Jr. 2000. Preventive services in a health maintenance organization: How well do pediatricians screen and educate adolescent patients? *Arch Pediatr Adolesc Med* 154 (2):173–79.

7. Blum, R. W., T. Beuhring, M. Wunderlich, and M. D. Resnick. 1996. Don't ask, they won't tell: The quality of adolescent health screening in five practice settings. *Am J Public Health* 86 (12):1767–72.

8. Advancing HIV prevention: New strategies for a changing epidemic—United States, 2003. *MMWR Morb Mortal Wkly Rep* 52 (15):329–32.

9. Grunbaum, J.A., L. Kann, S. Kinchen, J. Ross, J. Hawkins, R. Lowry, W. A. Harris, T. McManus, D. Chyen, and J. Collins. 2004. Youth risk behavior surveillance—United States, 2003. *MMWR Surveill Summ* 53 (2):1–96.

10. Warner, D. L. and R. A. Hatcher. 1994. A meta-analysis of condom effectiveness in reducing sexually transmitted HIV. *Soc Sci Med* 38 (8):1169–70.

11. Royce, R. A., A. Sena, W. Cates, Jr., and M. S. Cohen. 1997. Sexual transmission of HIV. *N Engl J Med* 336 (15):1072–78.

12. Varghese, B., J. E. Maher, T. A. Peterman, B. M. Branson, and R. W. Steketee. 2002. Reducing the risk of sexual HIV transmission: quantifying the per-act risk for HIV on the basis of choice of partner, sex act, and condom use. *Sex Transm Dis* 29 (1):38–43.

13. Hawkins K. B. and L. J. D'Angelo. 2005. "I was born with this?" Missed perinatal transmission of HIV infection in adolescents. *J Adolesc Health* 36(2):128.

14. D'Angelo, L. J., S. E. Abdalian, M. Sarr, N. Hoffman, and M. Belzer. 2001. Disclosure of serostatus by HIV infected youth: the experience of the REACH study. Reaching for Excellence in Adolescent Care and Health. *J Adolesc Health* 29 (3 Suppl):72–79.

15. English, A. and K. E. Kenney. 2003. *State minor consent laws: A summary* (2nd ed). Chapel Hill, NC: Center for Adolescent Health and Law.

16. DHHS. 2005. Guidelines for the use of antiretroviral agents in HIV-1-infected adults and adolescents. http://AIDSinfo.nih.gov.

17. Kaplan J. E., H. Masur, and K. K. Holmes. 2002. Guidelines for preventing opportunistic infections among HIV-infected persons. http://AIDSinfo.nih.gov.

18. Douglas, S. D., B. Rudy, L. Muenz, S. E. Starr, D. E. Campbell, C. Wilson, C. Holland, P. Crowley-Nowick, and S. H. Vermund. 2000. T-lymphocyte subsets in HIV-infected and high-risk HIV-uninfected adolescents: Retention of naive T lymphocytes in HIV-infected adolescents. The Adolescent Medicine HIV/AIDS Research Network. *Arch Pediatr Adolesc Med* 154 (4):375–80.

19. Goedert, J. J., C. M. Kessler, L. M. Aledort, R. J. Biggar, W. A. Andes, G. C. White, 2nd, J. E. Drummond, K. Vaidya, D. L. Mann, M. E. Eyster, and et al. 1989. A prospective study of human immunodeficiency virus type 1 infection and the development of AIDS in subjects with hemophilia. *N Engl J Med* 321 (17):1141–48.

Chapter 4

ADHERENCE TO MEDICATIONS FOR HIV: TEENS SAY, "TOO MANY, TOO BIG, TOO OFTEN"

Linda J. Koenig, Ph.D. and Pamela J. Bachanas, Ph.D.

Lindsay, Lindsay Is Sick in Bed

By Lindsay, 05/05/96

Chimi, chimi cocoa puffs, chimi chimi rye
Chimi, chimi cocoa puffs, chimi chimi rye
Lindsay, Lindsay is sick in bed.
She called the doctor and the doctor said
I've got the HIV virus (ding dong)
I've got the HIV virus (clap)
I've got the HIV virus (stamp your feet)
I've got to take a lot of medicine (ding dong)
I've got to take a lot of pills (stamp your feet)
I've got to take a lot of nasty stuff (clap)
Let's get the rhythm of the virus
Let's get the rhythm of the virus.
Put it all together and what do you got
Pills, medicine, virus, infection
Ding dong, clap, stamp, high dong
HIV gone, stamp, HIV gone.

Not long ago, the outlook for someone with HIV was poor. For many, HIV quickly progressed to the disease called AIDS and from there to death. But this changed in 1996, when powerful drugs to treat HIV became available. Combinations of these drugs are taken in a complex treatment plan called highly active antiretroviral therapy (HAART). HAART has helped many HIV-infected persons live relatively normal lives. When taken properly, HAART has markedly decreased the illness and death caused by HIV and has slowed or halted the progression from HIV infection to AIDS.[1,2] According to the Centers for Disease Control and Prevention, deaths from AIDS declined sharply between 1996 and 1997 (right after HAART became available) and then continued to decline each year through 2001. For people younger than 45 years, these gains continued through 2003.[3,4] From 1995 to 2002, people with AIDS began living longer; the later the year of diagnosis, the longer the survival times.[4]

Despite these successes and the widespread availability of HAART in the United States, many people have been unable to reap its full benefits. The reasons are complex but relate primarily to the challenging nature of the treatment itself combined with the unique features of HIV disease and the social context in which it exists.

In this chapter, we focus on the challenges of adherence to HAART. Adherence means taking the drugs exactly as prescribed, that is, taking every dose at the exact time it is to be taken, taking each dose in the exact way it is to be taken (e.g., on an empty stomach or with high-fat food), and storing the drugs properly (i.e., refrigerating them or not). We then discuss what makes adherence to HAART particularly difficult for teenagers. We describe the psychological and social developmental processes that may interfere with teens' adherence, and we present suggestions and strategies for helping teens adhere to their treatment plans. We end with a discussion of what is new and what we can look forward to in this rapidly evolving field.

WHY IS ADHERENCE TO HAART SO DIFFICULT?

Adhering to HAART is hard for many reasons. First, there are many pills to take (often a dozen or more), and they must be taken many times during the day. If the pills have special food requirements (i.e., need to be taken with or without food) and timing requirements (i.e., need to be taken at a certain time of the day), the number of dosing times per day is increased even more.[5] Second, HAART can cause debilitating side effects including nausea, diarrhea, and a general rundown feeling (called malaise). What makes it hard to deal with these side effects is that they are often prescribed before the person even has any symptoms of HIV disease; therefore people sometimes feel worse after taking HAART than before starting it.[6] If they start skipping doses, they start to feel better again, which makes it hard for them to justify continuing the therapy. Third, some people are afraid to take their medications in public for fear that doing so will reveal that they have HIV. Having HIV still carries stigma, especially for teens, who are concerned about how they are perceived in social situations and about being rejected by their peers. Consequently, if they need to be out in public, some people will not take their medications or even carry their pills with them. Last, a disproportionate number of people with HIV/AIDS are already struggling with a number of social burdens such as poverty, violence, homelessness, discrimination, substance abuse, and mental health problems. People dealing with such social stressors may not consider treatment for HIV to be their highest priority.[7] Studies have shown that people are less likely to adhere to HAART if they do not have much education, live in poor or unstable housing, do not have health insurance, or are substance abusers.[8–10] Being homeless or living in transitional housing does not mean that a person won't adhere to HAART,[11] but it does make it more difficult to take pills on a regular basis.

WHY IS ADHERENCE TO HAART SO CRITICAL?

To understand why adherence is such a critical issue in HIV treatment, it is important to understand how the virus works and how the drugs work. The virus works by attacking CD4 (or T-helper) cells. These cells usually help protect the body against infection, so when these cells are attacked by the virus, the immune system loses its ability to fight infection or becomes deficient (hence, the name *human immunodeficiency virus)*. The virus then uses CD4 cells to replicate (make copies of) itself, producing a large number of viral copies. The number of viral copies in a person's blood is called *viral load* and is another measure of that person's stage of HIV infection. Viral load can be used to predict what may happen to that person in terms of disease course and survival time.

The drugs used to treat HIV act in two ways. First, they minimize the virus replication process—in the best case, to a number of viral copies too low to be detected by current laboratory tests (called an undetectable viral load). Second, they reduce destruction of CD4 cells, allowing the immune system to work better and slowing the progression of disease. HAART includes drugs from several different classes: nucleoside reverse transcriptase inhibitors (NRTIs), non-nucleoside reverse transcriptase inhibitors (NNRTIs), and protease inhibitors (PIs).

It is necessary to take all three types of drugs because each one acts on a different stage in the replication process of the virus. If all three drugs are not taken in combination, more CD4 cells can be destroyed or more viral copies can be produced. Also, every missed dose gives the virus a chance to undergo changes (called mutations) that make it resistant to certain classes of drugs. When this happens, HAART will no longer work and viral load will increase. When a whole class of drugs stops working against HIV, a patient's options for future therapy can become limited. It is easy to see how poor adherence to HAART can affect not only the health of the person who is not adhering but also the health of others as resistant strains of HIV are passed on to them.[12,13]

Fortunately, new drugs, called fusion inhibitors, are being approved. And new HAART regimens (combinations of drugs and dosing schedules) are available, although the likelihood of a long-lasting response decreases every time the HAART regimen is changed.[14]

HOW WELL DO PEOPLE ADHERE TO HAART?

First let's ask how strictly a person needs to adhere to HAART in order for it to work. The answer is—very strictly. One of the cruel ironies of HAART is that not only is it hard to take exactly as prescribed, but it is also unforgiving of error. For HAART to work, it requires near perfect (95%) adherence. Compare this to treatment for other chronic diseases, in which 80% adherence (e.g., taking four of every five doses) is good enough. For HAART to work (i.e., to keep the virus from replicating), patients must take 95% or more of their prescribed doses.[15] This is not to say that less-than-perfect adherence will not do any good,[16] but studies have shown that the more adherence drops below this level, the less likely it is that viral load will be controlled.[15] Excellent explanations of HIV disease, treatment, and adherence can be found at the following Web sites: www.thebody.com, www.aidsinfo.nih.gov; www.projinf.org, and www.who/int/chronic_conditions/adherencereport/en/.

Now that we've established that 95% adherence to HAART is crucial, let's examine how well people are actually doing. In the AIDS Clinical Trial Group, where these combination drug treatments were first tested, average adherence ranged from 73% to 89%.[17] It is important to note that eligibility for this study was highly selective, resulting in an exceptionally motivated and adherent group of participants. In general clinic settings, rates as low as 67% have been found, even among patients who are relatively well educated and of moderate income.[18] In clinics serving a high proportion of indigent patients, average adherence ranged from 73% to 89%.[17]

It is also important to note that those who have the most trouble adhering may be those most likely to quit therapy altogether. For example, one study at an inner-city clinic serving a mostly indigent population found that 27% of patients starting their first HAART regimen dropped out of clinic care within the first 6 months of treatment.[19] In a study of people who had marginal or no housing, 31% stopped taking HAART during the 12-month follow-up period. Of those who quit, adherence at the last check was only 51%, compared with 74% for those who continued taking HAART.[11]

Adherence is a dynamic behavior, which means it changes over time in response to different individual and social circumstances.[20] Even those who do a good job of adhering at one point in time may not do so well at another. This has been shown in the Treatment Adherence Demonstration Project. At the beginning of the study, 35% reported being nonadherent (nonperfect adherence over the past three days), but at one of the three assessments over the next six months, as many as 54% reported being nonadherent.[21]

To again stress the importance of adherence for maintaining health, we mention one report comparing adherence and viral load. In this study, at each of four follow up visits, participants reported their adherence to HAART. Of those who reported adherence at all four visits, a higher percentage had a nondetectable viral load. As the number of follow-up visits at which participants reported adherence decreased, the number with a nondetectable viral load also decreased. Specifically, of those who reported adherence at all four follow-up visits, 72% had a nondetectable viral load; of those reporting adherence at three visits 66% had a nondetectable viral load; of those reporting adherence at two visits, 41% had a nondetectable viral load; of those reporting adherence at one visit, 35% had a nondetectable viral load; and of those reporting adherence at no visits, 13% had a nondetectable viral load.[22]

HOW WELL DO YOUTH ADHERE TO HAART?

Challenging enough for adults, adherence to HAART may be even more challenging for youth. A number of studies confirm that adherence to HAART is quite low among youth who acquired HIV as a result of their own behaviors (sex or drug use), as opposed to acquiring it from their mothers or a medical procedure. One study of 23 HIV infected teens, ages 13 to 21, just before and soon after HAART became available (1993–1998) indicated that although 78% of teens had been prescribed drugs for their HIV, only 28% were adherent. In this case, adherence was determined by clinician note that the patient reported having missed one or more weeks of medication or reported on two or more visits missing their medication schedule.[23] In another small study, this one of 31 teens and young adults ages 15 through 24 years, only 58% were 90% adherent (that is, took at least 90% of their prescribed doses); the proportion adherent increased to 87% when the definition of *adherence* was expanded to include those who took at least 75% of their doses. In a larger sample of 85 substance-abusing teens and young adults ages 16 to 29 years who had been prescribed HAART, only 61% reported having taken at least 90% of their medications over the last three days.[24]

Confirming the findings from these small to moderate-size samples are those from a large study done by the National Institute of Child Health and Human Development. This study, called REACH (Reaching for Excellence in Adolescent Care and Health), examined HIV-infected youth, ages 12 to 19 years, who acquired HIV as a result of behavior and who were receiving care at 16 locations in 13 U.S. cities. Among 161 HIV-infected youth who were prescribed HAART, 7% could not correctly identify the names of the drugs or how often they were to take them. Another 11% reported that they never took at least one of their drugs. Although 83% reported that they took all of their medicines at least some of the time, only 50% of these teens were fully adherent (i.e., took most or all of their medicines over the past month). Thus, of the entire study sample, only 41% of teens reported that they had taken most or all of their doses during the past month.[25] Later, the REACH investigators used a larger sample of 231 HIV-infected youth and found that 69% had been adherent during the past month.[26] Using a more strict definition of *full adherence,* the REACH investigators reported that only 28.3% reported having missed no doses during the past month.[27]

For teens, perhaps an even larger issue than missing doses is not taking any at all. Although we don't have much information on exactly what proportion of teens are prescribed HAART, it does appear that most are offered it and a large proportion have tried taking it. One study of mostly (70%) male adolescents and young adults ages 14 to 29 showed that 84% had been offered HAART and that 77% had tried it.[28]

Studies have also shown the difficulty teens have with continuing to take their HAART medications. A study of substance-abusing adolescents and young adults showed that only 50% were taking HAART at the start of the study although most had taken some type of antiretroviral therapy during their lifetime.[29] In the Adolescents Living with HIV/AIDS (Alpha) study of 59 adolescents and young adults (ages 14 to 24) who had received a diagnosis of HIV during their teen years, 58% had tried taking HAART, but only 32% were taking it at the time of the assessment. Among those who had ever taken any type of antiretroviral therapy (HAART or other), 47% had stopped taking it by 6 months, and 74% by 12 months. Of those who stopped, 79% had not restarted by the time of the study.[30]

We have limited data about teens' adherence to HAART over time. We do know, however, that it is exceptionally difficult for teens to keep taking their medications. The REACH study examined 65 participants who were adherent at the start of the study (reporting that they took most or all of their medications during the past month) and who attended at least four consecutive follow-up visits (every three months). The average time for these youth to become nonadherent was 12 months. Moreover, over a 12-month period, of the 35 participants whose viral load was undetectable at the start, viral load increased to a detectable level for 17 (48.5%), and the increases were significantly correlated with self-reported adherence to HAART.[26] Similar findings emerged from a study of 55 substance-abusing teens and young adults. Participants were significantly less likely to be taking HAART after 15 months; of those who had been taking HAART at the start of the study, 50% were no longer taking it. The same study showed that only 13% of those who had not been taking HAART when the study began had started it at the 15-month follow-up visit.[29]

WHAT KEEPS TEENS FROM ADHERING TO HAART?

For teenagers with any chronic illness, adhering to treatment is particularly challenging, for developmental and psychosocial reasons. Developmentally, teens often feel invincible, immortal, like they are living in the moment, and not realizing the long-term consequences of their actions.[31] Treatment for HIV presents additional challenges. Most teens who were infected as a result of their behavior may be prescribed therapy before they have any symptoms or feel sick. There are no incentives for them to adhere because the medications don't make them feel better, and they often feel worse. Similarly, they don't feel any worse if they stop taking or inconsistently take their medications; this lack of immediate negative consequences reinforces their feeling of invincibility. In addition, unpleasant side effects may play into their tendencies to make short-term choices, such as stopping their medications after a few days or weeks. Helping teens focus on the long-term health consequences of their choices is a significant challenge for providers, counselors, and teens' support systems.

Psychosocial, mental health, and substance-use problems, common among youth with HIV, may also make it difficult for teens to adhere to HAART.[32] In studies comparing demographically and socially similar youth with and without HIV infection, those with HIV infection were significantly more likely to have been sexually abused, to have practiced unprotected sex with casual partners, to have had sex under the influence of drugs, to have engaged in anal sex and sex for money, to have had another sexually transmitted disease, and to have used several different kinds of illicit drugs. HIV-infected youth also have multiple problem behaviors and consequences, including incarceration, psychiatric hospitalization, dropping out of school, and not living at home.[33–37] In one study of HIV-infected youth, 53% had had a diagnosis of psychiatric illness before their HIV diagnosis, and 82% reported having used substances. Also, 85% met criteria for a current psychiatric diagnosis, and 44% met criteria for a depressive disorder.[38] High rates of emotional disturbance (e.g., significant levels of depression [27%] and anxiety [34%]) and substance use (e.g., alcohol [70%] and marijuana [59%]) were reported in a sample of newly infected teens.[33] High rates of substance use (63% alcohol, 41% marijuana, 36% hard drugs [e.g., cocaine, heroin]) were found in another study.[39] These factors place HIV-infected youth at significant risk for psychological adjustment problems: developing new ones, continuing with current problems, or worsening existing problems.

Chronic substance use and mental health issues have been shown to make it hard for HIV-infected adolescents and adults to obtain regular medical care and adhere to medication regimens.[25,40,41] For example, for REACH participants, depression and substance use were significantly associated with decreased adherence, both during the time period in which the participant was depressed and using substances, as well as later.[25,26] These findings highlight the importance of assessing teens' emotional and behavioral functioning, as well as their coping strategies, when making a treatment plan.

Fiona*

Fiona is a 19-year-old African American woman who received a diagnosis of HIV shortly after giving birth to her daughter. She was very good about showing up for HIV clinic appointments for both herself and her baby. Neither her daughter nor her daughter's father was infected with HIV. Fiona had a low CD4 count and high viral load and was prescribed HAART after completing the clinic's education protocol with the nurse practitioner. When Fiona was seen by the clinic psychologist for an initial evaluation, she was tearful, sad, depressed, and admitted to having suicidal thoughts. However, she stated that she would not act on those thoughts because she needed to be around to care for her daughter. Fiona continued to show symptoms of depression (poor sleep, loss of interest in outside activities, weight gain, depressed mood, etc.) at subsequent visits. She also admitted to taking less than 50% of her HAART because she couldn't tolerate the side effects and would forget many of her doses.

After consultation with the nurse practitioner, it was agreed that Fiona would stop taking HAART at that time because she was more likely creating viral resistance than effectively treating her HIV disease. After two months of therapy sessions, Fiona agreed to take medication for her depression. Within three to four weeks, she began to feel noticeably better, her mood improved, she felt more energetic, she was crying less, and she felt better about trying to cope with her HIV diagnosis. Fiona continued to attend therapy sessions once or twice a month, where she slowly began the painful journey of coming to terms with her HIV diagnosis and its effects on her new family. Fiona's boyfriend was supportive and remained with Fiona and her baby throughout her journey. Fiona realized that she was not ready to cope with the magnitude of her illness and its potential implications for her and her daughter's future, much less embrace her treatment.

With the help of medication and counseling, Fiona was able to work through some of these issues, get some relief from her depression, and get to a stronger place where she could more firmly commit to taking HAART and adhering closely to her regimen. Her next attempt to take HAART was many months

---

* The details of cases have been changed to protect the identity of individuals.

later, but this time she was much more successful, as she was feeling both emotionally and physically stronger and better able to cope with the challenges of taking HAART.

Managing a life-threatening and socially stigmatized illness is emotionally difficult and challenging for adults. It is even more difficult for adolescents, who are more vulnerable and less prepared to deal with a health crisis of this magnitude, much less deal with it alone. Having peers' acceptance and support is perhaps more important during adolescence than during any other developmental period. Yet because they fear rejection, abandonment, and stigma, many teens do not tell their family, friends, or partners of their HIV status. This may explain why many HIV-infected adolescents in the Alpha study reported that no one reminded them of (25%) or brought or accompanied them to (53%) their clinic appointments.[30] Many teens avoid treatment and care, fearing it will expose their HIV status; they cope with their illness without support of friends or family. This is particularly concerning, especially in light of several studies that have shown that HIV-infected persons who have better social support adhere better to medications and clinic appointments.[28,42,43] Moreover, HIV-infected youth may be alienated from or abandoned by their families as a result of their sexual identity or HIV status. For example, 54% of Alpha study participants did not live with their parents.[30] Unstable or inconsistent housing is common; teens frequently move between the homes of their family members and partners. This instability makes it difficult for them to keep appointments, pick up medications before they run out, and adhere correctly to HAART.[23] Further, it often renders efforts by clinics (e.g., reminder calls, letters) unsuccessful, as contact information changes. In addition, teens who have not told people they are living with that they have HIV find it difficult to keep medications around and remember to take them regularly while at the same time trying to hide them.

Jane

Jane is an 18-year-old African American woman who received a diagnosis of HIV while pregnant. Her baby boy, Robert, was diagnosed with HIV infection shortly after he was born, and both mother and child received care in the adolescent and pediatric HIV clinics. Jane and her son lived with her mother, Josephine. Jane felt certain that if Josephine learned of her and Robert's HIV status, she would put them out of her house, leaving them nowhere to go. In addition, she felt ashamed of her own diagnosis and scared and sad for her son who would also have to live with this illness. Jane decided while still in the hospital that she would wait to tell her mother until she felt better prepared to deal with her and Robert's situation. Robert was soon placed on medications, which Jane explained to her mother were for treatment of sickle cell disease.

Josephine was helpful with the baby and helped give him his medication. Jane refused medication for herself, as she was not ready to tell her mother that she had HIV.

Jane and Robert were seen somewhat regularly for follow-up evaluation; however, it was noted that Jane always seemed sad and withdrawn during the clinic visits. When questioned about her coping and emotional functioning, Jane admitted to being depressed but refused any intervention. Further, she resisted multiple attempts by clinic staff to encourage her to disclose her status to her mother or another family member for support. Jane continued to struggle with coming to terms with her and her son's diagnoses and illnesses alone, which perpetuated her feelings of isolation, sadness, and depression.

During Jane's clinic visits, a peer counselor began talking with her about her situation. Over time, Jane began to open up to this person and shared her feelings of shame, loneliness, sadness, and alienation. The peer counselor was able to tell Jane how she told her own mother that she had HIV and how her mother was much more supportive than she had predicted. In addition, the counselor told Jane how important it had been to be able to confide in one or two close friends or family members. Over the next year, Jane slowly gathered the courage to tell her mother about the HIV. She was in noticeably better spirits during subsequent clinic visits and was clearly coping much better with her situation with the love and support of a family member. Further, her mother allowed them to remain in her home and began attending Robert's clinic visits with her.

Youth with HIV tend to have less structured and more chaotic schedules than adults, with both school and work, making adherence more challenging. Further, youth may not want to (and in some school situations, may not be allowed to) carry their medications with them at school or work (and must come to a nurse to get medications). Other teens do not work or attend school and have no set routine, which also makes adherence challenging. In the Alpha study, only 50% of adolescents under age 19 were attending school, and less than a third of those over age 19 were attending a GED program, vocational training, or college program. Similarly, only 20% of teens reported working full or part time.[30] In studies of why teens have trouble adhering, reasons for missing medication doses were "forgot," "had a change in daily routine," "busy with other things," and "slept through the dose.[24,27,44] Teens who do not link taking their medications with regular daily activities clearly have a lot of trouble adhering to their regimens and need extra help coming up with strategies for taking their medications on schedule.

Marcus

Marcus is an 18-year-old African American man who received an HIV diagnosis when he was 15. Marcus's mother has a long history of chronic substance abuse, and Marcus has lived with other family members (grandmother, aunts, sisters, cousins) most of his life. He dropped out of school shortly after learning his HIV diagnosis, as he felt that he no longer fit in. Marcus reported that he plans to get his GED; however, he has not made any progress toward taking the prep classes or the test. Since joining the adolescent HIV clinic shortly after his diagnosis, Marcus has had two jobs, from which he was soon (two to four weeks) fired. He said that he has trouble getting along with his supervisors. Marcus moves between family members' homes every two to three months. When asked why he moves so frequently, he says that he gets "tired" of living where he is, or his family gets "tired" of having him live there. Marcus also says that he frequently stays with friends, although he is vague about telling the clinic staff who his friends are, and he cannot be contacted when there.

After several years of going to the clinic, Marcus's doctor recommended that he begin HAART. Marcus agreed and said that he was ready to begin medications because he didn't want to become ill. However, Marcus faced many barriers, such as having no health insurance or money to pay for the medications and having to apply for and wait to qualify for the Ryan White public drug assistance program. Once Marcus began the medications, he had significant side effects and felt very ill. Being ill was difficult for him because many of his family members that he lived with did not know his diagnosis and did not understand why he was so sick. After he got through this initial period, he continued to struggle to take his medicines on schedule. Because he did not work or go to school, his daily schedule was unpredictable and often erratic. He would frequently stay up all night, sleep through doses of his medication, and forget to take them when he did get up. Given that he would often stay over at a friend's house, he was often without his medication and would miss doses in the evening or morning. Sometimes he would stay away from home for several days without his medication and miss several days of doses. Marcus would not plan ahead and would often run out of his medication before he could get it refilled. He would also call the clinic social worker and report that he did not have transportation or bus fare to get to the clinic to get refills. Marcus's family was often neither supportive nor helpful, as they either did not know his status and its importance, or they felt that he was not contributing financially to the household and they were not willing to give him money. Further, Marcus did not have a steady partner or friend that he confided in for support, so he was dealing with his HIV on his own.

Like many other young people coping with this disease, Marcus made several attempts to take HAART and had difficulty adhering consistently each time. Despite understanding the magnitude of his illness and the importance of treating it before he became too ill, Marcus had a great deal of difficulty adapting his chaotic and unstructured lifestyle to the complex schedules and commitment needed to treat his HIV disease.

HOW CAN WE IMPROVE ADHERENCE?

Researchers and clinicians have learned a lot about the challenges patients face when trying to adhere to HAART and are working to find strategies to help them. Although adhering to the strategies can be difficult, many teens do find ways to take their medication and are experiencing the health benefits. Whether teen or adult, the first step to beginning therapy is getting ready to work taking medication into one's life. Readiness is not easily defined, but it generally involves preparing oneself cognitively, emotionally, motivationally, socially, and structurally to make the changes needed.[45]

Education is a key aspect of readiness. It is critically important that patients understand the nature of HIV disease—how the virus copies itself and how disease progression is measured—and how medications work. Patients need to understand what each class of medicine does, or at least that each plays a role in interrupting the replication process, so that they understand why one drug—perhaps the one that is most inconvenient or associated with the worse side effects—cannot be skipped. It is also important that patients understand the need for near-perfect adherence and the meaning of resistance. These issues are critical, particularly for teens whose lifestyle, circumstances, or social environment may not be structured enough to make it easy to take medication regularly. Unless they can maintain a certain level of adherence, some patients may be better off not taking medications at all. These patients may be better off waiting until they are more likely to achieve full adherence, so that they can avoid resistance and ensure that the medicines are available to work for them later. These concepts can be quite difficult to grasp and should be explained in their simplest form using a variety of techniques and materials (e.g., using pictures and analogies in addition to verbal and written explanations) to accommodate different learning styles and literacy levels.[46] Many clinics have developed education protocols that teens must complete before beginning medications, including educational materials and a test that must be completed with a nurse educator or a required number of appointments that must be kept.

A good patient-provider relationship is essential for good adherence. Trust is the foundation for all patient-provider interactions, but it is especially important when selecting a patient's first regimen.[47] Open communication helps the provider identify the regimen with a dosing schedule that best suits the patient's lifestyle. It also allows patients to feel comfortable telling their provider about any trouble they have adhering to the schedule. Good communication will help the provider consider possible solutions, for example, suggesting medications to combat side effects or changing the regimen to allow for different dosing times. Because youth may view providers as authority figures and have difficulty standing up to them or disagreeing with them, it often takes a lot of work on the part of the health care team to empower adolescents to be proactive and have an open relationship with their providers.

Before beginning HAART, patients should discuss with their provider their daily activities, both weekdays and weekends, so that a dosing schedule can be tailored for them. Scheduling doses near a recurring activity will limit forgetting. A trial run using a medication surrogate (e.g., M&M's, jelly beans, vitamins) is sometimes useful. Each dose of the surrogate should be recorded along with any difficulties encountered while taking it. Based on this trial run, a list of anticipated problems can be developed and strategies designed to overcome them. Preparation for taking one's first regimen is important; those who have never taken antiretroviral medication have the best chances for a positive response and lasting improvement.[48] It is also important to continue to talk about the identified problems (barriers) and strategies, as new barriers will emerge over time. Issues that affect initial adherence may be quite different from those that affect long-term adherence.[19]

As previously described, many HIV-infected adolescents are socially isolated from families and friends. Readiness for HAART also involves accepting and coming to grips with a disease that is still potentially fatal and carries tremendous social stigma. This can be particularly difficult for teens, not only because of their young age and developing cognitive capacity, but because many have yet to come to grips with issues such as sexual identity, disinterested or abusive parents, and substance abuse. These issues, which put them at risk for HIV in the first place, must be confronted in the process of accepting their HIV diagnosis.[49] Some programs encourage patients to identify a treatment buddy who will accompany them to their clinic visits, go through the education process with them, and remind them to take their medicines and keep their appointments.[50] Support groups can be helpful, allowing teens to talk about what works in terms of taking medication and telling others that they have HIV. Group members can support each other outside of the group, volunteering to call each other for encouragement and support during difficult times. Support groups reduce isolation and stigma for many teens, as they realize they are not the only ones struggling with these issues.

Adherence counseling and medical treatment for youth with HIV must be part of a more comprehensive system of care that includes mental health and social services. Individual counseling is helpful for teens less comfortable discussing their issues or concerns in a group or for teens needing more one-on-one help coming up with problem-solving strategies. Individual therapy is recommended for teens with more serious mental health or substance abuse issues. Social work services are needed for teens with legal, financial, educational, or housing issues.

WHAT ARE SOME ADHERENCE INTERVENTION PROGRAMS FOR YOUTH?

To date, only four adherence interventions designed for HIV-infected youth have been described: TREAT (Therapeutic Regimens Enhancing Adherence in Teens), a pilot program using peer groups, Adolescent Impact, and Teens Linked to Care.

TREAT is an eight-week intervention based on the stages of change model.[51,52] It was designed to prepare teens who had never taken medication for their HIV to successfully take HAART. People must first be willing to recognize a problem before they can think about it and then prepare to make the behavioral changes needed. The TREAT program identifies a teen's stage of readiness and focuses interventions on that stage to get the teen to the action stage in which they begin taking HAART. The program was well received by the 79 young participants, and the materials helped program staff successfully identify each teen's stage of readiness. However, among youth not eligible for the TREAT program because they were already taking HAART, 40% were found to be at stages of readiness that did not match with their treatment status. Thus it is important that teens not be denied access to medications because they do not meet readiness criteria. Evaluation of the program, however, showed that, for teens who received the full TREAT intervention, the activities helped them move through the early stages, and most began treatment with HAART.[49]

The next two programs used teen peer groups to improve adherence. The first program is the only intervention to involve family members. It combined peer groups (7–8 youth participants) with groups for family members or a treatment buddy (14–16 participants). Participants discussed things like the dynamics of HIV, why they should take therapy, how to manage side effects, and how to communicate with doctors. Most (78%) of the 23 participants completed the 12-week intervention, and 91% reported increased adherence. Four had improved immune functioning at six-month follow up evaluation, and two of four participants who had not been taking any medication began taking HAART. Participants said that what they gained most from the group were connectedness and decreased isolation. The second program, called Adolescent Impact, combines peer group sessions with one-on-one counseling sessions (12 sessions altogether) to improve adherence and reduce sexual transmission risk.[53] The clinical trial evaluating this intervention is still in progress, so outcome data are not yet available, but reports indicate that patient satisfaction with the groups is high.[54] Among 81 youth infected either by their mother (perinatally infected) or as a result of their behavior, average attendance at the seven group sessions was 71%, which is high for this hard-to-engage population; most (57%) reported that it was the groups (as opposed to the individual sessions) that were most likely to help them take care of their HIV.[55]

The fourth intervention, a modification of the group-based intervention, called Teens Linked to Care (TLC), is the only adherence intervention to be have been evaluated in a clinical trial. Because of poor attendance, the effective TLC intervention[56] was modified to be delivered as one-to-one counseling, offered either in person or by phone, for teens and young adults. Six of 18 sessions addressed health improvement including taking, and improving adherence to, antiretroviral therapy (an issue not as important during the original TLC, which began before HAART was available). Although the intervention had a positive effect on decreasing risk behaviors, it did not seem to improve medication use or adherence.[29]

HOW CAN TECHNOLOGY IMPROVE ADHERENCE?

For adults and adolescents, the number one reason for missed medications is forgetting.[5,57,58] Numerous tools and devices—low tech and high tech—are available to help patients; some may fit better into a patient's lifestyle than others. Dosette pillboxes enable patients to organize medications into compartments for specified times of the day or week. Pharmacies can also bundle each day's medications into blister packs, which groups together all of the doses for each day or each week so the patient doesn't have to do it. A quick glance at the container will show patients whether all of their doses have been taken that day. Similarly, the MEMS® cap—a pill bottle monitoring device that uses microprocessor technology to record each time the bottle is opened—has a version called Smart Cap. In addition to tracking bottle openings, Smart Cap gives patients two cues to improve adherence: number of times the bottle was opened that day and number of hours since it was last opened. These types of cues help the patient know whether a dose is due or whether all doses have been taken for that day.[50]

Programmed beepers, alarm watches, and pagers[58,59] are popular. Of five devices offered to teens (i.e., dosette pillboxes, dummy beepers, calendars, wristwatches with multiple alarms, and gym bags [presumably to hide medications]), youth chose the multiple alarm watch as the best device for improving adherence.[58] Many youth, however, don't want a beeper going off in public, drawing attention and risking questions that could lead to people finding out that they have HIV. As high-tech electronics become more common in the world of teens, however, adherence reminders can be discretely embedded in commonly used devices. For example, teens in the Adolescent Impact study

are given a Palm Zire™ personal digital assistant on which On-Time RX®
software is loaded.[60] In addition to giving password-protected reminders for
dosing times, it also reminds patients of remaining doses and refill times,
maintains a log of how the patient responded to the alarm (that is, took or
didn't take that dose), and stores personal health data and medical appointments. Moreover, using similar technology, On-Call RX® works with cell
phones—commonly used by teens—allowing patients to send and discretely
receive reminders in the form of text messages, numeric pages, or emails.
More information on this device is available at http://www.ontimerx.com/
mobile/index.asp.

WHAT'S NEW?

Teens present unique legal and ethical challenges for providers. Some laws
allow teens to obtain diagnosis and treatment for sexually transmitted infections without parental consent. The specifics of these laws vary from state to
state but are in place to encourage youth to seek treatment. Many youth get
tested for HIV and receive care and treatment under such laws, and some
providers may feel quite uncomfortable treating adolescents for a disease of
such magnitude without having some family member involved. Given the
importance of social support, special attention must be given to finding other
sources of support, providing assistance in disclosing to parents and other
family members, and addressing these complicated scenarios.

Although the focus of this chapter has been on teens infected as a result
of their behavior, a large number of youth who got their infection from their
mother (perinatally infected) are now surviving into adolescence.[61] There are
not many published reports about how well perinatally infected teens adhere
to HAART, but anecdotal reports indicate that adherence is also quite challenging for these long-term survivors. To date, few adherence-related counseling programs or interventions have served both perinatally and behaviorally
infected youth, but combining them may become more common as more perinatally infected teens are seen in adolescent HIV clinics.

Adherence has become a central issue in HIV care, not only because it is
linked to survival but because it has implications for other aspects of health.
Because risk for mother-to-child transmission is lowest when an HIV-infected
pregnant woman's viral load is low,[62] adherence to medication for pregnant
teens will be critical for the baby's health, as well as their own. In addition,
because risk for sexual transmission of HIV appears to be reduced when viral
load is low,[63] adherence is likely to become a more important aspect of prevention counseling.

HIV treatment itself is rapidly changing, and recent advances have dramatically simplified many of the regimens. Guidelines for medication use

and selection are updated regularly (found at www.aidsinfo.com) and contain information about a regimen's simplicity, as well as its strength. Twice daily dosing is now possible for most patients, and even some once-a-day combinations are widely available.[64] These regimens make adherence easier, but they may increase the negative effects of a single missed dose.[65] At the same time, recommendations for when to start therapy have also been evolving. Whereas once the motto was an aggressive "hit early, hit hard," current guidelines suggest a more cautious approach, as clinicians balance the positive effects of HAART with issues of tolerance, complications associated with long-term use, and preservation of future treatment options. Thus, although simpler regimens may lead to greater adherence among teens, it is unclear whether concern about long-term use may ultimately lead to more decisions to wait before beginning HAART. Nevertheless, options for treating and managing HIV disease are growing, and with them are the prospects for improved health and increased quality of life for many teens with HIV.

NOTE

The findings and conclusions in this chapter are those of the authors and do not necessarily represent the views of the Centers for Disease Control and Prevention.

REFERENCES

1. Palella, F. J., Jr., K. M. Delaney, A. C. Moorman, M. O. Loveless, J. Fuhrer, G. A. Satten, D. J. Aschman, and S. D. Holmberg. 1998. Declining morbidity and mortality among patients with advanced human immunodeficiency virus infection. HIV Outpatient Study Investigators. *N Engl J Med* 338 (13):853–60.

2. Jensen-Fangel, S., L. Pedersen, C. Pedersen, C. S. Larsen, P. Tauris, A. Moller, H. T. Sorensen, and N. Obel. 2004. Low mortality in HIV-infected patients starting highly active antiretroviral therapy: a comparison with the general population. *Aids* 18 (1):89–97.

3. Centers for Disease Control and Prevention. HIV/AIDS Surveillance Report, 2001. (13(2)). 2002. US Department of Health and Human Services, Centers for Disease Control and Prevention.

4. Centers for Disease Control and Prevention. HIV/AIDS Surveillance Report, 2003. (15). 2004. US Department of Health and Human Services, Centers for Disease Control and Prevention.

5. Chesney, M. A., J. Ickovics, F. M. Hecht, G. Sikipa, and J. Rabkin. 1999. Adherence: A necessity for successful HIV combination therapy. *AIDS* 13 Suppl A:S271–78.

6. Walsh, J. C., R. Horne, M. Dalton, A. P. Burgess, and B. G. Gazzard. 2001. Reasons for non-adherence to antiretroviral therapy: patients' perspectives provide evidence of multiple causes. *AIDS Care* 13 (6):709–20.

7. Remien, R. H., A. E. Hirky, M. O. Johnson, L. S. Weinhardt, D. Whittier, and G. M. Le. 2003. Adherence to medication treatment: a qualitative study of facilitators and barriers among a diverse sample of HIV+ men and women in four US cities. *AIDS Behav* 7 (1):61–72.

8. Broers, B., A. Morabia, and B. Hirschel. 1994. A cohort study of drug users' compliance with zidovudine treatment. *Arch Intern Med* 154 (10):1121–27.

9. Kleeberger, C. A., J. P. Phair, S. A. Strathdee, R. Detels, L. Kingsley, and L. P. Jacobson. 2001. Determinants of heterogeneous adherence to HIV-antiretroviral therapies in the Multicenter AIDS Cohort Study. *J Acquir Immune Defic Syndr* 26 (1):82–92.

10. Arnsten, J. H., P. A. Demas, R. W. Grant, M. N. Gourevitch, H. Farzadegan, A. A. Howard, and E. E. Schoenbaum. 2002. Impact of active drug use on antiretroviral therapy adherence and viral suppression in HIV-infected drug users. *J Gen Intern Med* 17 (5):377–81.

11. Moss, A. R., J. A. Hahn, S. Perry, E. D. Charlebois, D. Guzman, R. A. Clark, and D. R. Bangsberg. 2004. Adherence to highly active antiretroviral therapy in the homeless population in San Francisco: A prospective study. *Clin Infect Dis* 39 (8):1190–98.

12. Wainberg, M. A., and G. Friedland. 1998. Public health implications of antiretroviral therapy and HIV drug resistance. *JAMA* 279 (24):1977–83.

13. Altice, F.L., and G.H. Friedland. 1998. The era of adherence to HIV therapy. *Ann Intern Med* 129 (6):503–505.

14. Palella Jr, F. J., J. S. Chmiel, A. C. Moorman, and S. D. Holmberg. 2002. Durability and predictors of success of highly active antiretroviral therapy for ambulatory HIV-infected patients. *AIDS* 16 (12):1617–26.

15. Paterson, D. L., S. Swindells, J. Mohr, M. Brester, E. N. Vergis, C. Squier, M. M. Wagener, and N. Singh. 2000. Adherence to protease inhibitor therapy and outcomes in patients with HIV infection. *Ann Intern Med* 133 (1):21–30.

16. Bangsberg, D. R., and S. G. Deeks. 2002. Is average adherence to HIV antiretroviral therapy enough? *J Gen Intern Med* 17 (10):812–13.

17. Chesney, M. A., J. R. Ickovics, D. B. Chambers, A. L. Gifford, J. Neidig, B. Zwickl, and A. W. Wu. 2000. Self-reported adherence to antiretroviral medications among participants in HIV clinical trials: The AACTG adherence instruments. Patient Care Committee & Adherence Working Group of the Outcomes Committee of the Adult AIDS Clinical Trials Group (AACTG). *AIDS Care* 12 (3):255–66.

18. Deloria-Knoll, M., J. S. Chmiel, A. C. Moorman, K. C. Wood, S. D. Holmberg, and F. J. Palella. 2004. Factors related to and consequences of adherence to antiretroviral therapy in an ambulatory HIV-infected patient cohort. *AIDS Patient Care STDS* 18 (12):721–27.

19. Koenig, L. J., S. T. Varnell, T. J. Bush, M. Palmore, D. Stratford, and T. V. Ellerbrock. Randomized controlled trial of an intervention to prevent antiretroviral non-adherence among patients starting their first highly active antiretroviral therapies (HAART) regimen. Paper presented at the National HIV Prevention Conference. June 2005, Atlanta, GA.

20. Spire, B., S. Duran, M. Souville, C. Leport, F. Raffi, and J. P. Moatti. 2002. Adherence to highly active antiretroviral therapies (HAART) in HIV-infected patients: from a predictive to a dynamic approach. *Soc Sci Med* 54 (10):1481–96.

21. Tesoriero, J., T. French, L. Weiss, M. Waters, R. Finkelstein, and B. Agins. 2003. Stability of adherence to highly active antiretroviral therapy over time among clients enrolled in the treatment adherence demonstration project. *J Acquir Immune Defic Syndr* 33 (4):484–93.

22. Mannheimer, S., G. Friedland, J. Matts, C. Child, and M. Chesney. 2002. The consistency of adherence to antiretroviral therapy predicts biologic outcomes for human immunodeficiency virus-infected persons in clinical trials. *Clin Infect Dis* 34 (8):1115–21.

23. Martinez, J., D. Bell, R. Camacho, L. M. Henry-Reid, M. Bell, C. Watson, and F. Rodriguez. 2000. Adherence to antiviral drug regimens in HIV-infected adolescent

patients engaged in care in a comprehensive adolescent and young adult clinic. *J Natl Med Assoc* 92 (2):55–61.

24. Belzer, M. E., D. N. Fuchs, G. S. Luftman, and D. J. Tucker. 1999. Antiretroviral adherence issues among HIV-positive adolescents and young adults. *J Adolesc Health* 25 (5):316–19.

25. Murphy, D. A., C. M. Wilson, S. J. Durako, L. R. Muenz, and M. Belzer. 2001. Antiretroviral medication adherence among the REACH HIV-infected adolescent cohort in the USA. *AIDS Care* 13 (1):27–40.

26. Murphy, D. A., M. Belzer, S. J. Durako, M. Sarr, C. M. Wilson, and L. R. Muenz. 2005. Longitudinal antiretroviral adherence among adolescents infected with human immunodeficiency virus. *Arch Pediatr Adolesc Med* 159 (8):764–70.

27. Murphy, D. A., M. Sarr, S. J. Durako, A. B. Moscicki, C. M. Wilson, and L. R. Muenz. 2003. Barriers to HAART adherence among human immunodeficiency virus-infected adolescents. *Arch Pediatr Adolesc Med* 157 (3):249–55.

28. Comulada, W. S., D. T. Swendeman, M. J. Rotheram-Borus, K. M. Mattes, and R. E. Weiss. 2003. Use of HAART among young people living with HIV. *Am J Health Behav* 27 (4):389–400.

29. Rotheram-Borus, M. J., D. Swendeman, W. S. Comulada, R. E. Weiss, M. Lee, and M. Lightfoot. 2004. Prevention for substance-using HIV-positive young people: Telephone and in-person delivery. *J Acquir Immune Defic Syndr* 37 (Suppl 2):S68–77.

30. Bachanas, P. J., C. David, P. Demas, L. J. Koenig, M. Morris, Y. Wember, A. McWhorter, and A. Bell. 2004. Adherence challenges in HIV seropositive adolescents: Implications for interventions. Paper presented at the National Conference on Child Health Psychology. Charleston, SC.

31. La Greca, A. M. 1990. Issues in adherence with pediatric regimens. *J Pediatr Psychol* 15 (4):423–36.

32. Rotheram-Borus, M. J., D. A. Murphy, D. Swendeman, B. Chao, B. Chabon, S. Zhou, J. Birnbaum, and P. O'Hara. 1999. Substance use and its relationship to depression, anxiety, and isolation among youth living with HIV. *Int J Behav Med* 6 (4):293–311.

33. Bachanas, P. J., C. David-Ferdon, M. K. Morris, J. L Gess, and K. S. Myszka. Psychological adjustment, coping style, and social support in HIV infected adolescents and young adults. Unpublished Manuscript, 2006.

34. Dodds, S., T. Blakley, J. M. Lizzotte, L. B. Friedman, K. Shaw, J. Martinez, C. Siciliano, L. E. Walker, J. L. Sotheran, R. L. Sell, G. Botwinick, R. L. Johnson, and D. Bell. 2003. Retention, adherence, and compliance: special needs of HIV-infected adolescent girls and young women. *J Adolesc Health* 33 (2 Suppl):39–45.

35. Hein, K., R. Dell, D. Futterman, M. J. Rotheram-Borus, and N. Shaffer. 1995. Comparison of HIV+ and HIV- adolescents: risk factors and psychosocial determinants. *Pediatrics* 95 (1):96–104.

36. Kissinger, P., C. Fuller, R. A. Clark, and S. E. Abdalian. 1997. Psychosocial characteristics of HIV-infected adolescents in New Orleans. *J Adolesc Health* 20 (4):258.

37. Lynch, D. A., S. Krantz, J. M. Russell, L. L. Hornberger, and C. J. Van Ness. 2000. HIV infection: A retrospective analysis of adolescent high-risk behaviors. *J Pediatr Health Care* 14 (1):20–25.

38. Pao, M., M. Lyon, L. J. D'Angelo, W. B. Schuman, T. Tipnis, and D. A. Mrazek. 2000. Psychiatric diagnoses in adolescents seropositive for the human immunodeficiency virus. *Arch Pediatr Adolesc Med* 154 (3):240–44.

39. Rotheram-Borus, M., D. Murphy, C. Coleman, M. Kennedy, H. Reid, T. Cline, et al. 1997. Risk acts, health care, and medical adherence among HIV+ youths in care over time. *AIDS Behav* 1:43–52.

40. Catz, S. L., J. A. Kelly, L. M. Bogart, E. G. Benotsch, and T. L. McAuliffe. 2000. Patterns, correlates, and barriers to medication adherence among persons prescribed new treatments for HIV disease. *Health Psychol* 19 (2):124–33.

41. Tucker, J. S., M. A. Burnam, C. D. Sherbourne, F. Y. Kung, and A. L. Gifford. 2003. Substance use and mental health correlates of nonadherence to antiretroviral medications in a sample of patients with human immunodeficiency virus infection. *Am J Med* 114 (7):573–80.

42. Catz, S. L., J. B. McClure, G. N. Jones, and P. J. Brantley. 1999. Predictors of outpatient medical appointment attendance among persons with HIV. *AIDS Care* 11 (3):361–73.

43. Ammassari, A., M. P. Trotta, R. Murri, F. Castelli, P. Narciso, P. Noto, J. Vecchiet, A. D'Arminio Monforte, A. W. Wu, and A. Antinori. 2002. Correlates and predictors of adherence to highly active antiretroviral therapy: overview of published literature. *J Acquir Immune Defic Syndr* 31 (Suppl 3):S123–27.

44. Bachanas, P. J., H. Mirsalimi, J. Ries, R. Costa, and M. Sawyer. Psychosocial barriers to medical adherence in HIV-infected adolescents. Paper presented at the annual meeting of the American Psychological Association, August 2000. Washington, DC.

45. Fowler, M. E. 1998. Recognizing the phenomenon of readiness: concept analysis and case study. *J Assoc Nurses AIDS Care* 9 (3):72–76.

46. Kalichman, S. C., B. Ramachandran, and S. Catz. 1999. Adherence to combination antiretroviral therapies in HIV patients of low health literacy. *J Gen Intern Med* 14 (5):267–73.

47. Futterman, D., B. Chabon, and N. D. Hoffman. 2000. HIV and AIDS in adolescents. *Pediatr Clin North Am* 47 (1):171–88.

48. Palella Jr, F. J., J. S. Chmiel, A. C. Moorman, and S. D. Holmberg. 2002. Durability and predictors of success of highly active antiretroviral therapy for ambulatory HIV-infected patients. *AIDS* 16 (12):1617–26.

49. Rogers, A. S., S. Miller, D. A. Murphy, M. Tanney, and T. Fortune. 2001. The TREAT (Therapeutic Regimens Enhancing Adherence in Teens) program: Theory and preliminary results. *J Adolesc Health* 29 (3 Suppl):30–38.

50. Davies, G., L. J. Koenig, D. Stratford, M. Palmore, T. Bush, M. Golde, E. Malatino, M. Todd-Turner, and T. Ellerbrock. Overview and implementation of an intervention to prevent adherence failure among HIV-infected adults initiating antiretroviral therapy: Lessons learned from Project HEART. In press. *AIDS Care*.

51. Prochaska, J. O., and C. C. Diclemente. 1982. Transtheoretical therapy: Toward a more integrative model of change. *Psychotherapy: Theory, Research, and Practice* 19:276-88.

52. Prochaska, J. O., C. C. DiClemente, and J. C. Norcross. 1992. In search of how people change. Applications to addictive behaviors. *Am Psychol* 47 (9):1102–14.

53. Koenig, L. J., S. Chandwani, L. Peralta, R. R. Stein, and W. Barnes. Adolescent Impact: Conceptual basis for a developmentally targeted intervention to minimize sexual transmission risk and promote adherence to treatment and care among adolescents living with HIV/AIDS. Paper presented at the National HIV Prevention Conference. June 2005. Atlanta, GA.

54. LaGrange, R., M. Metcalf, S. Abramowitz, C. Trexler, and W. Barnes. Adolescent Impact: Preliminary findings on engaging and retaining HIV infected adolescents in care. Paper presented at the National HIV Prevention Conference. June 2005. Atlanta, GA.

55. Abramowitz, S., S. Chandwani, W. Barnes, R. LaGrange, and L. J. Koenig. Participant satisfaction with Adolescent Impact: A behavioral intervention for HIV positive youth. Posted presented at the annual meeting of the Society for Adolescent Medicine. 2006.

56. Rotheram-Borus, M. J., M. B. Lee, D. A. Murphy, D. Futterman, N. Duan, J. M. Birnbaum, and M. Lightfoot. 2001. Efficacy of a preventive intervention for youths living with HIV. *Am J Public Health* 91 (3):400–405.

57. Turner, B. J. 2002. Adherence to antiretroviral therapy by human immunodeficiency virus-infected patients. *J Infect Dis* 185 (Suppl 2):S143–51.

58. Lyon, M. E., C. Trexler, C. Akpan-Townsend, M. Pao, K. Selden, J. Fletcher, I. C. Addlestone, and L. J. D'Angelo. 2003. A family group approach to increasing adherence to therapy in HIV-infected youths: results of a pilot project. *AIDS Patient Care STDS* 17 (6):299–308.

59. Dunbar, P. J., D. Madigan, L. A. Grohskopf, D. Revere, J. Woodward, J. Minstrell, P. A. Frick, J. M. Simoni, and T. M. Hooton. 2003. A two-way messaging system to enhance antiretroviral adherence. *J Am Med Inform Assoc* 10 (1):11–15.

60. Metcalf, M., L. Orban, Y. Peele, S. Chandwani, L. J. Koenig, and L. Peralta. Can HIV-infected youth use personal digital assistant as an adherence tool? Submitted for presentation at the annual meeting of the Pediatric Academic Societies. San Francisco, CA. 2006.

61. McConnell, M. S., R. H. Byers, T. Frederick, V. B. Peters, K. L. Dominguez, T. Sukalac, A. E. Greenberg, H. W. Hsu, T. A. Rakusan, I. R. Ortiz, S. K. Melville, and M. G. Fowler. 2005. Trends in antiretroviral therapy use and survival rates for a large cohort of HIV-infected children and adolescents in the United States, 1989–2001. *J Acquir Immune Defic Syndr* 38 (4):488 94.

62. Bulterys, M., and M. G. Fowler. 2000. Prevention of HIV infection in children. *Pediatr Clin North Am* 47 (1):241–60.

63. Hosseinipour, M., M. S. Cohen, P. L. Vernazza, and A. D. Kashuba. 2002. Can antiretroviral therapy be used to prevent sexual transmission of human immunodeficiency virus type 1? *Clin Infect Dis* 34 (10):1391–95.

64. Rosenbach, K. A., R. Allison, and J. P. Nadler. 2002. Daily dosing of highly active antiretroviral therapy. *Clin Infect Dis* 34 (5):686–92.

65. Parienti, J. J., R. Verdon, and C. Bazin. 2001. Once-daily regimen may increase drug holidays. *J Infect Dis* 183 (10):1539–40.

Chapter 5

NEW TREATMENTS FOR HIV: WHAT THE FUTURE HOLDS

Ligia Peralta, M.D.

Skin, Bones, and Children's Clothes

By Kelly, 02/04/02

AIDS, anorexic, annoying,
Boost
Clothes too big
You're just skin and bones
Children's clothes
Diarrhea, drinks, drink, drink
Eat, eat more, eat again, eat all the time,
    don't stop eating!

Feeds, fatty foods, fiber
Frustrating
You're just skin and bones
Gain, gain more, gain mass
Hurry, hate being so skinny
I'm trying!

Loss of legs, loss of butt, clothes too loose
Maddening, find that magnesium
Pressures, potassium, will getting sick be my fault?
Scales, different scales, Scandi Shakes,
Use that G-Tube
Weight loss, more weight loss, where is my body going?
Anorexia, aggravating, annoying, AIDS

Treatment of HIV has undergone a great many changes over time and is still evolving. Since its discovery in 1981, treatment has grown from mere treatment of opportunistic infections to prevention of viral replication. The most common treatment used today, highly active antiretroviral therapy (HAART), focuses on the enzymes that the virus uses to replicate or make copies of itself. Although HAART is not always effective and requires strict adherence, it is still the most frequently prescribed treatment regimen. Researchers are experimenting with new ways of attacking the virus, but none have yet reached mainstream medicine. As our knowledge of the virus increases, so will the treatment options.

This chapter reviews some of the promising new drugs, such as entry inhibitors, their mechanisms of action and early clinical experience, and vaccines.

THE HISTORY OF HIV TREATMENT

The first treatment of HIV did not focus on the virus itself. In the early stages of the virus's discovery, clinicians knew too little about it to fight it. Instead, they focused on fighting the opportunistic infections, or diseases caused by the lowered level of immunity associated with HIV, to prolong the lives of those afflicted.[1,2]

The first HIV medications focused on blocking the production of enzymes that the virus needed to reproduce inside the cell and spread: reverse transcriptase and protease.[2] The year 1987 marked the arrival of the first medication approved for the treatment of HIV, zidovudine (ZDV, or AZT). This nucleoside reverse transcriptase inhibitor (NRTI) yielded promising results at first, but it failed to generate long-term results in fighting off the advancement of the disease. The same would hold true for subsequent medications of the same type. Even the use of serial monotherapy (changing medications to another of the same type) provided disappointing results. Later, clinicians added the use of non-nucleoside reverse transcriptase inhibitors to the medication arsenal, but results were still inadequate.[1]

In the mid 1990s, protease inhibitors (PI) entered the medication regimens of HIV patients. Clinicians soon discovered that, although none of these medications worked well individually, in combination they were extremely effective. Thus began the use of HAART, which included two NRTIs and one PI in its regimen. With proper medication adherence, patients with HIV could now live for years without developing AIDS.[1,3]

THE FUTURE OF HIV MEDICATIONS

HAART is effective in slowing or halting viral replication, but it has no effect on the virus when it is latent. Some newer treatments focus on immunization, blocking of the enzyme that allows HIV to integrate with a cell, and a medication that destroys inactive forms of HIV. The last is the most promising idea for HIV patients, as it is the only possibility for complete removal of the virus from the body. Lifetime control of viral replication requires lifetime therapy unless researchers can find a mechanism to clear viral reservoirs and/or mount a suppressive anti-HIV-1 immune response (e.g., by immunization).[2,3–6]

Treatment failure is always a concern when treating youth who may have difficulty disclosing their status and managing their medications openly.

In one such case, a 16-year-old HIV-infected boy's virus became suppressed (undetectable viral load) at the beginning of antiretroviral therapy; but years later, his CD4 count dropped and his viral load climbed to more than 50,000. During this period, medications were changed several times and his genotyping testing indicated he had resistance to the three most commonly used classes of drugs. What's more, he often forgot to take his antiretroviral medications for fear of being discovered to have HIV, which resulted in lower levels of suppressive therapy and a cause of treatment failure. In the end, he had exhausted his treatment options.

BLOCKING TRANSMISSION OF THE VIRUS: A BRIDGE BETWEEN HAART AND VACCINES

Protease inhibitors and highly active antiretroviral therapy first came about in 1996. Since then, drugs have been developed that attack the HIV virus at all stages of its life cycle and older approved drugs are being simplified and developed into better formulations.

All three drug classes have seen improvements; a new NRTI (Tenofovir) has been developed, and, in 2003, a new class that inhibits HIV entry into the cell, different from the existing HIV therapies now in the pharmacy, was approved. This class represents an important shift in HIV research and development and provides hope for those who are drug resistant and experiencing a multitude of toxicities. For those patients who have exhausted their drug treatment options, the first member of this class approved by the U.S. Food and Drug Administration (FDA) is being used primarily as a component of salvage therapy. There are other products that, when they come of age, may push this class closer to the forefront.[3–9]

In the absence of a vaccine to protect against HIV infection, this new class of drugs that prevents the very earliest stage of HIV infection—as opposed to current drugs that prevent HIV replication—should be assessed as a public health intervention.

ENTRY INHIBITORS

Entry inhibitors are a new class of antiretroviral drugs that act to prevent HIV penetration of CD4 cells. Entry is required for HIV to infect the cells. Blocking HIV entry means the virus does not penetrate the CD4 cells and

Figure 5.1
HIV Entry: Sites of Action of the Newer Entry Inhibitors

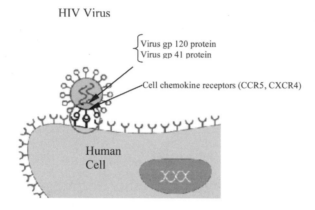

The HIV virus binds with the receptors on the CD4 cell. New entry inhibitors bind to parts of HIV, while others bind to parts of the CD4 cell that HIV needs for entering the cell.

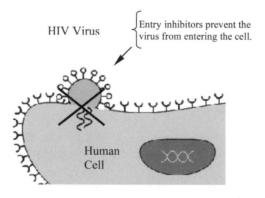

The HIV particle then fuses itself to the cell membrane and the virus enters the cell. The HIV virus binds with the receptors on the CD4 cell. New entry inhibitors bind to parts of HIV; others bind to parts of the CD4 cell that HIV needs for entering the cell. The HIV particle then fuses itself to the cell membrane an the virus enters the cell.

therefore is unable to infect them. These drugs work in different ways: some bind to parts of HIV, and others bind to parts of the cell (Figure 5.1).

While still in the experimental stages, these medications will completely block infection of the cell and viral replication, as this can only happen once the virus is inside the cell.[2] More important, they work on a separate part of the virus's life cycle having little or no potential for resistance from the current drug regimens that work after the virus enters the cell. Should these medications prove effective, ideally, they may be able to completely replace current HAART regimens. In addition, as patients may have fewer pills to take, they will be more likely to adhere to their medications.[3,5,6,9]

MECHANISMS OF ACTION AND USE

Although grouped as *entry* inhibitors, some of these new medications block the proteins on the HIV's surface called gp120 or gp41. Others block the CD4 cell's surface protein receptors also called CCR5 or CXCR4 receptors. The virus needs a series of interactions with these proteins and receptors before entering the cell. These different areas and interactions have caused these drugs to be subclassified as (1) attachment inhibitors, (2) chemokine receptor antagonists, or (3) fusion inhibitors.[5]

At the earliest stage, the virus requires interaction of its surface gp120 protein with the surface of the cell. The first subclass, *attachment inhibitors*, binds to that protein and blocks this interaction. Once the first interaction has occurred, successful entry requires a second interaction between a separate site on the virus gp120 protein and either of the chemokine receptors in the cell surface (CCR5 or CXCR4). The second drug subclass, *chemokine receptor antagonists*, blocks this second interaction, preventing the formation of a protein complex and thereby stopping the virus at the cell surface. The third required level of interaction for entry into the cell involves interaction of gp41, another virus protein, with the cell. The third drug subclass, *fusion inhibitors*, consists of simple proteins that bind to the gp41 virus protein, thus preventing this third level of interaction. Of all the subclasses, only one entry inhibitor, a fusion inhibitor, has been approved by the FDA in March of 2003: enfuvirtide (ENF or T-20). It is an injectable medication that must be used in combination with other anti-HIV drugs. The most common side effect associated with ENF is painful and persistent injection site reactions. They occur in 98% of people who take the drug. Most are mild to moderate pain or discomfort, although 10% are severe and require prescribed pain relief.[5–7]

Apart from ENF, there is little clinical experience with these new antiretroviral compounds. ENF has been found to be highly effective in treatment-experienced patients with resistance to some of the currently available agents, but the attachment inhibitors and chemokine antagonists in Phase II trials have potential as more versatile drugs that might be useful in earlier stages of infection. For example, the chemokine receptor antagonists may have the potential to prevent HIV transmission when used either as vaginal or anal compounds to reduce the infectivity of microbes (microbicides) or as a prophylaxis before or after exposure to HIV. Therefore these agents are also being considered as potential agents to prevent sexual transmission.[10]

Development of chemokine antagonist drugs that block two types of receptors has been the most popular. In particular, blockage of CCR5 receptors appears to be a potential low-risk intervention, as this receptor is unnecessary for life. Humans who lack CCR5 receptor at the cell surface as a result of a genetic mutation have no apparent health problems but have a relative resistance to HIV infection as described in a cohort of highly HIV sexually exposed but uninfected individuals.[11] The importance of considering these products as potential agents to prevent sexual transmission is also supported by animal studies.[10] For example, the role of CCR5 in allowing for HIV transmission has been demonstrated in macaques.[12] The mucosal surface of the genital tract is thought to favor the HIV virus, as this environment is rich in white cells expressing CCR5 receptors.[10] In addition, the HIV virus that has special attraction for CCR5 is the predominant HIV strain found at the time of being infected and in most early infections.[13] Other advantages of these drugs over the current injectable entry inhibitor are their potential use as oral medications coupled with favorable absorption and metabolism of the drug at a well-tolerated and safe dose.[14–16] This raises the possibility that some of these drugs may be used once a day in the future.

Although these are promising medications, there are still many questions about the development of resistance to these new drugs. There is evidence of the development of test tube resistance that may alter binding to CCR5, but little is known about these mutations and the changes that may result.[17] Based on this information and on the recommendation that antiretroviral monotherapy is not currently recommended in HIV management, it is unlikely that entry inhibitors will be used as single medications. Therefore studies are required to address the question of which other classes will be best used in combination. Although monotherapy is not recommended for HIV treatment, the demonstration that limited courses of monotherapy with zidovudine are capable of blocking maternal to child transmission should lead to trials of these drugs to reduce perinatal and sexual transmission.

THE HISTORY OF HIV VACCINE DEVELOPMENT

Another treatment route that experts have aggressively pursued in recent years is the development of an HIV vaccine. Vaccines are one of the two public health interventions that have had the greatest impact on the world's health, the other one being clean water. Vaccines stimulate the body's immune system to provide protection against infection or disease and are considered the most cost-effective public health intervention to prevent illness or death for millions of individuals every year. HIV/AIDS is spreading at an alarming pace, with a record 4.8 million estimated new infections in 2003, and 50% of those infections occur in young people under age 25 worldwide. At the current rate, there will be 45 million new infections by 2010 and nearly 70 million more deaths by 2020. Besides causing massive human suffering and loss of life, the disease is affecting the stability of nations, creating labor shortages and making orphans of an entire generation of children. Meanwhile, vaccines against HIV are being developed, and they are in various stages of clinical trial but at present, none have proven effective.[18,19]

Vaccines have historically taken many years to develop, and HIV vaccines are not going to be an exception. For example, a vaccine to prevent *Haemophilus influenzae*, bacteria that causes children's infection in the blood and the membrane covering the brain, was discovered after 92 years of research. It took 89 years to develop the "whooping cough" (pertussis) vaccine. In recent times, the process has been expedited, and it took 47 years to develop a polio vaccine, 42 years for the measles, and only 16 years to develop the hepatitis B vaccine approved in 1981. Although vaccine research has made progress in shortening the length of time between the discovery of infection and the advent of a preventive vaccine, the challenging task of developing an HIV/AIDS vaccine will likely be a lengthy process.[18,20]

CHALLENGES IN DEVELOPING AN HIV VACCINE

AIDS researchers have carefully detailed how the virus destroys the immune system, but they have yet to find out which immune responses can protect against infection. The virus replicates so quickly and makes so many mutations during the process that vaccines can't possibly protect against all types of HIV. The virus also has developed sophisticated mechanisms to avoid immune attack, covering up its surface protein to hide vulnerable sites from antibodies and producing proteins that disturb production of other immune defenses.[19]

UNDERSTANDING HIV VACCINES: WHAT IS AN HIV VACCINE?

Although an effective HIV vaccine has not yet been developed, many important observations and breakthroughs have been made since the mid-1980s. For example, monkey experiments have shown that vaccines can protect animals from a simian virus, a relative of HIV. Studies have identified people who repeatedly exposed themselves to HIV but remained uninfected, suggesting that some people have immune responses to stop the virus. A small percentage of people who become infected seem to suffer no damage, and others suppress the virus for a decade or more before showing damage to their immune systems.[21–24] In addition, scientists have found that some rare proteins released from the cells (antibodies) work powerfully against the virus in test tube experiments.[25–28]

At the beginning of HIV vaccine development, scientists identified the protein on the surface of the virus (gp120) as the region that attaches to human cells. Therefore vaccines were initially designed to trigger production of infection-fighting proteins (antibodies) against this and other HIV surface proteins. The approach seemed promising because HIV uses the surface protein to enter onto white blood cells and establish an infection. This finding led to studies to develop a vaccine based on genetically engineered gp120 and the larger protein gp160 to prevent the acquisition of infection. This was the approach taken by a biotechnology company called VaxGen in designing AIDSVax, the only HIV vaccine that made it to a large clinical trial in two decades. In February 2003, after more than a decade of work, VaxGen scientists announced the results of the first Phase II trial to test the efficacy of their vaccine. Unexpectedly, AIDS-Vax, did not prevent HIV infection in the study cohort as a whole.[20,21]

Table 5.1
Types of Current Experimental HIV Vaccines

Type	Description
Peptide vaccine	Made of tiny pieces of proteins from the HIV virus
Recombinant sub-unit protein vaccine	Made of bigger pieces of proteins that are on the surface of the HIV virus. Examples of these proteins are gp 120, gp 140, or gp 160 produced by genetic engineering
Live vector vaccine	Non-HIV viruses are engineered to carry genes encoding HIV proteins. This type of vaccine most resembles the HIV virus. The genes are inserted into a bacterium or virus that does not cause disease in humans (vector), which carries them into the body's cells. The genes in turn produce proteins that are normally found on the surface of the HIV virus. Many vaccines used today, like the smallpox vaccine, use this approach.
DNA vaccine	Uses copies of a small number of HIV genes, which are inserted into pieces of DNA. The HIV genes will produce proteins very similar to the ones from real HIV.
Vaccine combination	Uses any two vaccines, one after another, to create a stronger immune response. Often referred to as "prime-boost strategy."
Virus-like particle vaccine (pseudovirion vaccine)	Noninfectious HIV look-alike that has one or more, but not all, HIV proteins

Source: Cohen, J. 2005. Public health. Gates Foundation picks winners in Grand Challenges in Global Health. *Science* 309 (5731):33–35.

Although this vaccine failed to provide protection against infection, researchers learned some critical lessons and continued working on new products. Currently, 34 candidate HIV vaccines are in the early phases of human clinical trials in 19 countries.

In general, researchers have new strategies that may lead to an effective HIV vaccine. Scientists take small parts of the HIV virus and alter them in a laboratory to create synthetic copies. As was the case of the earliest experimental vaccines, the current ones do not use whole or live HIV. Therefore the vaccines cannot cause HIV or AIDS. The vaccines being tested should produce either antibodies or stimulate special white cells able to kill infected cells (cytotoxic T-lymphocyte cells or CTLs) to fight infection (Table 5.1).[21,22,27,28]

POSSIBLE VACCINE RESULTS

An HIV vaccine may be totally successful in preventing infection, creating what is known as *sterilizing immunity*. Sterilizing immunity may be possible in certain groups of the population or up to 100% of the population. In another scenario, a vaccine may not prevent the infection, but decrease the possibility of HIV transmission from an infected individual to another person. Yet another possibility is that a vaccine may slow the process of infection, so that even if a person becomes HIV infected, the vaccine helps that individual remain healthier longer. This is the concept of therapeutic vaccines.

Although scientists are still searching for a preventive vaccine, two new therapeutic HIV vaccine studies are currently underway. These vaccines do not work the same way as typical vaccines that prevent infection. Instead, they work to stimulate special white cells that are capable of both identifying and killing HIV-infected cells. In turn, this acts to prevent, or at least limit, viral replication and delay the progression of HIV.[28,29]

VACCINE SAFETY: HOW ARE VACCINES TESTED?

HIV vaccine candidates are evaluated in a series of clinical trials known as Phase I, II, and III (Table 5.2).

Vaccine research is a long process that begins with basic laboratory research and product development, including animal experimentation performed in academic and pharmaceutical industry laboratories. The next step is to test these products on healthy human volunteers through sequential phases. Phase I and II trials provide data on the safety of the candidate vaccines and on their ability to induce immune responses specific to HIV. These trials are carried out on small numbers of volunteers (50–200 per trial). Depending on the results obtained, candidate vaccines can proceed to large-scale Phase III trials designed to obtain definitive information about their efficacy in inducing protection against HIV infection or

Table 5.2

Stages of Vaccine Testing in Humans

Phase	Number of Participants	Primary Rationale
I	20–100	Safety
II	Hundreds	Safety and immune response (required for Phase III)
IIb	2,000–5,000	Intermediate trial
III	Thousands	Safety and Effectiveness (required before licensure)

AIDS. For scientific reasons, Phase III trials are carried out in populations with a high incidence of HIV infection, involving thousands of volunteers. This phase is required for FDA approval and licensure.[19,29]

An intermediate trial, Phase IIb, is designed to identify those vaccines that merit a Phase III trial. This intermediate study is designed to determine whether the type of vaccine being tested will be effective. It is not designed to establish the efficacy of a particular candidate vaccine, as in Phase III, but rather to help researchers decide if this product is worth testing in the larger and costlier Phase III trial. The number of volunteers required for such trials is smaller, around 2,000 to 5,000 volunteers as compared to more than 10,000 for Phase III trials. Phase IIb trials therefore are much easier to design and manage, and as fewer doses of vaccine are required, these trials are also much faster to implement. Of importance, they may also provide researchers with information about the immune response generated by the vaccine that causes it to be effective. For safety reasons, studies in adolescents are usually limited to Phase IIb and III trials, once the safety data are available from adult Phase I and II trials.[19,29]

In 2003, a group of world-leading scientists proposed and established the Global HIV Vaccine Enterprise, a consortium to accelerate HIV vaccine discovery by developing a blueprint, which for the first time identifies key research priorities. The blueprint includes new approaches (1) to address the major scientific barriers to an HIV vaccine, (2) to host more clinical trials and train more researchers in affected countries, (3) to increase private-sector investment in research and development, and (4) for local leaders to encourage volunteers to participate in studies.[29,30]

CONCLUSION

Treatment for HIV has undergone a great many changes over time and is still evolving. The new drugs described here have yet to reach mainstream medicine; however, as our knowledge of the virus increases, so will the treatment options. Today, those first diagnosed with HIV have more options than those first diagnosed 20 years ago. Current treatments continue to extend the lives of those infected with HIV. Furthermore, the development of new drugs such as entry inhibitors and potential HIV vaccines offer continued improvements in treatment.

The availability of a safe, highly effective and accessible preventive HIV vaccine would be a valuable complement to other preventive interventions to reduce transmission of the virus. HIV immunization strategies could reach populations where other interventions are not sufficiently effective. Also, it could be used as treatment interventions when combined with antiretroviral therapies, resulting in lower treatments costs and increasing long-term efficacy.

Preventing the transmission of HIV/AIDS by discovering and making accessible an effective vaccine must be a combined worldwide effort of governments, the private sector, academia, and communities. With this collaboration and safe participation of individuals in clinical trials, in another 20 years, the prevention and treatment options for HIV will be superior to the ones available today.

REFERENCES

1. Bartlett, J. G. 2004. Antiretroviral therapy. In *A Guide to Primary Care of People with HIV/AIDS*, ed. J. G. Bartlett et al. Rockville: U.S. Department of Health and Human Services, Health Resources and Services Administration, HIV/AIDS Bureau.

2. Hospital Infection Control. 2004. The evolution of antiretroviral therapy: Applying clinical trial data to optimize HAART in the management of HIV. http://www.hiconline.com/hivsupplement.htm.

3. Sande, M. A., and A. Ronald. 2004. Treatment of HIV/AIDS: Do the dilemmas only increase? *JAMA* 292 (2):266–68.

4. Dybul, M., A. S. Fauci, J. G. Bartlett, J. E. Kaplan, and A. K. Pau. 2002. Guidelines for using antiretroviral agents among HIV-infected adults and adolescents. *Ann Intern Med* 137 (5 Pt 2):381–433.

5. Starr-Spires, L. D., and R. G. Collman. 2002. HIV-1 entry and entry inhibitors as therapeutic agents. *Clin Lab Med* 22 (3):681–701.

6. Hunt, M. 2004. Basic viology: Definitions, classification, morphology, and chemistry. *Virology.* http://pathmicro.med.sc.edu/mhunt/intro-vir.htm.

7. Condra, J. H., M. D. Miller, D. J. Hazuda, and E. A. Emini. 2002. Potential new therapies for the treatment of HIV-1 infection. *Annu Rev Med* 53:541–55.

8. National Institutes of Health. 2004. Treatment of HIV infection. http://www.niaid.nih.gov/factsheets/treat-hiv.htm.

9. Department of Health and Human Services. 2005. Guidelines for the use of anti-riretoviral agents in HIV-1-infected adults and adolescents. http://www.aidsinfo.nih.gov/guidelines/adult/AA_040705.pdf.

10. Shattock, R. J., and J. P. Moore. 2003. Inhibiting sexual transmission of HIV-1 infection. *Nat Rev Microbiol* 1 (1):25–34.

11.   McNicholl, J. M., D. K. Smith, S. H. Qari, and T. Hodge. 1997. Host genes and HIV: The role of the chemokine receptor gene CCR5 and its allele. *Emerg Infect Dis* 3 (3):261–71.

12.   Veazey, R. S., R. J. Shattock, M. Pope, J. C. Kirijan, J. Jones, Q. Hu, T. Ketas, P. A. Marx, P. J. Klasse, D. R. Burton, and J. P. Moore. 2003. Prevention of virus transmission to macaque monkeys by a vaginally applied monoclonal antibody to HIV-1 gp120. *Nat Med* 9 (3):343–46.

13.   van't Wout, A. B., N. A. Kootstra, G. A. Mulder-Kampinga, N. Albrecht-van Lent, H. J. Scherpbier, J. Veenstra, K. Boer, R. A. Coutinho, F. Miedema, and H. Schuitemaker. 1994. Macrophage-tropic variants initiate human immunodeficiency virus type 1 infection after sexual, parenteral, and vertical transmission. *J Clin Invest* 94 (5):2060–67.

14.   Schutten, M., C. A. van Baalen, C. Guillon, R. C. Huisman, P. H. Boers, K. Sintnicolaas, R. A. Gruters, and A. D. Osterhaus. 2001. Macrophage tropism of human immunodeficiency virus type 1 facilitates in vivo escape from cytotoxic T-lymphocyte pressure. *J Virol* 75 (6):2706–709.

15.   Lalezari, J., M. Thompson, P. Kumar, P. Piliero, R. Davey, K. Patterson, A. Shachoy-Clark, K. Adkison, J. Demarest, Y. Lou, M. Berrey, and S. Piscitelli. 2005. Antiviral activity and safety of 873140, a novel CCR5 antagonist, during short-term monotherapy in HIV-infected adults. *AIDS* 19 (14):1443–48.

16.   Demarest J., K. Adkison, S. Sparks, A. Shachoy-Clark, K. Schell, S. Reddy, L. Fang, K. O'Mara, S. Shibayama, and S. Piscitelli. 2004. Single and multiple dose escalation study to investigate the safety, pharmacokinetics, and receptor binding of GW873140, a novel CCR5 receptor antagonist, in healthy subjects. Abstract 130, CROI 2004.

17.   Moore, J. P., and R. W. Doms. 2003. The entry of entry inhibitors: a fusion of science and medicine. *Proc Natl Acad Sci U S A* 100 (19):10598–602.

18.   World Health Organization. HIV vaccines. http://www.who.int/vaccines-diseases/history/history.shtml.

19.   UNAIDS. 2004. Report on the global AIDS epidemic. July 2004.

20.   Gallo, R. C. 2005. HIV/AIDS research after HAART. *Res Initiat Treat Action* 11 (1):39–41.

21.   Berman, P. W., T. J. Gregory, L. Riddle, G. R. Nakamura, M. A. Champe, J. P. Porter, F. M. Wurm, R. D. Hershberg, E. K. Cobb, and J. W. Eichberg. 1990. Protection of chimpanzees from infection by HIV-1 after vaccination with recombinant glycoprotein gp120 but not gp160. *Nature* 345 (6276):622–25.

22.   Connor, R. I., B. T. Korber, B. S. Graham, B. H. Hahn, D. D. Ho, B. D. Walker, A. U. Neumann, S. H. Vermund, J. Mestecky, S. Jackson, E. Fenamore, Y. Cao, F. Gao, S. Kalams, K. J. Kunstman, D. McDonald, N. McWilliams, A. Trkola, J. P. Moore, and S. M. Wolinsky. 1998. Immunological and virological analyses of persons infected by human immunodeficiency virus type 1 while participating in trials of recombinant gp120 subunit vaccines. *J Virol* 72 (2):1552–76.

23.   McCutchan, F. E. 2000. Understanding the genetic diversity of HIV-1. *AIDS* 14 (Suppl 3):S31–44.

24.   Peeters, M., and P. M. Sharp. 2000. Genetic diversity of HIV-1: the moving target. *AIDS* 14 (Suppl 3):S129–40.

25.   Poignard, P., R. Sabbe, G. R. Picchio, M. Wang, R. J. Gulizia, H. Katinger, P. W. Parren, D. E. Mosier, and D. R. Burton. 1999. Neutralizing antibodies have limited effects on the control of established HIV-1 infection in vivo. *Immunity* 10 (4):431–38.

26. Romano, L., G. Venturi, S. Giomi, L. Pippi, P. E. Valensin, and M. Zazzi. 2002. Development and significance of resistance to protease inhibitors in HIV-1-infected adults under triple-drug therapy in clinical practice. *J Med Virol* 66 (2):143–50.

27. Kennedy, D., and C. Norman. 2005. What don't we know? *Science* 309 (5731):75.

28. Cohen, J. 2005. Is an effective HIV vaccine feasible? *Science* 309 (5731):99.

29. NIAID. HIV vaccines. http://www.niaid.nih.gov/daids/vaccine/default.htm.

30. Cohen, J. 2005. Public health. Gates Foundation picks winners in Grand Challenges in Global Health. *Science* 309 (5731):33–35.

The HIV virus binds with the receptors on the CD4 cell. New entry inhibitors bind to parts of HIV; others bind to parts of the CD4 cell that HIV needs for entering the cell. The HIV particle then fuses itself to the cell membrane and the virus enters the cell.

Part II
MATTERS OF MIND

Chapter 6

LEARNING TO LIVE WITH AN EPIDEMIC: REDUCING STIGMA AND INCREASING SAFE AND SENSITIVE SOCIALIZING WITH PERSONS WITH HIV

Beatrice J. Krauss, Ph.D., Christopher Godfrey, M.A., Joanne O'Day, M.A., Elizabeth Freidin, B.A., and Robert Kaplan, Ph.D.

Don't Judge
By Michael Dowling

Why do we judge
Our fellow man
Why do we group others
Why shouldn't people be able to have
the freedom of self-expression
The freedom to be
Themselves
Without being judged
Why?
Because there's only one person

Some have called this a century of emerging infectious illnesses for the United States: Lyme disease, Hanta virus (a viral infection that emerged in the South-west and was carried by small rodents), and HIV, to name a few.[1] As with other initially unfamiliar illnesses (e.g., cancer in the 1930s), at first we didn't know how to react to people with HIV—quarantine was suggested, for example. As we are learning to live with an HIV epidemic, however, the lessons we learn can be applied to other emergent illnesses. Some lessons we have already learned from illnesses with which we are familiar.

When an infectious illness is familiar, time-limited, and not deadly, we generally feel comfortable being around someone who has it, and we behave accordingly. For example, if a friend or family member has a cold, we joke about the sneezing or the runny nose; we suggest home remedies like chicken soup, juice, and a lot of rest; and we offer sympathy. To protect each other, the person with the cold covers his or her mouth when coughing or sneezing, and we both wash our hands after touching.

In contrast, serious and emerging illnesses—that is, illnesses that are new and about which we don't know very much—may tax our social and protective skills. Imagine that you learn that a friend or family member is gravely ill and has a condition about which you've heard only bits and pieces. When you ask questions, people don't want to talk about it. By listening in on conversations and hearing the news, you learn that other people can catch it but you don't learn how; that a person might be embarrassed if people knew they had it but you're not sure why; that it has sets of symptoms that vary over time and between different people but no one knows exactly why that occurs; and that a person is likely to have it the rest of his or her life. Would you know how to act day to day if you were around someone who has it? Would you joke and suggest chicken soup? Would you offer sympathy? Would using tissues to cover coughs and sneezes, and washing your hands be enough? If the illness is new, and people don't want to talk about it, how would you know what to do?

For example, if your brother has a cold, eats only part of his breakfast, and offers the rest of his bacon and eggs to you, you would know not to eat it. But what if he has HIV? Would you or wouldn't you accept the food? If you thought about it for a moment, would you then accept it? Why? Would you know what to say about your decision? What if you learn your brother had an infection of thrush in his mouth, as well as HIV when you had breakfast with him?

This situation actually happened. As you will find out as you read this chapter, it was handled sensitively and sensibly by a sibling who knew very little about general medicine, infectious disease or thrush, and only a little about HIV. He did, however, know a lot about empathy and kindness and how his brother was feeling. It represents the kind of daily challenge that youth and families of the Lower East Side of New York City have faced since the early 1980s, as they deal with a growing and changing HIV epidemic that has affected their families and their neighborhood in many significant ways.[2]

New York City residents have been living with the HIV epidemic since the first U.S. cases were identified in 1981.[3] Although in New York City the rate of HIV has varied over time and from neighborhood to neighborhood, throughout the duration of the U.S. epidemic, about one quarter of the people with HIV have lived in New York City.[4] Further, the face of the New York City epidemic has changed over time; some risks have diminished or disappeared, others have persisted, and the populations associated

with them have changed accordingly: early in the epidemic, hemophiliacs, transfusion recipients, or others who received untested blood or blood
products; men who had sex with men; some of the babies of HIV-infected
mothers who became infected with HIV before treatments to prevent
mother-to-child transmission during pregnancy and delivery and after
birth were introduced; health care workers and others who received needle
sticks before postexposure treatment was available to help prevent infection; and then injection drug users and the sexual partners of injection
drug users. Now the New York City epidemic is described as a "mixed"
heterosexual/homosexual/injection drug use epidemic, and the population
most at risk at the turn of the twenty-first century is young women of
color.[5,6]

Since the HIV epidemic began, much has changed. We first learned about
AIDS, but then learned that AIDS is only the later stage of a much longer
illness, HIV infection, which is caused by the human immunodeficiency virus.
Increasingly sensitive tests have been developed for HIV antibodies and for
the presence of HIV itself. Treatments have improved for HIV infection and
for the diseases and conditions associated with the decreased immune function
that accompanies it, and for the special set of illnesses called AIDS-defining
illnesses (for example, *Pneumocystis carinii* pneumonia) that characterize the
severe immune deficiency of AIDS. We continue to learn more about how
HIV attacks the body's immune system. But with all this new information con-
stantly developing, how does someone who may have a friend, family member,
or classmate with HIV keep up? How do you learn that information so that
you can behave in a kind, safe, and sensitive manner toward someone you know
who has HIV?

Since 1994, the lead author, Dr. Krauss, has been studying and working with
youth and families in a New York City neighborhood, where about 10% of
the adults and adolescents have HIV.[7] We initially entered the neighborhood
to assist in strengthening parents' and guardians' roles as health educators of
their children to help *prevent* HIV (Parent/Preadolescent Training for HIV
Prevention, PATH). However, the adults and youth quickly let us know that
they thought that it was equally important to learn how to interact comfortably
daily with friends and family living with HIV.

The rest of this chapter summarizes the best that she has learned from
them about living with HIV, and what her discipline, social psychology,
has contributed to the dialogue between social scientists interested in HIV
and the community members living with the HIV epidemic. One of the
major contributions of social psychology concerns the concept of "stigma,"
reacting differently toward someone because of a brand or a label, for
example, a person with HIV. Stigma has far-reaching effects. In the case of
HIV, stigmatizing someone—that is, behaving unkindly and insensitively

toward them—can negatively affect their health, including their mental health, and, ultimately, the health of all of us.

THE HEALTH EFFECTS OF STIGMA

Stigma

The word *stigma* derives from Greek and Latin roots, which indicated first a tattoo, then more generally a brand or mark, on someone who was either a criminal or a slave; thus, the noun *stigma* came to connote a visible mark of infamy or disgrace or lowered status. Perhaps one of the most famous of such marks is Hester Prynne's scarlet "A" in Nathaniel Hawthorne's *The Scarlet Letter*. Also, because people tended to treat badly someone with such a mark, the verb *stigmatize* came to mean to reproach, censure, or blame.[8] Thus, stigmatization (the act of stigmatizing or of being stigmatized) can lead to avoidance and censure of someone by others. Yet because much of our identity depends on how people react to us[9] (for example, if people avoid you, you begin to wonder if something is the matter with you), stigmatization can also lead to self-blame and shame in the person being stigmatized. In fact, the best known social scientist writing about stigma states that it leads to a "spoiled identity."[10] The identity we thought we had is "spoiled" or tainted or marred by the stigma and therefore is no longer whole and complete—like a formerly perfect fruit with bruises.

AIDS and HIV Infection: Our Images Lag Behind a Dynamic, Ever-Changing Epidemic

Without treatment, AIDS takes place, on average, 10 to 11 years after HIV infection first occurs and lasts 9 months to 2 years. Thus, even in the worst-case scenario—that is, no treatment—AIDS generally occurs during the last 10% of the disease course of HIV infection.[11] Furthermore, new treatments have delayed the onset of AIDS dramatically. In fact, some individuals with HIV infection may never progress to AIDS, although we don't know this for sure yet because an important treatment breakthrough, highly active antiretroviral therapy (HAART), was introduced only in 1996–1997, too soon for us to be able to tell if it can actually stop the onset of AIDS.

Because in the United States we knew about AIDS before we discovered the human immunodeficiency virus and before we understood the course of HIV infection, that initial emphasis on AIDS still leads some of us to substitute images of AIDS (or even the word *AIDS*) for all of HIV infection. Thus, some people still think that everyone infected with HIV has visible "marks" or a changed appearance, even though that actually happens only when people have AIDS, and then only to some of them. For example, some people with AIDS have raised purplish splotches on the skin from Kaposi's sarcoma, a rare form of cancer that sometimes occurs in those with severely compromised immune systems, although it can also occur in elderly Jewish men of Eastern European origin. Others have lost a lot of weight from a wasting disease—one of the conditions considered an AIDS-defining illness—associated with the presence of the HIV virus. Think of the appearance of the character played by the actor Tom Hanks in the movie *Philadelphia*. Although some people with AIDS may have these visible changes, most people with HIV will not. They look completely healthy; however, they can still be stigmatized.

Invisible "Brands"

The "mark" of an illness does not need to be physically visible for someone to be stigmatized. It need be nothing more than a label that in one way or another evokes reproach or blame. Because the transmission of HIV is often associated with sexual or drug use behavior, even though these behaviors are extremely common in the United States and around the world (where, in fact, HIV is largely a heterosexual epidemic),[12] it remains easy to discredit someone by saying she has HIV or AIDS. Some examples will help make this clear; in each case, just saying "HIV" or "AIDS" becomes an insult. Among the taunts reported by the youth of the Lower East Side to the lead author during her study are:[13]

"I don't like you, anyway. You skinny girls have AIDS."

"The alphabet only has 23 letters. You and Magic Johnson got HIV."

"I love you, you love me, Barney [the children's show dinosaur character] gave you HIV."

In these cases, the taunts were meant to be personal and hurtful. In the first case, a girl had just turned down a boy's invitation to go out; in the second, a family member had HIV and the taunt implied everyone in the family was "branded" with HIV. The last taunt revised and changed a harmless jingle from a children's TV show into a personal attack on a youth whose image was soft and warm like the dinosaur, Barney.

The youth at whom these taunts were aimed may or may not have actually had HIV. But imagine the impact if he or she did, or if a relative or friend did. In fact, because most people with HIV have no visible marks, we often don't know when we are around someone who has it. That means that individuals with HIV may well be looking and listening when such situations occur. They may well be deciding to whom it is safe to disclose their HIV status; from whom they might receive some social support, understanding, or assistance; and whom it is best to avoid.[14] Because these people look healthy, we won't know they have HIV, but imagine how remarks like these would make them feel. They probably wouldn't feel like telling very many people; maybe they wouldn't feel like telling anyone at all.

The Spreading Effects of Being Stigmatized

Shame and the experience, or even expectation, of reproach lead people to stay away from others and to become socially isolated. Why be around someone if you think that person is going to make you feel bad or if you think there is something wrong with you? Therefore stigma and social isolation go hand in hand. Stigma has been associated with increased depression,[15–17] and has been found to make it less likely that someone with HIV will enter treatment or, if treated, will keep appointments and take medicines as scheduled.[18] In fact, many people go out of their neighborhood to get tested or treated for HIV, to places where it is unlikely anyone knows them, because they are afraid of the rumors that may be spread about them or their illness if they are recognized going to a place where medical care for HIV is provided. This makes their medical care more time-consuming and burdensome.

Because HIV is a virus that mutates (and takes only three days to do so), avoiding treatment or skipping medicines makes it more likely that new or new drug-resistant strains of it will emerge.[19] To illustrate, most HIV medications interfere with the life cycle of HIV. If a person stops taking such medicine, the viruses that survived partial treatment multiply, making it less likely that treatment will work in the future. A case in New York City, discovered in 2004, woke everyone up. An individual was found to have a rapidly progressing form of HIV that went from infection to AIDS in a matter of months; in addition, it responded only to one very new HIV medication and was resistant to about 20 others. It is believed that the person caught a mutated and resistant virus.[19] Therefore it is good for the health of everyone to encourage someone who has been potentially exposed to HIV through a risk behavior to get tested for it and, if found to be HIV positive, to enter treatment and to stay with it. That will happen much more readily if people feel safe going for testing and treatment, and if they feel supported in taking their medicines. It will be much more difficult if people with HIV feel unsupported and stigmatized.

But the person with HIV is not the only one affected by stigma. Stigma also spreads to their loved ones, including children and caregivers, when they see that the person with HIV is treated badly or when they themselves are treated badly merely because they are associated with that person.[20–25] In fact, each of the authors has been asked at least once, "Why are you studying a disease like HIV?"

Stigma can even prevent us from seeing the HIV epidemic. For example, data from the New York City Department of Health and Mental Hygiene indicate that about 10% of the adult/adolescent population in the Lower East Side of New York City has HIV. But many of the people who live there don't know they are HIV-positive. Most adults in our study know someone with HIV; just under half (46%) of the children, ages 10 to 13, are certain they know two or three people with HIV, more than 26% of whom had died.[7] But because people are not talking openly, they don't know that other people in their neighborhood also know people with HIV. They think they're the only ones. In fact, no one seems to be able to accurately estimate the size of the epidemic in their neighborhood.

This silence is especially poignant when you understand who the people with HIV are. About 75% of the youth in our study who said that they know someone with HIV described the person with HIV who is closest to them as extended family (e.g., aunts, uncles, cousins) or as family friends (e.g., parent's friend); about 21% described that person as immediate family (e.g., father, mother, step-parent, brother, sister); and only about 4% described that person as a neighbor or acquaintance.[7] What that means is that for many people, the HIV epidemic is profoundly personal, whether or not they themselves have it. Sadly, many of them are experiencing that epidemic alone.[13]

Stigma hurts all of us because it keeps us from talking openly about HIV, about the prevention of HIV, about testing for HIV, about treatment of HIV, about people with HIV, about HIV risk behaviors, and even about the stigma associated with HIV. As one young woman from the Lower East Side put it:

"I just want to know why everyone is treating my uncle so badly. He's sick and people are mean to him."

UNDERSTANDING WHERE HIV STIGMA COMES FROM

Fear of Transmission and Awkward Interactions

Most researchers believe HIV stigma arises from misperceptions about casual household or social transmission[2,18]; people are afraid they will catch HIV during routine daily interactions. But, as the remainder of this chapter indicates, there are other reasons for stigma and avoidance besides unrealistic or inaccurate fears of transmission. However, those fears are important to discuss; if you are close to someone with HIV, chances are that daily interaction is pretty common, and it's important to know why it is almost impossible to transmit HIV through this kind of contact so that both you and the person with HIV can feel more comfortable.

For example, in the Lower East Side, youth who had been with someone with HIV in the last month reported their top eight interactions (Table 6.1).[7]

Table 6.1
Interactions with People Living with HIV

Activity with a Person Living with HIV	Percent of Youth Reporting the Activity
Hug	54.2%
Give a compliment to	52.5%
Kiss	45.8%
Shake hands	45.8%
Have dinner together	39.0%
Play games together	35.6%
Listen to fears and concerns	33.9%
Run errands for	32.2%

Some of these activities are fairly intimate; others are fairly routine; all occurred regularly. Yet these youth were only somewhat comfortable doing them. They expressed a high level of unrealistic worry about HIV on a questionnaire, scoring, on average, "worry a lot," across more than 20 different activities, including being with a person with HIV or talking about sickness. Their highest worries, however, were: "someone I know has HIV and hasn't told me," and "someone I know will get HIV," again underscoring the upset caused by failing to talk openly about HIV; some believed family members had HIV or would get it, but they were afraid to ask about it. They also showed low knowledge about it, getting correct only 68% of the items on a 50-item HIV knowledge test. What they missed was important: for example, most did not know that there were treatments to help prevent transmission of HIV from an HIV-infected pregnant woman to her child; some believed they could get HIV from mosquitoes that had bitten an infected person.[26] Worse, their worry and their lack of knowledge fed into one another: worry may have caused them to avoid information about HIV, and lack of knowledge may have contributed to feeling worried when they didn't need to be.[26] And their worries were not only about "catching HIV"; they were worried about even being around someone with HIV or talking about sickness. In other words, although youth and people with HIV interacted regularly, the youth were not completely comfortable doing so. They were relatively uninformed and worried.

Some authors have called this discomfort *interactional awkwardness*; people who are uninformed but well intentioned are not sure how they are supposed to feel and behave when they are around someone with HIV—that is, if they even know that they are around someone with HIV. They are afraid that they may give incorrect advice, say the wrong thing, ask the wrong question, try too hard to be nice, do something stupid, show their discomfort, hurt someone's feelings, or expose the person with HIV or themselves to danger.

This is a two-way street. The person with HIV also may be feeling awkward. He or she may not want to burden others with his or her problems, may want just to socialize and not talk about the illness, or may worry about how others will react if they find out about it. One man from the Lower East Side who had multiple sclerosis said, "I got so tired of explaining my illness and its symptoms to everybody that I finally just told everyone I had AIDS. That was something they understood. I hoped they would just stop asking questions and go away."

As this man's story illustrates, awkwardness often arises in the United States when dealing with people with *any* serious illness.[14,27-29] When you don't feel comfortable, you either work it out or stay away. If you stay away, you often figure out reasons for doing so which won't hurt your own identity. That is, you figure out reasons that help you keep a positive image of yourself—as kind and decent, for example, or, in rare cases, as a "tough" person who doesn't care. If you feel you are "kind and decent" and stay away from people with HIV ("I'm not bothering them"), imagine how they then feel? We'll look at some of the reasons people give themselves that maintain stigma and a positive self-image, and then explore strategies for overcoming stigma, and the fear, avoidance, and interactional awkwardness that may precede, accompany, or follow stigma.

Factors Underlying Fear and Avoidance

Fears of catching HIV or hurting the person with HIV, by themselves, are probably not enough to motivate stigmatization and activate the subsequent fear and avoidance of people with HIV. Social psychologists have found that for heightened fear and avoidance to occur, fear needs to be combined with a feeling that one has little power or control over what is feared.[30,31] That is, because they have insufficient or incorrect knowledge, people are afraid that they might get HIV or endanger or hurt a person living with it, *and* they feel that they do not have the skills to prevent this from occurring.

Also, it is easier to remain fearful and avoidant if the feared individuals are seen as distinctly different from one's self or from the groups with which one identifies.[32] HIV becomes "their" problem and not "ours," so of course we don't need to get involved. Indeed, thinking about in-groups and out-groups, "us" and "them," is such a common way of approaching problems before we deal with them more deeply that every one of us has probably done this. The only trouble is that the virus doesn't do an interview to find out what groups an individual belongs to before it infects someone. It doesn't say:

"Excuse me, I'm conducting a survey and would like to ask you some questions: Is this your first sexual experience or have you been sleeping around? Are you injecting illegal drugs or sharing syringes for your diabetes medications with other family members? Do others think of you as a nice, clean, neat person? Are you a white, gay male ... Oh, sorry, that was last year. Are you a young woman of color? Do you live inside or outside the United States? Do you look healthy or ill? Congratulations, you have answered my questions correctly. You qualify. According to my checklist, here, I can now infect you and skip everybody else."

It sounds silly and it is silly. But if we accuse someone of thinking in terms of "us" versus "them" in a harsh way, we may "brand" or stigmatize that person as uncaring or unthinking—the very sort of thing we are trying to overcome. How, then, do we combat this kind of thinking?

Reducing Stigma and Out-Group—Based Avoidance

First, all of us have complex identities that can't easily be placed into just one category; this is just as true whether or not any of us have HIV. A person may be a brother, a friend, a teacher's assistant, a member of a band, and a pretty good soccer player, and that person may or may not have HIV. Out-group biases—"people with HIV" versus "us"—are more difficult to maintain if we begin to *cross categories*[33,34] of identification when we talk—that is, if we realize that all of us belong to more than one identity category, and that we share different identity categories with different people (for example, friend, sibling, interested in sports as well as experiencing a serious illness, which we probably all will at some point in our lives). In fact, we can cross-categorize HIV infection by calling it one of a number of infectious conditions the way we did at the beginning of this chapter. We can even cross-categorize a poorly functioning immune system (also called immunodeficiency); it can be a symptom of HIV, but it is also experienced by people undergoing transplants (they take medicine to suppress their immune systems so that their bodies won't reject the transplant), by people undergoing chemotherapy for cancer or other conditions (many chemotherapies affect immune function), or by people born with a defective immune system, to name just a few.

Think about the many groups to which you belong and how many different people belong to at least one of those same groups. Cross-categorization often diminishes our tendencies to make in-group versus out-group distinctions. Also, it helps us to begin to experience emotions on behalf of a group with which we do not belong; we still have reason to identify with members of that group because we share other group memberships with many of those same people.[35]

Reducing Stigma through Reducing Fear of "Catching HIV"

Knowing How HIV Is Transmitted

As you have read in other chapters in this book, HIV is relatively difficult to transmit. It has been transmitted by only four bodily fluids—blood, semen, vaginal secretions, and breast milk; and even when transmitted, infection will occur only if a sufficient quantity of the virus enters the body through a "portal of entry" (for example, broken skin, or torn or scratched mucous membranes).

Knowing Why HIV Is Not Transmitted in Other Bodily Fluids

Saliva has an insufficient quantity of HIV cells in it for infection to occur, and the HIV cells in tears and sweat are largely dead.

More Important—Knowing How to Deal with the Most Complicated Situations

When we told the youth of the Lower East Side about how HIV is, and is not, transmitted, some of the reactions of older youth who had relatives with HIV were:[36]

> "Yes, but don't people with HIV sometimes have TB and other things you could catch?"
>
> "Yeah, but my older brother uses my toothbrush all the time. He has hepatitis C and HIV. I know he isn't supposed to, because of hep C, not because of HIV. I'm more worried about how to talk to him about this and about hep C than I am about catching HIV."
>
> "Yeah, but isn't it true, because the immune system of someone with HIV isn't working right, they have to worry about catching all kinds of things from us? More than we have to worry about catching something from them?"

The youth were right in every case.

We quickly came to understand that we had to cross-categorize the disease HIV with *all infectious diseases*—that is, hepatitis C, colds, TB, to name just a few—as well as with conditions that affect the immune system as we did previously. This helps break down the concept of HIV as a disease apart from all others, acknowledges that a person with HIV may have more than one condition (called co-occurring conditions in medicine), and that, because of likely decreased immune function, such a person is at increased risk of catching illnesses from others.

Further, some with HIV don't even know that they have it. It is estimated that, in the United States in 2005, about one-quarter of people with HIV are untested.[37] Throughout, we have been talking about people with HIV as if everyone who has HIV knows it; but not everyone does. To truly prevent this epidemic from spreading further, we should be talking about "people," any of whom may potentially have or get HIV if they perform a risk behavior or are exposed to HIV, and any of whom may be susceptible to other diseases if they are exposed to them, whether or not they already have HIV. In fact, many conditions—most of the hepatitises, many sexually transmitted infections, certainly a cold—are much easier to transmit than HIV. So, to stop epidemics and to protect people, maybe we should be behaving as if anyone could be infected with anything. We have stopped talking about the HIV epidemic in isolation, and about "us" versus "them" "risk groups," such as injection drug users or gay men or health care workers. Instead we have begun talking about many conditions together and about risk behaviors. For example, HIV can be passed by injecting medicines with dirty needles, not just with illegal drug use; this focuses attention on transmission modalities rather than on populations. We arrived here through the social psychological principle of cross-categorization, combined with accurate medical knowledge.

Universal Protection—Universal Precautions

Everyone who works in a hospital has to learn a set of procedures called *universal precautions* that prevent the transmission of *all infectious diseases*. Following these precautions means that you wash your hands before and after contact with others, and that you put a barrier between people and bodily fluids—latex gloves for blood, urine, and feces; goggles if eyes could be splashed; a mask if coughing or sneezing is likely; a gown if clothing is likely to get soiled; don't touch the sharp end of needles or instruments and dispose of used "sharps" in appropriate containers. In fact, these precautions are to be followed in all interactions with patients, for there is often no way to know whether or not dangerous germs are on anyone's skin or if bodily fluids are infected. And most hospitals tell employees to stay away from others if they have a persistent cough or rash.

If we take these precautions down just a notch, most of them sound very much like the home health habits our parents and grandparents have taught us—cover your mouth when you sneeze, wash your hands before eating, cover a sore or cut with a Band-Aid, if you have the flu or the measles stay away from others until you aren't contagious, if colds are going around wash your hands often, be careful around sharp tools or instruments. Such habits protect the person with HIV from getting illnesses from others and also protect others from some forms of blood-to-blood transmission of HIV. All you have to add to this list to greatly reduce HIV transmission is that if you are sexually active, use latex or polyurethane male or female condoms (or use dental dams) as barriers against vaginal secretions and semen or preseminal fluid in order to protect against some, but not all, sexually transmitted infections, of which HIV is one; if you have a baby and are nursing and have HIV, use formula instead of breast milk; and, if you are pregnant and have HIV, go to a doctor who will use special procedures (medicine before and after delivery, cesarean-section) to help prevent transmission to your child during pregnancy or childbirth.

In the study we have been conducting on the Lower East Side, we randomly selected some parents (i.e., male and female guardians, as well as mothers and fathers) and gave them workshops to help them better understand HIV and other medical conditions. We chose parents because they are the major socialization agents for their children; we wanted to know if teaching them would affect the attitude and behaviors of their children, ages 10–13, and if so, how. But we also know that knowledge is not enough; people need to learn how to put that knowledge into practice through acquisition of new skills to transmit it effectively to others and to change their own behaviors. Therefore in these parent workshops, we not only provided them with knowledge (e.g., about universal precautions), we let them practice teaching that knowledge to others, practice skills, and practice using their judgment about what skills to use for over a dozen possible neighborhood scenarios. For example, when discussing universal precautions, it's not enough to tell people to be careful of used syringes; you have to tell them what to do and let them practice it: pick the syringe up from the back using a paper cup to grab it, put it in an unpiercable container like a Gatorade jar, seal the jar with duct tape, and take it to a local hospital, clinic, or pharmacy where it can be disposed of properly.[13]

A Challenge: Should the Brother Eat the Eggs?

Now you know about transmission and some methods of prevention. Remember our story at the beginning of the chapter? One brother has HIV (and thrush) and offers his other brother the rest of his half-eaten scrambled eggs.[2] Let's call the brothers Harry, who has HIV and thrush, and Joe. Now that you've learned about transmission, can you answer the question: Should Joe eat the eggs? When I asked a room full of public health and infectious disease specialists, the conversation went something like this:

> —Nearly all of us have the buds for thrush in our mouths, but our intact immune systems protect us. Joe can safely eat the eggs.
> —Yes, but asthma is common in that neighborhood. Does Joe have asthma? Does he use an inhaler? Asthma medications often contain steroids that alter the immune function in the mouth. If that is the case, Joe should not eat the eggs.
> —We forgot about Harry. Do we know everything we need to know about Joe's health? What if Harry lets Joe eat some eggs and then takes them back to finish them? What if Joe had a cold or cough or some other infectious condition? Or something more serious? Wouldn't he be endangering Harry?
> —And, of course, I want to know if Joe has HIV. He may be one of the ones who has it and hasn't been tested. If that's the case then he surely shouldn't eat the eggs. The thrush poses a danger to him.

It went on and on. Could Joe be a drug user, could he have one of the infections that are more common in injection drug users? Was Harry taking his medications? What are the odds for each of these things? Are you ready to throw up your hands and quit? So were we, until Joe provided the perfect—and simple—solution:

I really didn't want to eat the eggs. I wasn't hungry. But I didn't want to hurt [Harry's] feelings. I knew HIV isn't transmitted in saliva. So I said to him "Look. I know you have to be careful. You can't go eating off everyone's plate. You have to protect yourself in case someone is sick and doesn't know it. It's tough. I don't want you to feel alone in this. So I am going to be careful along with you. O.K.?"

Joe didn't eat the eggs, but his reasoning took in Harry's viewpoint and the adjustments Harry had to make because of his HIV. All Joe really knew was that HIV could affect the immune system and that Harry had to be careful of catching things. He didn't need much more detailed knowledge.

Harry was grateful for Joe's statement and for his behavior. As this story demonstrates, knowledge and understanding of the biology of transmission are not sufficient to inform our interactions with people with HIV. There needs to be sensitivity and kindness as well as safety. Although Joe didn't have that much accurate information about HIV transmission, he knew how to be sensitive and kind by understanding and appreciating Harry's adjustments to HIV.

Reducing Interactional Awkwardness

From hearing about this experience and others, we quickly learned that the best experts on how people with HIV like to be treated are people with HIV and their loved ones who know that they have it and who treat them sensitively and respectfully. In fact, more than a decade ago, caregivers and people with HIV sketched out what they considered to be helpful and unhelpful behaviors.[38] Table 6.2 lists a few of the 22 behaviors they mentioned. All have stood the test of time.

In our study, we made exercises and group activities using the expanded list of behaviors, both helpful and unhelpful. We have used this list in several different ways with many different groups of people, including parents in HIV-affected communities in the United States and abroad, men returning from jail to communities with large numbers of people with HIV, and staff of a major metropolitan hospital. In some cases, we asked volunteers to act out examples from the list so that everyone could see and experience the effects (for example, "We're all going bowling. You look too tired to come. Bye." "Wait . . . gee . . . thanks a lot.") In other cases, we substituted the phrase "someone with an illness" for "person with HIV," and then asked to what illness these behaviors applied. In all cases, we promoted a discussion that concluded, with very little prodding from us, that not only do these behaviors apply to illnesses in general, they apply to how friends and considerate people treat each other for other situations and problems.

Table 6.2
Helpful and Unhelpful Behaviors

Helpful Behaviors	Unhelpful Behaviors
Spending time with the person with HIV in social, relaxing enjoyable activities	Leaving him or her alone and excluded from social activities
Being natural with the person with HIV in the same way one always was	Never talking or saying what you feel about HIV/AIDS or acting in a phony cheerful manner
Being nice to the person with HIV's friends and family; this eases the person with HIV's sense that the illness causes pain and burdens to loved ones	Making rude or insensitive comments or being impolite, such as making fun of symptoms, smoking in his or her presence or not allowing him or her to be alone
Serving as a trusted friend and listening with understanding as if you could be in their shoes	Putting down the way the person with HIV is handling HIV or giving unwanted advice on how he or she should act

Making Appropriate Behavior the Norm

Finally, fear, stigma, and avoidance are reduced when appropriate behavior is promoted through strong expectations, local norms, or even by law.[30] In New York State, for example, strong laws prevent people from discriminating against individuals with HIV in the workplace or in housing, and prevent care providers from disclosing that a person has HIV without that person's permission.[7,13] People with HIV are also covered nationally under the federal Americans with Disabilities Act, which provides some protections and outlines appropriate accommodations for people with disabilities, and which considers HIV infection to be a disability.

Some organizations go beyond compliance with the law. We worked with a major metropolitan New York City hospital to normalize the appropriate ways to interact with people with HIV and the loved ones who accompany them to appointments by conducting a brief training of nearly 950 nonclinical staff (e.g., security guards, receptionists, janitors, housekeepers) based on the principles outlined in this chapter. We called the training "Positive and caring support for people with HIV/AIDS in your families, communities and workplace." The institutional support for the training was evident in that the chief executive officer of the hospital took it, just like everyone else. The challenge was that 50% of the hospital's staff was foreign born, coming from at least five far-flung parts of the world, each with different experiences and thoughts about the HIV epidemic. Yet data from post-training evaluations suggest that it was successful; participants reported that they felt more comfortable about likely daily activities with someone with HIV. Some wrote spontaneously about the changes they would like to make in their daily interactions at work. One person even wrote, "I'll try to be nicer to people who *may* have HIV." It is a lovely statement, because the writer doesn't assume that he can tell who has it and who doesn't. It is likely, then, that laws and training can change attitude and behavior toward persons with HIV.

THE EFFECTS OF PARENT TRAINING ON YOUTH COMFORT INTERACTING WITH PEOPLE WITH HIV: A COMMUNITY INTERVENTION TO DESTIGMATIZE HIV[7]

Can changed attitudes and behaviors be carried across the generations to youth and children? With the help of colleagues at Cornell University,[39] we designed and evaluated an intervention to strengthen the ability of parents in the Lower East Side of New York City to be HIV/sexually transmitted infections/substance use/hepatitis/unintended pregnancy health educators of their own children. As you recall, we called it the Parent/Preadolescent Training for HIV Prevention, or PATH. More than 200 parents and their 10- to 13-year-old children participated in PATH, with families selected at random from public housing units, and some parents randomly selected for in-depth training.

One of the PATH modules focused on safe and sensitive socializing with persons with HIV[13] and formed the basis for everything discussed in this chapter. This module included the following aims: (1) overcome fear, (2) understand transmission of HIV *and* other illnesses, (3) open up a dialogue with a person with HIV about mutual safety, (4) have that dialogue in a way that overcomes interactional awkwardness, and (5) increase resources and skills for each of these aims. You can see how the following activities embody the broad aims we've discussed here.

The module had nine activities designed to: (1) clarify messages about HIV risks; (2) encourage understanding of how different infectious diseases, including HIV, are transmitted; (3) promote mastery of universal precautions for all infectious diseases; (4) practice interacting in a caring manner with a person with HIV; (5) promote understanding of the issues facing families living with HIV; (6) increase knowledge about what persons living with HIV (and most people generally) consider to be negative and positive social support; (7) give practice answering difficult questions about illnesses in general and about HIV in particular; (8) provide an opportunity to map the HIV-related resources in the local community; and (9) present the laws (and their rationale) about HIV privacy, confidentiality, and nondiscrimination.

The module contained these activities:

1. Role-playing parents or children talking about HIV risk, with a third person acting as an observer/coach to improve parent-child communication by learning coaching and reflection skills (which help individuals to view their behaviors as if they were an outside "coach" and to think about the effects those behaviors have on others).

2. A presentation by the facilitators about infectious disease transmission, followed by group processing of a true-false quiz concerning myths and facts about HIV, TB, and other infectious diseases.

3. Practicing universal precautions in situations that may occur in the neighborhood (for example, finding a discarded syringe), accompanied by an illustrated take-home handout about how to properly deal with them.

4. Group processing of how to react to common neighborhood social situations where a person with HIV may be present (see Figure 6.1 for an illustration of such a scene).

5. A video about family life and HIV.

6. Group discussion of the list of helpful and unhelpful behaviors, produced by people with HIV and their caregivers, that we discussed in Table 6.2.

7. Role-playing parents in a family where someone may have HIV whose children are bombarding them with difficult questions about it and about other illnesses that are infectious, stigmatized, life-threatening, or have difficult treatment regimens, followed by processing of how it felt to be the parent or child.

8. Joint construction of a map of HIV-related resources in the neighborhood, accompanied by a local resource guide.

9. Presentation and discussion of best practices and of local, state, and federal laws concerning HIV privacy, confidentiality and nondiscrimination Figure 6.1).

Training the parents had a profound impact on the attitudes and behaviors of the youth that was far beyond our expectations; children of trained parents significantly increased their reported comfort interacting with a person with HIV from before their parents' training to six months later. Comfort with 14 of 22 daily activities with persons with HIV changed for the better, including sharing a soda or beverage (they now know to use two containers); kissing (on unbroken skin); letting a person with HIV cook dinner for you; washing clothes together; letting him/her babysit you; swimming in a pool together; having dinner together; hugging; playing one-on-one basketball; going to the movies together; helping him/her get medicines; going with him/her to medical appointments; listening to his/her fears and concerns; helping with errands. The only areas where they didn't change were activities for which the youth were already comfortable (e.g., shaking hands) or activities that put the person with HIV into a dependent relationship to them (e.g., feeding him/her). In contrast, youth whose parents had not taken the training increased comfort on only one activity: "going to the movies together."

Figure 6.1
For More Than a Dozen Neighborhood Scenes, Parents Are Asked "Someone Here Has HIV; How Could They Be Supported in a Safe and Sensitive Manner?"

For all children who had interacted with a person with HIV in the last month, greater comfort predicted an increased number of recent activities together even after factoring in how close they were to the person with HIV and the number of persons with HIV they had ever known.

Anecdotes reported by trained parents and youth indicate further how the training affected daily life. Before the training, nearly all conversations concerning HIV took the form of a query by a child, a warning by a parent, and a reassurance by the child—"How do people get HIV?" "Don't do sex or drugs or you'll die." "I won't." For these parents, messages improved. They were specific, accurate, and in the child's life context: "You can only get HIV through blood-to-blood contact, or through some other bodily fluids we can talk about, mostly through sex or drugs. It's not easy to get. When your uncle comes to dinner tonight, it's OK to hug him."

One trained parent reported, "I've introduced my child to his uncle with HIV now. He never knew him before."

The fear and social isolation likely produced by stigma were undone in this case.

Finally, there was a truly unexpected result. It seems that just being enrolled in a project about HIV and taking questionnaires about it, as did every parent, trained or untrained, as well as every child, before they began the study and again six months later, opened up talk about HIV. Across more than 200 families and six months of involvement with the PATH project, about 11% of the children lowered their estimate of the number of persons with HIV they thought they knew by about two people, regardless of whether or not their parents were trained. Many told us that they were relieved to learn that some relatives they suspected had HIV did not have it—addressing one of their greatest worries—"someone I know has HIV and hasn't told me."

CONCLUSIONS

Our work suggests it is possible to address and reduce HIV-related stigma by confronting fears, increasing skills, and acknowledging the complexity of people, diseases, and the situations people face. Diseases are complex, people are complex, and the situations people with HIV and their loved ones face together are complex. That complexity means that we must break down our simple categorizations and think more broadly. But the knowledge, skills, and comfort required to do this and to face difficult situations are not complex; they follow simple principles and rules. It seems that all of them—knowledge, skills, comfort, or interactional ease—not just one or two, are required to combat HIV and HIV-related stigma and improve the health of all of us. It is not just people with HIV who have to make adjustments; everyone does.

ACKNOWLEDGMENTS

The authors thank the parents and children of the Lower East Side for their generous and continuing contributions to reducing HIV-related stigma. We also thank Ms. Sylwia Hodorek for her research assistance, as well as Ms. Maria Rodriguez. Parts of this chapter were drawn from a forthcoming research article to be published in the *Journal of Pediatric Psychology*. The authors thank the National Institute of Mental Health for their continued support of the PATH project (MH53834).

REFERENCES

1. Garrett, L. 1994. *The Coming Plague: Newly Emerging Diseases In A World Out of Balance.* New York: Farrar, Strauss and Giroux.

2. Krauss, B. J., L. Goldsamt, E. Bula, and R. Sember. 1997. The white researcher in the multicultural community: Lessons in HIV prevention education learned in the field. *J Health Educ* 28(6):67–71.

3. DeVita, V., S. Hellman, and S. Rosenberg, eds. 1997. *AIDS: Etiology, Diagnosis, Treatment and Prevention.* 4th ed. Philadelphia: Lippincott-Raven.

4.   Centers for Disease Control and Prevention. 2005. MMWRs on HIV/AIDS and surveillance: Trends in HIV/AIDS diagnoses—33 states, 2001–2004. 54(45):1149–53. http://www.cdc.gov/hiv/pubs/mmwr/Surveillance.htm. Accessed Nov.18, 2005.

5.   Chu, S. Y. and J. W. Curran. 1997. Epidemiology of human immunodeficiency virus infection in the United States. In *AIDS: Etiology, Diagnosis, Treatment and Prevention*, ed. V. T. Devita, S. Hellman, and S. A. Rosenberg, 4th ed. Philadelphia: Lippincott-Raven Publishers.

6.   Preventing HIV/AIDS in adolescents. National Commission on AIDS. 1994. *J Sch Health* 64 (1):39–51.

7.   Krauss, B. J., C. C. Godfrey, J. O'Day, and E. Freidin. 2006. Hugging my uncle: The impact of a parent training on children's comfort interacting with persons living with HIV. *J Pediatr Psychol.*

8.   Houghton Mifflin Company. 2001. *The American Heritage Dictionary of the English Language*, 4th ed. Surrey, England: Delta Publishing.

9.   Rawls, J. 1971. *A Theory of Justice*. Boston: Harvard University Press.

10.   Goffman, E. 1963. *Stigma: Notes on the Management of Spoiled Identity*. New York: Simon and Schuster.

11.   Pantaleo, G., et al. 1997. Immunopathogenesis of Human Immunodeficiency Virus infection. In *AIDS: Etiology, Diagnosis, Ttreatment and Prevention*, eds. V. T. Devita, S. Hellman, and S. A. Rosenberg. 4th ed, 75–88. Philadelphia: Lippincott-Raven Publishers.

12.   UNAIDS: The Joint United Nations Programme on HIV/AIDS. 2004 Report on the Global AIDS Epidemic: Executive Summary. http://www.unaids.org/bang-kok2004/GAR2004_html/ExecSummary_en/ExecSumm_00_en.htm. (Accessed 23 November 2005).

13.   Krauss, B. J., et al. 2000. Saving our children from a silent epidemic: The PATH program for parents and pre-adolescents. In *Working with Families in the Era of HIV/AIDS*, eds. W. Pequegnat and J. Szapocznik, 89–112. Thousand Oaks: Sage.

14.   Siegel, K., and B. J. Krauss. 1991. Living with HIV infection: Adaptive tasks of seropositive gay men. *J Health Soc Behav* 32 (1):17–32.

15.   Hack, K. L., A. M. Somlai, J. A. Kelly, and S. C. Kalichman. 1997. Women living with HIV/AIDS: The dual challenge of being a patient and caregiver. *Health Soc Work* 22:53-62.

16.   Lichtenstein, B., M. K. Laska, and J. M. Clair. 2002. Chronic sorrow in the HIV-positive patient: Issues of race, gender, and social support. *AIDS Patient Care STDS* 16 (1):27–38.

17.   Schrimshaw, E. W. 2003. Relationship-specific unsupportive social interactions and depressive symptoms among women living with HIV/AIDS: Direct and moderating effects. *J Behav Med* 26 (4):297–313.

18.   Herek, G. M., J. P. Capitanio, and K. F. Widaman. 2002. HIV-related stigma and knowledge in the United States: prevalence and trends, 1991–1999. *Am J Public Health* 92 (3):371–77.

19.   Das-Douglas, M. 2005. Primary drug resistant HIV: A brief overview. Presented at the Annual Conference Planning Meeting of the National Institute of Mental Health Consortium of Family Grantees, Brooklyn, NY.

20.   Baker, S., M. Sudit, and E. Litwak. 1998. Caregiver burden and coping strategies used by informal caregivers of minority women living with HIV/AIDS. *Abnf J* 9 (3):56–60.

21.   Demi, A. 1997. Effects of resources and stressors on burden and depression of family members who provide care for an HIV-infected woman. *J Family Psychol* 11:35–48.

22.   Draimin, B H., et al. 1999. A troubled present, an uncertain future: Well adolescents in families with AIDS. *Journal of HIV/AIDS Prevention and Education for Adolescents and Children* 3:37–50.

23. Gewirtz, A. and S. Gossart-Walker. 2000. Home-based treatment for children and families affected by HIV and AIDS. Dealing with stigma, secrecy, disclosure, and loss. *Child Adolesc Psychiatr Clin N Am* 9 (2):313–30.

24. Poindexter, C. C. 2002. 'It don't matter what people say as long as I love you': Experiencing stigma when raising an HIV-infected grandchild. *J Ment Health Aging* Winter:331–48.

25. Roth, J., R. Siegel, and S. Black. 1994. Identifying the mental health needs of children living in families with AIDS or HIV infection. *Community Ment Health J* 30:581–93.

26. Krauss, B. J., C. Godfrey, J. O'Day, J. Pride, and M. Donaire. 2000. Now I can learn about HIV—Effects of a parent training on children's practical HIV knowledge and HIV worries: A randomized trial in an HIV-affected neighborhood [Abstract]. *XIV World AIDS Conference, Conference Record* (2 July 2000):170.

27. Fife, B. L. and E. R. Wright. 2000. The dimensionality of stigma: A comparison of its impact on the self of persons with HIV/AIDS and cancer. *J Health Soc Behav* 41 (1):50–67.

28. Fleishman, J. A., C. D. Sherbourne, S. Crystal, R. L. Collins, G. N. Marshall, M. Kelly, S. A. Bozzette, M. F. Shapiro, and R. D. Hays. 2000. Coping, conflictual social interactions, social support, and mood among HIV-infected persons. HCSUS Consortium. *Am J Community Psychol* 28 (4):421–53.

29. Link, B. G., J. Mirotznik, and F. T. Cullen. 1991. The effectiveness of stigma coping orientations: Can negative consequences of mental illness labeling be avoided? *J Health Soc Behav* 32 (3):302–20.

30. Brewer, M. 2003. *Intergroup Relations*. Philadelphia: Open University Press.

31. Smith, C. A. and R. S. Lazarus. 1990. Emotion and adaptation. In *Handbook of Personality: Theory and Research*, ed. L. A. Pervin, 609–637. New York: Guilford Press.

32. Tajfel, H. 1969. Cognitive aspects of prejudice. *J Biosoc Sci* Suppl 1:173–91.

33. Hewstone, M., M. R. Islam, and C. M. Judd. 1993. Models of crossed categorization and intergroup relations. *J Pers Soc Psychol* 64 (5):779–93.

34. Messick, D. M. and D. M. Mackie. 1989. Intergroup relations. *Annu Rev Psychol* 40:45–81.

35. Mackie, D. M., T. Devos, and E. R. Smith. 2000. Intergroup emotions: Explaining offensive action tendencies in an intergroup context. *J Pers Soc Psychol* 79 (4): 602–16.

36. Krauss, B. J. 1997. HIV education for teens and preteens in a high-seroprevalence inner-city neighborhood. *Fam Soc* (November-December):579–91.

37. Centers for Disease Control and Prevention. HIV Testing Among Populations at risk for HIV Infection—Nine States. November 1995-December 1996. http://www.cdc.gov/.mmwr/PDF/wk/mm4750.pdfCDC.

38. Hays, R. B., L. McKusick, R. Pollack, R. Hilliard, C. Hoff, and T. J. Coates. 1993. Disclosing HIV seropositivity to significant others. *AIDS* 7 (3):425–31.

39. Tiffany, J., D. Tobias, A. Raqib, and J. Ziegler. 1993. *Talking with Kids about AIDS: A Program for Parents and Other Adults Who Care (manual)*. New York: Cornell University.

Chapter 7

HIV DISCLOSURE: WHO KNOWS? WHO NEEDS TO KNOW? CLINICAL AND ETHICAL CONSIDERATIONS

Lori Wiener, Ph.D. and Maureen E. Lyon, Ph.D., A.B.P.P.

Friends

By Deanna

I want them
I need them
everyone does
without friends
the world would end
at least my life would feel
so empty and blue
friendships help bring
happiness, it's true
My life was a secret
from all who I knew
for 13 years I lied
to everyone I knew
Then one day I told
cause I couldn't be me
I said I've got a disease
it's called HIV
No one believed me
at least that day
so I said it again
in a different way
Now the word was out
that this kid had AIDS
so many questions
so many afraid

Now they understand
that I am okay
and I have more friends
it's much better this way
When living a lie
it was hard to be
myself or relaxed
in my friends company
Today I am happy
for what I have done
I told the truth
And now I can have fun
The kids in school
I can now see
they care for me
as a friend
with HIV

As increasing numbers of HIV-infected children are surviving well into their adolescent and young adult years,[1,2] the management of diagnosis disclosure becomes a crucial component of medical, psychological, and social care.[3,4] Disclosure of HIV status is complex with uncertain consequences and unique considerations for each individual. In this chapter we first examine how adolescents learn of their diagnosis. This process differs for adolescents who have acquired their infection at birth or early in life, compared with adolescents who have acquired HIV through sexual contact. Next, we propose guidelines for professionals to facilitate disclosure to patients and for patients to facilitate disclosure to others. Then we discuss ethical guidelines for health care providers using the HIV Ethical Decision Making Model.[5] Complications when the patient is a minor and in institutional settings, such as the workplace, schools, and emergency rooms, are also examined. Finally, we discuss ways to help youth living with HIV make conscious choices about having children that include both partners and their health care provider to ensure the best possible outcome for the new family.

LEARNING THE DIAGNOSIS

Early in the epidemic HIV-infected children born with HIV were told little about their disease. With poor survival expected, it was thought to be in the child's best interest to protect him/her from the emotional burdens and societal prejudices that his/her parents faced.* Change began with dramatic

---

* For the purposes of this discussion, "parents" refers to caregivers who might be grandparents or guardians.

improvements in mortality and morbidity. With puberty, the likelihood of sexual activity made it critical for adolescents to know the truth to protect others from the virus. With increasing autonomy and independence, the need to take medications as prescribed made it critical for adolescents to be fully informed to protect themselves from the virus. There was also an increasing risk that adolescents would learn their diagnosis by chance, potentially damaging trust in their caregiver and health care provider.

As HIV positive children lived into adolescence, policy and practice began to change. This culminated in 1999, when the American Academy of Pediatrics' Committee on Pediatric AIDS published a report[6] endorsing disclosure to older children and adolescents as beneficial and ethically appropriate. Within treatment centers, as children's immunologic status stabilized or improved, conversations about disclosure of diagnosis became an important focus of care. "Should we tell the truth?" was no longer a choice.

Prevalence of Disclosure: Parent to Child

Depending on the study, between 10% and 75% of children over the age of seven know their HIV diagnosis.[7-10] With rare exceptions all adolescents living with HIV are told about their HIV infection. Different sample sizes, demographic factors, and disease status account for some of the discrepancy in these findings. There are also regional and programmatic practices and policies that account for these differences.

Predictors of Disclosure

Research suggests that children living with HIV are more likely to be told their diagnosis the older they are. Other predictors of disclosure are higher child IQ, increased parent-rated child anxiety, higher medication dose frequency, a recent major life event, and greater family expressiveness.[7,10,11]

Patterns of Disclosure: Parent to Child

Patterns of disclosure vary from complete disclosure, in which the child learns the name of the illness (HIV and/or AIDS), disease-specific information and how the child acquired the disease; to partial disclosure, in which the child learns that he or she has a virus that is affecting the immune system.[12] Many children who receive partial disclosure are told of the need to take medicine to keep their virus at bay, and often how their virus can be transmitted, without the term HIV or AIDS being used. Sometimes deception occurs when the nature of the illness is hidden behind another condition, such as asthma or cancer. Complete nondisclosure occurs when there is no communication about the illness or the caregiver denies that a disease exists.

Researchers at the National Institutes of Health[7] found that 75% (N = 99) of the children in their setting on average had been told their diagnosis by the age of 7 1/2 years. Of those who knew, however, 35% followed the disclosure pattern of deceptive information being given by their caregiver. Recent studies confirm that a significant minority of children receive only partial information about the diagnosis from their parents.[8,9] In all, 45% of these children reported "not being surprised" when told their diagnosis; 11% reported that their lives had gotten better after learning the diagnosis; 49% felt their lives had not changed much, and 30% felt their lives changed for the worse since learning their diagnosis. Also, 65% of the children felt like they were told at the right time and 86% by the right person.

Disclosure Outcomes: Patient Reports

Children who were told their diagnosis usually reported good outcomes. They had better self-esteem and were less likely to be depressed than children who did not know their diagnosis.[14,15] HIV-infected children who learned their diagnosis and who lived in a supportive environment also report positive psychosocial adjustment.[16] In a study of psychiatric disorders, a more severe end of the clinical spectrum of behavior and mood, children who knew their diagnosis were no more likely to have a psychiatric problem than those who did not know their HIV status.[9]

In a study of children who reported sharing their diagnosis on television shows and in newspapers, those children who went public were less likely to feel competent, compared to those who did know their diagnosis and did not go public.[11] This is the only study of its kind and suggests that adolescents and families should be cautious when making this choice.

Impact of Disclosure: Clinical Observations

Clinicians report positive outcomes associated with disclosure including the promotion of trust, improved adherence, enhanced support services, open family communication, and better long-term health and emotional well-being[6,10,16] when the timing of disclosure was sensitive to their cognitive development. Children with HIV are at risk for significant cognitive impairment. Developmental data suggest specific problems with processing speed, memory, and other measures of executive planning and judgment. Although the adolescent may be able to meet "mature minor" criteria for "competence," observations of "adolescent onset dementia" impairment of executive abilities, combined with the observation of deteriorating function in adolescence point to the need for careful consideration about earlier disclosure and development of new models for support of comprehension of HIV-related information as children age.[17]

Disclosure is most correctly thought of as a process. Table 7.1 provides guidelines for health care providers to assist the parent/guardian in disclosing the HIV diagnosis to a child or adolescent who has been infected since birth or early childhood.[13]

Table 7.1
Guidelines for Disclosure

Step One—Preparation

- Have a meeting with the parent/caregivers involved in the decision-making process. Staff members that the family trusts should be present.
- Address the importance of disclosure and ascertain whether the family has a plan in mind. Respect the intensity of feelings about this issue. Obtain feedback on the child's anticipated response. Explore the child's level of knowledge and his or her emotional stability and maturity.
- If the family is ready to disclose, guide them in various ways of approaching disclosure (see Step Two).
- If the family is not ready, encourage them to begin using words that they can build on later, such as *immune problems*, *virus*, or *infection*. Provide books for the family to read with the child on viruses. Strengthen the family through education and support and schedule a follow-up meeting. Let the family know that you will meet with them on a regular basis to help guide them through the disclosure process and to support the child and family after disclosure. Respect the family's timing, but strongly encourage the family not to lie to the child if he or she asks directly about having HIV, unless significant, identifiable safety concerns render the decision to disclose inadvisable. Also remind the family to avoid disclosure during an argument or in anger.

Step Two—Disclosure

- In advance, have the family think through or write out how they want the conversation to go. They need to give careful consideration to what message they want their child to walk away with. Encourage the family to begin with "Do you remember" to include information about the child's life, medications, and/or procedures so that the child is reminded of past events before introducing new facts.
- Have the family choose a place where the child will be most comfortable to talk openly.
- Provide the family with questions the child may ask so they are prepared with answers. Such questions include "How long have you known this?"; "Who else has the virus?"; "Will I die?"; "Can I ever have children?"; "Who can I tell?"; "Why me?"; and "Who else knows?"
- Encourage having present only the people with whom the child is most comfortable. The health care provider may offer to facilitate this meeting,

(Continued)

Table 7.1
Guidelines for Disclosure (Continued)

---

but if at all possible, preparation should be done in advance so that the family can share the information on their own.

- Medical facts should be kept to a minimum (immunology, virology, the effectiveness of therapy) and hope should be reinforced. Silence as well as questions need to be accepted. The child should be told that nothing has changed except a name is now being given to what he or she has been living with. The child also needs to hear that he or she didn't do or say anything to cause the disease and that the family will always remain by the child's side.
- If the diagnosis is to be kept a secret, it is important that the child is given the names of people to talk to, such as a health care provider, another child living with HIV, and/or a family friend. Stating, "You can't tell anyone," makes the child feel ashamed and guilty.
- Provide the child with a journal or diary to record questions, thoughts, and feelings. If appropriate, provide books about children living with HIV.
- Schedule a follow-up meeting.

Step Three—After Disclosure

- Provide individual and family follow-up meetings two weeks after disclosure and again every two to four weeks for the first six months to assess the impact of disclosure, answer questions, and to help foster support between the child and family.
- Ask the child to tell you what he or she has learned about the virus. In this way, misconceptions can be clarified. Writing and art may be useful techniques.
- Assess changes in emotional well-being and provide the family with information about symptoms that could indicate the need for more intensive intervention.
- Support parents for having disclosed the diagnosis and, if interested and available, refer them to a parents' support group. Encourage them to think about the emotional needs of the other children in the family in the disclosure process.
- Remind parents that disclosure is not a one-time event. Ongoing communication will be needed. Ask parents what other supports they feel would be helpful to them and their child. Provide information about HIV camp programs for HIV-infected and affected youth.

Source: Wiener, L.S. 2004. Disclosure. In *Textbook of Pediatric HIV Care*, ed. S.L. Zeichner and J.S. Read, 667–71. Cambridge: Cambridge University Press.

Thinking ahead about reasons for telling or not telling is one of the best ways to prepare for disclosure. Medical staff and family members of adolescents should support disclosure as a process, encouraging appropriate timing, organization of support systems, and culturally sensitive language. They can also support the youth

Table 7.2
Guidelines for Disclosure for Adolescents

Here are a few questions those who support adolescents in the disclosure process can help them ask and answer:

- Why do you want to tell them?
- Why do you feel they need to know?
- Will they understand the importance of keeping it to themselves?
- What are the advantages of telling them?
- What are the disadvantages of telling them?
- How realistic are your expectations?
- Are you likely to regret having told them?

In the future, are you likely to regret not having told them sooner?

by being open with them about the challenges, as well as the advantages of disclosure. Table 7.2 provides guidelines to help adolescents decide who they should tell.

Prevalence and Patterns of Disclosure: Teen to Others

Who teens tell and what effect their telling has on friends, employers, potential partners, and sexual partners are not well studied.[13,18–20] In a year-long study of 64 children who told their HIV diagnosis to friends, the children who disclosed had significantly greater immune functioning (higher CD4 cell %), than children who had not yet told their HIV status to friends. This effect remained significant even when the child's age and level of medication (protease inhibitors) were statistically controlled.[21]

In the nationwide REACH (Reaching for Excellence in Adolescent Care and Health) study of 317 behaviorally infected adolescents, adolescents were more likely to disclose their HIV status to their mothers than to their fathers (77% vs. 47%).[13] Among behaviorally infected adolescents, length of time since diagnosis and Hispanic ethnicity are associated with disclosure to mothers.[13]

The more social support teens had the more likely they were to tell a parent. They were also more willing to disclose their status to sexual partners who were also HIV-positive.

Among adolescents infected since early childhood, the majority chose not to share their status with others (guardian already knew). However, adolescents who decided to tell other family members, friends, and romantic partners were more likely to receive social support and have a good social self-concept, fewer problem behaviors, more classmate support, and fewer post-traumatic stress symptoms, such as intrusive thoughts and avoidant behaviors.[4,20,21]

Clinical impressions suggest that adolescents infected at birth become sexually active later than uninfected children in comparable age ranges. One possible explanation is that perinatal HIV infection appears to delay pubertal development in children and adolescents.[22] Delay in pubertal development may influence adult height[23] and psychosocial development of a child, and even add to social stigma of HIV disease. Psychologically, delayed puberty, like delayed growth, is an issue for these youth as they are greatly concerned about their appearance and how their bodies compare to those of their peers. Like other chronically ill pediatric patients who have diminished skeletal growth and delayed puberty, HIV-infected children and adolescents may be more distressed about their actual or perceived pubertal delay than about their underlying chronic illness.[22] These have important implications for clinical practice. For example, a 15-year-old HIV-infected teen may report no interest in dating or becoming sexually active. This could result in a deemphasis on their need for sex education. The pregnancies of several adolescents infected since birth underscores the importance of information and sex education, even at the age of 18, when providers may assume the teen has "heard it all." Without proper education on transmission prevention, these long-term survivors are a potential source of HIV transmission.[24] Clearly, sexual activity and disclosure of one's status leads to ethical challenges and underscores the importance of an adolescent developing a code of sexual ethics. This is consistent with Erikson's[25] description of adolescence as a time when adolescents consolidate a moral code of living.

Ethics as a discipline invites us to use reasoned analytic and critical approaches and precedents to answer questions about how we ought to behave in given situations and why. The clinical and psychosocial profile of HIV-infected adolescents is often complex and emotion-laden. Accordingly, conflict or uncertainty about when and how to disclose one's HIV status can ensue. Stepping back to critically examine and discuss each situation can be clarifying and in itself empowering.[26]

ETHICS AND DISCLOSURE

Health care providers working with HIV-positive adolescents and young adults benefit from having a working model for arriving at sound ethical decisions when coping with HIV-related issues of disclosure in clinical practice. When the individual is an adolescent minor, ethical issues are even more challenging. Fortunately, the American Psychological Association (APA), Office on AIDS, has developed a curriculum, *Ethical Issues and HIV/AIDS: A Multi-Disciplinary Mental Health Services Curriculum,* to meet these challenges. The curricula teach a process for arriving at sound ethical decision making. APA's HIV Office for Psychology Education has trained hundreds of psychologists nationwide to teach the curriculum.[5] Although not HIV-specific, another resource is The Center for Ethical Practice. The Center provides consultation and training for mental health professionals, which focuses on ethical decision making when working with adolescents.[27] This process of ethical decision making can be applied to the painful ethical dilemmas that arise when conflicts exist when trying to determine the best interest of the HIV positive adolescent, the law, ethical principles, privacy rights, and public health.

A discussion of the model developed under the guidance of APA's Office on AIDS[5] is presented here with the permission of the authors. Although several models could be used for ethical decision making, we chose this one because it has been tested and accepted by psychologists working with HIV-positive clients.

ETHICAL DECISION MAKING: A MODEL

A model for ethical decision making is a process that assumes that there are no right or wrong answers. Ethics sometimes conflict with the law. Nine steps are involved:[5]

1.   Pause and identify your personal response to the case.
2.   Review the facts of the case.
3.   Conceptualize an initial plan based on clinical issues.
4.   Consult your agency's policies and your professional codes.
5.   Analyze your plan based on the five ethical principles listed in Table 7.3.
6.   Identify the legal issues.
7.   Refine your plan so that it:

- Is most congruent with your personal values.
- Advances clinical interests as much as possible.
- Permits you to operate within agency policies and professional ethics codes.
- Minimizes harm to client and relevant others.
- Maximizes all other ethical principles to extent possible.
- Allows you to operate within the law.

8.   Choose a course of action and share it with your client.
9.   Implement course of action: Monitor and discuss outcomes.

FIVE ETHICAL PRINCIPLES

The five ethical principles are well known to medical ethicists and are derived from a long Western history of philosophy starting with the Greeks and early

Table 7.3
Five Ethical Principles

Autonomy—The Right to Self-Rule:

- The right to do what you want as long as you do not interfere with the welfare of others.
- The right to free choice
- Autonomy presumes the client is mentally competent to make his or her own decisions.

Beneficence—Benefit Others:

- As helping professionals, we have an obligation to improve and enhance the welfare of our clients, even when that might inconvenience us as providers.
- When other considerations are equal, we must presume the welfare of the client is our primary consideration.

Nonmaleficence—Do Not Harm:

- Avoid inflicting physical or psychological harm to others.
- Avoid actions that might put others at risk of harm.

Fidelity—Be Faithful:

- Keep promises.
- Tell the truth.
- Be respectful of our clients in order to build and maintain their trust.

Justice—Be Fair:

- Treat all of our clients fairly.
- Ensure that each receives his or her due portion of our time and energy.
- Justice presumes impartiality, reciprocity, and equality.

Violating these principles, whether they are in conflict with each other or because a "higher moral purpose" might be served—places a strong burden on the individual to provide an ethical rationale for rejecting the principle.

Source: Karen S. Kitchner. Ethical principles and decisions in student affairs. *Applied Ethics in Student Services*. ed. J.H. Cannon and R. D. Brown. pp. 17–29. New Directions in Student Services, No. 30. San Francisco: Jossey Bass.

Romans (Table 7.3). What follows is a case illustrating ethical challenges with respect to confidentiality and disclosure.

Joe**

Joe is a 14-year-old African American with HIV who acquired his infection after a sexual assault by a male friend of his mother. Joe's mother and

---

** The details of cases have been changed to protect the identity of individuals.

grandmother abused alcohol and drugs. Joe was removed from his home and was placed in the foster care system. While the court was making a decision about appropriate placement for him, Joe was invited to join an after-school group for at-risk teens in the Adolescent Clinic. Joe's HIV status was known to the group leader who was part of his health care team, but not to the members of the group. The purpose of the group was to educate adolescents about sexual behaviors, contraception, pregnancy, and disease prevention in order to decrease risky behaviors and to improve health. Joe made friends easily and was readily accepted into the group. Joe was a bright youngster who attended a local magnet school. Joe became friends with a boy his age in the group, Dwight. About six weeks into the group, Dwight revealed to the group leader that he and Joe had had oral sex with one another. Joe was upset.

Do you need to breach Joe's confidentiality? Does Dwight's need to find out about his HIV status and his risk of infection from Joe supersede his right to confidentiality? How does the fact that Joe is a minor affect your analysis? Which of the five ethical principles apply to this case? Do any of these ethical principles conflict? Answer these questions by performing an ethical analysis using the APA model.

The APA decision-making model can lead to different but equally ethical decisions. It is the process of following the model that will lead to an ethical decision that is clinically sound and legally defensible, regardless of what your decision actually is. Using this model can also help to prevent burnout and harm to oneself and to one's client. It can also increase confidence in one's decisions.

See Table 7.4 on Confidentiality and Disclosure: The Pitfalls of Working with Minors for guidelines specific to working with adolescent minors, keeping these issues in mind as the model is applied to this case.

LEGAL CONSIDERATIONS: CONFIDENTIALITY VERSUS DISCLOSURE BY HEALTH CARE PROVIDERS

What are a licensed health care provider's obligations with regard to confidentiality of HIV-positive patients' diagnosis? What are a provider's responsibilities with regard to duty to warn and duty to protect the rights of others from harm? Laws differ from state to state. Health care providers have an obligation to know the law in the state in which they practice and to be aware that the law may differ greatly even within a small geographical area. For example, in Virginia a physician has a legal right to notify a spouse of their husband/wife's HIV status, but not any other sexual partner. The Department of Public Health has the authority to disclose HIV status to a spouse. In Virginia law [VA. Code Ann. 32.1–289.2 (1989) and

Table 7.4
Confidentiality and Disclosure: Pitfalls in Working with Minors

A. You do not clarify your positions up front.

B. You are lacking in relevant information.

- What are the statutes of your state with regard to minor's right to consent to mental health treatment and to medical treatment "as an adult?"
- Legal requirements re/disclosure are more specific for particular issues (e.g., federal regulations for any state agency that receives federal funds).

A. You fail to anticipate/recognize conflicts of interest between "vested parties."

- Can you work effectively with a minor client without establishing a good relationship with the child's parent/guardian?
- Different belief systems lead to different priorities: Do you believe your obligation re/confidentiality is to the child client, or is it to the family?

B. You do not have *clear positions or policies* regarding confidentiality and disclosure.

- What do you believe about the "rights" of a minor client?
- Can you establish a good therapeutic relationship with a minor *even if you offer limited confidentiality?*
- What do you believe about the "rights" of the parent/guardian?

C. You do not have a developmental model re: when and how to involve minors in treatment planning and decisions.

- Research children ages 12 to 15 have an understanding of confidentiality.
- The goal of disclosure is not just to obtain consent, but to ensure understanding.
- Your goal is not just to avoid disclosure, but rather to establish a working relationship in which clients can take the lead in sharing or consenting to have shared information. This process includes:

  o Explaining clearly the reason for disclosure.
  o Exploring the likely consequences and repercussions of the disclosure.
  o Discussing how to proceed so that negative consequences are minimized and potential benefits are maximized.

D. You do not have a working model for assessing risk.

Source: Sherry Kraft, Ph.D. and Mary Alice Fisher, Ph.D., *The Center for Ethical Practice*, Charlottesville, VA. www.CenterForEthicalParctice.org.

VA. Code Ann. 18.2–67.4:1 (2004)], it is a felony to know one's HIV status and to have unprotected sex without disclosing one's HIV status, even if the infected person uses a condom.

In nearby Maryland, a physician and other licensed heath care providers may use their informed medical judgment about disclosing a patient's HIV status to sexual partners. The physician or other licensed heath care provider will not be liable either way. In Maryland [Md. Ann. Health Gen 18–601.1 (1989)] exposing another person to HIV is a misdemeanor, and the infected person is subject to a $2,500 fine or imprisonment for up to three years.

In contrast, in Washington D.C., there is no law regarding disclosure or duty to warn. This means that physicians and health care providers have an obligation to keep a patient's information confidential. In case law, a suit was brought by a spouse against a local hospital for not disclosing her spouse's positive HIV status. The court upheld the right to privacy of the HIV-positive patient and the obligation of the health care providers to protect the privacy of the HIV-positive patient.[28]

Fortunately or unfortunately, these laws change over time.[29] Readers should consult with local advocacy groups and their local Department of Health for up-to-date information. A Web site funded by the Centers for Disease and Control and Prevention (CDC) lists the laws in all 50 states www.hivcriminallaw.org. The work of Gostin and Hodge in 2000[30] discusses HIV partner counseling and referral services and the handling of willful exposure cases, when an HIV-positive person intends to cause harm by intentionally infecting another person. This scholarly report discusses the CDC and other governmental policies and procedures. The report also discusses the issues of privacy and the right to know from a legal and ethical perspective, as well as the powers and duties to protect individuals and the public health.

INSTITUTIONAL CONSIDERATIONS: WORK, DISCLOSURE, AND THE AMERICANS WITH DISABILITIES ACT

On June 25, 1998, the U.S. Supreme Court ruled in *Bragdon v. Abbott* that HIV disease falls within the scope of the Americans with Disabilities Act (ADA) for protection from discrimination. Generally, the ADA prohibits discrimination in employment and places of public accommodations by employers, hospitals, physicians, other health care workers, and others.*** The Court recognized that impairment from HIV can affect a host of other life activities

***See the home page for the ADA at http://www.usdoj.gov/crt/ada/adahom1.htm or call 1–800–514–1301 (voice) or 1–800–514–0383 (TTD) for answers to general and technical questions. Equal Employment Opportunity Commission 1-800-669-4000.

that may be supported by the ADA. Legal experts say the ADA does offer protection to HIV-infected workers, and these employees should seek reasonable accommodation at their workplaces whenever possible and necessary.[31] Despite this good news, there is evidence that at least some HIV-infected patients have postponed antiretroviral treatment or taken early leave from their work, rather than disclose their HIV status.

Adolescents do not need to volunteer their HIV status during the hiring process, or after they are hired, if they do not need accommodations. Once hired for a job, however, they will need to be honest about their health on any insurance forms they are asked to complete about their health. Generally speaking the application of the law with regard to confidentiality is highly dependent on the facts of the case. The American Civil Liberties Union provides guidance at http://www.aclu.org/HIVAIDS/HIVAIDS.

Adolescents should also be informed that they will not be eligible for military service. The military excludes individuals with any medical illness, such as asthma, and including HIV. Individuals infected with HIV while in the military, however, will not necessarily be discharged if they are able to maintain a state of good health. HIV-positive adolescents are eligible for training through Job Corps, provided that they reveal their HIV status when asked, either on forms or during the interview process. There have been a number of adolescents whose failure to be honest about their HIV status during the application process resulted in the loss of the opportunity to join Job Corps.

Conversations with employers about AIDS and disability can be difficult. If an accommodation is needed, generally it is the responsibility of the employee to tell this to the employer. Adolescents should be encouraged to talk with their health care provider, before taking the conversation to work. Their health care provider can best describe how AIDS may affect their work and can provide a note outlining the diagnosis and any time off or workplace accommodations that will be needed. Generally speaking, less is best in these situations. Employers should have needed information, but the adolescent should be able to protect their privacy and dignity. The same process holds true for adolescents completing their physicals for their college applications.

INSTITUTIONAL CONSIDERATIONS: PUBLIC SCHOOLS—WHO NEEDS TO KNOW?

Fear of discrimination is often what prevents a parent from disclosing their child's HIV status to the school, or an adolescent from disclosing HIV status to the teachers or classmates.[32] Federal policy directly addresses the issue of discrimination in public schools. The U.S. Department of Education, Office for Civil Rights (OCR) in Washington, D.C., writes the regulations and administers the policy on the school placement of children with AIDS under Section 504 of the Rehabilitation Act of 1973. OCR policy clearly protects individuals infected by AIDS and prohibits discrimination against children with AIDS as qualified handicapped persons. OCR policy states that most children with AIDS can attend school in the regular classroom without restrictions.

Federal policy does not address the issue of who in a public school needs to know a child's HIV status. This is left to state laws and policies, which differ from state to state. Some state laws and school board policies require that a student's HIV status be disclosed to school personnel. Students, parents, health care providers, and school personnel should find out if their school has a policy and if their state has a law about disclosure of HIV status to school personnel. For example, the state of Illinois's AIDS Confidentiality Act under "Notification of School" states that if a school-age child is reported to the Illinois Department of Public Health or any local health department as having been diagnosed with HIV, the agency must notify the principal of the school where the child is enrolled (http://www.illinoislegalaid.org/).

In contrast, the New York State Legislature passed a law that HIV status does not require disclosure, unless it is relevant to the health of the infected individual or to the development of an appropriate educational program (http://www.emsc.nysed.gov/sss/HIV/Policy_Implementation_Package). The New York law is consistent with the advice of the CDC.[32]

State laws also differ with respect to playing sports at school. For example, Tennessee's State Board of Education recently changed its policy to allow students living with HIV to play school sports (http://www.thebody.com/cdc/news_updates_2005/apr22_05). The National Association of School Psychologists has a position paper with recommendations regarding disclosure in schools[33] (http://www.nasponline.org/information/pospaper_aids.html). The document, "Someone at School Has AIDS: A Guide to Developing Policies for Student and School Staff Members Who are Infected with HIV,"[34] provides a guide to helping schools develop or revise existing policies to deal effectively with HIV in schools (http://www.nasbe.org).

It is unusual for parents to voluntarily disclose their child's HIV status to school officials or classmates.[35] The effect of the fears of discrimination[36] can be seen in the contrast with parents of children with other chronic illnesses who want their child's school to be informed and for the physician to provide this information.[37] When parents of children with HIV do disclose their child's HIV status, they are most likely to inform the school nurse.[38] Benefits of disclosure include having the school nurse administer medications and monitor medication side effects, as well as informing parents when there is an outbreak of infectious disease. An informed teacher can reinforce an Individual Education Plan, assess educational goals, be flexible with assignments due during times of medical appointments and hospitalizations, and observe possible physical or emotional problems.

The health care team can also help families decide who needs to know at school. This begins by making sure that parents know that their adolescent has a right to an education, regardless of illness severity. Sometimes a meeting is needed in which a health care provider accompanies a parent and an adolescent to the school to let teachers, the principal, and the school nurse know of the educational, emotional, and health care needs of a particular adolescent.[37] Health care providers reinforce the message that adolescents living with HIV should prepare for young adulthood.[38]

INSTITUTIONAL CONSIDERATIONS: EMERGENCY ROOMS

A study of 124 emergency room visits by HIV-positive adolescents found that in 38% of the visits, there was no note in the medical record that the patient was HIV-positive.[39] This is worrisome on two counts: first, 45 of these visits involved potential health care worker exposure to the HIV virus; second, 11 of the visits involved medical management decisions, which would have been different if the health care provider had known the adolescents' HIV status. Although all health care workers need to consistently practice universal precautions, this is a risky situation for HIV-positive adolescents who may receive less than optimal diagnostic workup or treatment for their presenting illness. Some patients may have assumed that the emergency room staff had access to their records, which was not true at the time of this study period, 1986–1996. HIV-positive adolescents should be instructed to disclose their HIV status when they present to the emergency room. In high-prevalence areas, health care providers in the emergency room should be trained to ask about the HIV status of patients as part of the routine workup.

DISCLOSURE AND DESIRE FOR A CHILD

With the benefit of highly active antiretroviral treatment (HAART), particularly when it is started before pregnancy and the benefit of cesarean section, the risk of transmission of HIV to a child through pregnancy (perinatal transmission rate) has been reduced to an overall rate of 0.99% in 2001–2002 from a rate of 5.1% in 1997–1998,[40] from the highest rate of 78% in 1993.[41] Elective cesarean section delivery was associated with a significant reduction in transmission rates, averaging 40%, independent of HIV viral load and maternal treatment with antiretroviral agents.[41] With new technologies and treatment, the risk of transmission of HIV to an uninfected partner has also been minimized.

There are differences in the way that knowledge about HIV transmission through pregnancy is given to HIV-positive persons of reproductive age. In some HIV clinics, HIV-positive persons are rarely given medical advice on reproduction,[42,43] even though a significant proportion of HIV-infected individuals express a wish for parenthood. In contrast, several European fertility clinics have experience in providing both intrauterine inseminations and in vitro fertilization to couples to achieve pregnancy where the male is HIV-infected and the female is uninfected, without HIV transmission to the uninfected female partner.[43,44]

There is little evidence that knowledge of HIV status is having a significant impact on decisions about pregnancy. Rates of pregnancy and abortion are similar for HIV-negative and -positive women.[45,46] Although pregnancies may be unplanned, most HIV-positive women (70%) report that the most important reason for carrying pregnancy to term was the desire for a child.[47] Little data are available regarding adolescents and pregnancy. In a study of 75 perinatally infected young women, however, six females became pregnant and, of those, three individuals had more than one pregnancy. The average age of first conception was 17.2 years. Compared to their community peers, adolescents infected at birth with HIV were more likely to become pregnant (14% vs. 11.8%).[48]

Our clinical experience suggests that HIV-positive adolescents and young women, especially those who are not engaged in medical care or who are "lost to care," are afraid to disclose their HIV status to an obstetrician/gynecologist. They fear the disapproval, judgment, and anger that they expect their doctor to have toward them, because of their pregnancy. They may also fear that an abortion will be recommended. This may have the unintended consequence of keeping them from seeking care early in their pregnancy. They often also fear disclosure of their diagnosis to their loved one. Sometimes, it is the fear that the disclosure will end the relationship. Other times, it is fear of violence because of their betrayal of the trust of their partner. Also present is the fear that they have infected their partner.

Adolescents and youth have a basic human right to all information and services related to their reproductive health.[49] Yet, national laws and international agreements often are neglected or are unrecognized.[49] Even in the United States, there is resistance to reproductive techniques that would decrease the risk of HIV transmission to a loved one, even for adults.[50] Still, others have argued that the primary ethical concern is the autonomy of the HIV-positive person to make decisions about having a child and that, for this reason, fertility services should never be denied to people with HIV/AIDS, particularly given that techniques and treatments are available to minimize harm to the uninfected partner.[51]

Gloria

Gloria was a behaviorally infected, HIV-positive 14 year old when she began treatment in the Adolescent Clinic of a children's hospital setting. She and her family knew her diagnosis. When she was 17 years old, her aunt noticed that she was pregnant and pressured her to terminate her pregnancy, which Gloria did reluctantly. Gloria was in psychotherapy at the time for treatment of a somato-form disorder, with multiple physical symptoms with no known medical cause. She believed her HIV was a punishment from God for her bad behavior. Her family agreed. Shortly after her abortion, Gloria became "lost to treatment."

At the age of 22, Gloria tracked down her former therapist in a private prac-tice setting and asked if she could schedule an appointment. On the phone she reported that she had a job, her own apartment, and was attending college part-time. What she did not reveal was that she was six months pregnant—too late to get an abortion. She had not received medical care, or antiretroviral medication, since leaving the Adolescent Clinic. She also had not disclosed her HIV status to her boyfriend, Chris. Chris was violent, an attribute she initially thought was protective. Although Gloria reported a good relationship with Chris, she also reported that, when provoked, he would beat her.

The first session focused on linking Gloria with medical care through the public health system of a small city, which had a specialty HIV clinic. Gloria kept her appointment. The obstetrician was furious with her and referred her to a surgeon to perform a cesarean section at the time of delivery to reduce the risk of transmission to the baby. Gloria was started on antiretroviral medications, which she reported taking with 100% adherence.

The next few sessions focused on ways to disclose her HIV status to Chris. He planned to be at the birth. Because of her worry that he might become vio-lent, finding a safe place and a safe context for the disclosure was discussed. The disclosure could take place in her doctor's office or in her therapist's office or in the presence of her family (her aunt and older brother). She could then suggest to him that he also get tested. In the end Gloria decided to tell Chris on her own. She chose a time when he would not be studying for exams and when he was sober. She also alerted her aunt, who agreed to come to her apartment that evening, as if she had just stopped by spontaneously. Although Gloria was afraid, she garnered her courage and tearfully said she had something important to tell him. She was surprised by Chris's response, "We all have to die of something someday." He revealed that he was afraid she was going to tell him that the baby was not his or that there was something wrong with the baby. She assured him that the baby was his and that she was now taking medication to protect the baby. She also told him that the doctor planned to do a cesarean section, which would also protect the baby. She asked Chris to get tested and let him know that her doctor agreed to test him the next time she went in for a checkup. She told him that she was would take very good care of his child, whether or not the child was infected with HIV, and whether or not he decided to stay with her.

This story had a good outcome. Gloria's baby and Chris were HIV-negative. Two years later, Gloria sent her therapist an email. She described the gratitude she felt toward Chris, even though he was no longer a part of her life. She had very much wanted to have a child, but she was too conflicted with fear of infecting Chris, fear of infecting a child, and her desire to have a child, to make this choice consciously.

HIV-positive adolescents and youth have a fundamental need and desire to reproduce. Under these circumstances, it is best to take a nonjudgmental approach to reproductive decision making, which respects an adolescent's autonomy.[51] The empowerment of young people to promote and safeguard their rights to access sexual and reproductive health information and services may enable them to act on their own behalf to gain access to the information and services they need to make informed choices.[49] Without such an approach, HIV-positive adolescents may avoid contact with the health care system, endangering not only their lives, but also the lives of their loved ones and children. Fertility intentions and sexual relations need to be addressed consistently by health care providers.[51]

CONCLUSION

The issue of disclosure strikes at the heart of all persons infected and affected by HIV. HIV disease presents increasing challenges to adolescents, their parents, and health care providers because of the uncertain disease outcome, associated stigma, and frequent ethical challenges.[52] Most adolescents benefit from the assistance available to them through a comprehensive multidisciplinary care team approach that is tailored to their developmental needs and social circumstances and includes culturally sensitive counseling and supportive intervention programs around disclosure, prevention of disease transmission, and treatment options. Enabling adolescents to find meaning in life, praising their survival skills, and tapping new sources of psychic strength, courage, and resiliency are the essence of this demanding yet rewarding work.

REFERENCES

1. Gortmaker, S. L., M. Hughes, J. Cervia, M. Brady, G. M. Johnson, G. R. Seage, 3rd, L. Y. Song, W. M. Dankner, and J. M. Oleske. 2001. Effect of combination therapy including protease inhibitors on mortality among children and adolescents infected with HIV-1. *N Engl J Med* 345 (21):1522–28.

2. Berk, D. R., M. S. Falkovitz-Halpern, D. W. Hill, C. Albin, A. Arrieta, J. M. Bork, D. Cohan, B. Nilson, A. Petru, J. Ruiz, P. S. Weintrub, W. Wenman, and Y. A. Maldonado.

2005. Temporal trends in early clinical manifestations of perinatal HIV infection in a population-based cohort. *JAMA* 293 (18):2221–231.

3. Lipson M. 1993. Disclosure within families. *AIDS Clin Care* 5:43–44.

4. Wiener, L. S., and H. B. Battles. 2006. Untangling the web: a close look at diagnosis disclosure among HIV-infected adolescents. *J Adolesc Health* 38 (3):307–309.

5. Jue, S., T. Eversole, and J. R. Anderson. 2000. *Ethical Issues and HIV/AIDS Mental Health Services.* Washington, DC: American Psychological Association. For further information, resources, trainers and participants should consult the American Psychological Association's HIV and Ethics Resource Manual from the APA Office on AIDS, 750 First Street, NE, Washington, DC 20002–4242: phone (202) 336–6052.

6. Disclosure of illness status to children and adolescents with HIV infection. American Academy of Pediatrics Committee on Pediatrics AIDS. 1999. *Pediatrics* 103 (1): 164–66.

7. Wiener, L. S., H. B. Battles, N. Heilman, C. K. Sigelman, and P. A. Pizzo. 1996. Factors associated with disclosure of diagnosis to children with HIV/AIDS. *Pediatr AIDS HIV Infect* 7 (5):310–24.

8. Flanagan-Klygis, E., L. F. Ross, J. Lantos, J. Frader, and R. Yogev. 2001. Disclosing the diagnosis of HIV in pediatrics. *J Clin Ethics* 12 (2):150–57.

9. Lester, P., M. Chesney, M. Cooke, R. Weiss, P. Whalley, B. Perez, D. Glidden, A. Petru, A. Dorenbaum, and D. Wara. 2002. When the time comes to talk about HIV: Factors associated with diagnostic disclosure and emotional distress in HIV-infected children. *J Acquir Immune Defic Syndr* 31 (3):309–17.

10. Mellins C, E. Brackis-Cott, C. Dolezal, A. Richards, S. W. Nicholas, and E. J. Abrams. 2002. Patterns of HIV status disclosure to perinatally HIV-infected children and subsequent mental health outcomes. *Clin Child Psychol Psych* 7(1):101–14.

11. Wiener, L. S., H. B. Battles, and N. Heilman. 2000. Public disclosure of a child's HIV infection: Impact on children and families. *AIDS Patient Care STDS* 14 (9):485–97.

12. D'Angelo, L. J., S. E. Abdalian, M. Sarr, N. Hoffman, and M. Belzer. 2001. Disclosure of serostatus by HIV infected youth: the experience of the REACH study. Reaching for Excellence in Adolescent Care and Health. *J Adolesc Health* 29 (3 Suppl):72–79.

13. Wiener, L. S. 2004. Disclosure. In *Textbook of Pediatric HIV Care,* ed. S. L. Zeichner and J. S. Read, 667–71. Cambridge: Cambridge University Press.

14. Bacha, T., L. Smith, and E. C. Pomeroy. 1998. Exploration of knowledge of diagnosis and depression in children ages 9–12 with HIV infection. Paper presented at the XII International Conference on AIDS.

15. Blasini, I. C., C. Cruz, L. Ortiz, I. Salabarria, and N. Scalley. 1998. Disclosure model for pediatric patients living with HIV. Paper presented at the XII International Conference on AIDS.

16. Wiener, L. 1998. Helping a parent with HIV tell his or her children. In *HIV and Social Work: A Practitioner's Guide,* ed. D. Aronstein and B. Thompson, 327–38. Binghamton, NY: Haworth Press.

17. Armstrong, D. W., E. J. Levy, B. Briery, E. Vazquez, M. Merritt-Jensen, K. Miloslavich, and C. Mitchell. 2002. Merging of neuroscience, psychosocial functioning, and bioethics in pediatric HIV. Paper presented at the110th Annual American Psychological Association, Chicago, Illinois.

18. Lyon, M., C. Brasseux, and L. J. D'Angelo. 1999. Who should I tell? Disclosure of HIV status by infected adolescents. *J Adolesc Health* 24:20.

19. Rotheram-Borus, M. J., and S. Miller. 1998. Secondary prevention for youths living with HIV. *AIDS Care* 10 (1):17–34.

20. Battles, H. B., and L. S. Wiener. 2002. From adolescence through young adulthood: Psychosocial adjustment associated with long-term survival of HIV. *J Adolesc Health* 30 (3):161–68.

21. Sherman, B. F., G. A. Bonanno, L. S. Wiener, and H. B. Battles. 2000. When children tell their friends they have AIDS: possible consequences for psychological well-being and disease progression. *Psychosom Med* 62 (2):238–47.

22. Buchacz, K., A. D. Rogol, J. C. Lindsey, C. M. Wilson, M. D. Hughes, G. R. Seage, 3rd, J. M. Oleske, and A. S. Rogers. 2003. Delayed onset of pubertal development in children and adolescents with perinatally acquired HIV infection. *J Acquir Immune Defic Syndr* 33 (1):56–65.

23. Biro, F. M., R. P. McMahon, R. Striegel-Moore, P. B. Crawford, E. Obarzanek, J. A. Morrison, B. A. Barton, and F. Falkner. 2001. Impact of timing of pubertal maturation on growth in black and white female adolescents: The National Heart, Lung, and Blood Institute Growth and Health Study. *J Pediatr* 138 (5):636–43.

24. Frederick, T., P. Thomas, L. Mascola, H. W. Hsu, T. Rakusan, C. Mapson, J. Weedon, and J. Bertolli. 2000. Human immunodeficiency virus-infected adolescents: A descriptive study of older children in New York City, Los Angeles County, Massachusetts and Washington, DC. *Pediatr Infect Dis J* 19 (6):551–55.

25. Erikson E. 1963. *Childhood and Society* 2nd ed. New York: Norton.

26. Wiener, L., A. Septimus, and C. Grady. 1998. Psychological support and ethical issues for the child and family. In *Pediatric AIDS: The Challenge of HIV Infection in Infants, Children, and Adolescents*, ed. P. A. Pizzo and C. M. Wilfert, 3rd ed. Baltimore: Williams & Wilkins.

27. The Center for Ethical Practice, 934 E. Jefferson St., Charlottesville, VA 22902. Mary Alice Fisher, Ph. D. Director. Phone: 434–971–1841. www.CenterForEthicalPractice.org.

28. Bruner, Daniel, Esq. (Director of Legal Services, Whitman Walker Clinic, Washington DC), In discussion with the author, January, 2005.

29. Lazzarini, Z., S. Bray, and S. Burris. 2002. Evaluating the impact of criminal laws on HIV risk behavior. *J Law Med Ethics* 30 (2):239–53.

30. Gostin, L. O., and J. G. Hodge. 2002. HIV partner counseling and referral services-handling cases of willful exposure. August 30, 2000. www.publichealth.law.net

31. Here's a look at status of court rulings on ADA. First key decision involved HIV-infected person. 2001. *AIDS Alert* 16 (2):18, 23–24.

32. Education and foster care of children infected with human T-lymphotropic virus type III/lymphadenopathy-associated virus. 1985. *MMWR Morb Mortal Wkly Rep* 34 (34):517–21.

33. National Association of School Psychologists. 2005. Position Statement on HIV/AIDS. http://www.naspaonline.org/information/pospaper_aids.html.

34. Bodgen, J., K. Fraser, C. Veg, and J. Aschcroft. 2001. *Someone At School Has AIDS: A Complete Guide to Education Policies Concerning HIV Infection.* Alexandria, VA: National Association of State Boards of Education:

35. Massachusetts Department of Public Health. 1997. Most parents are hesitant to tell school about child's HIV. *AIDS Policy Law* 12(14):4.

36. Cohen, J., C. Reddington, D. Jacobs, R. Meade, D. Picard, K. Singleton, D. Smith, M. B. Caldwell, A. DeMaria, and H. W. Hsu. 1997. School-related issues among HIV-infected children. *Pediatrics* 100 (1):E8.

37. Andrews, S. G. 1991. Informing schools about children's chronic illnesses: Parents' opinions. *Pediatrics* 88 (2):306–11.

38. Wiener, L., Havens, J., and Ng, W. 200_ Psychosocial challenges in pediatric HIV infection. In *Medical Management of AIDS in Children*. Philadelphia: W. B. Saunders Company.

39. Fanburg, J. T., and J. D'Angelo L. 1999. Inaccurate documentation of HIV-positive status in adolescents visiting an urban emergency department. *J Adolesc Health* 25 (5):354–57.

40. Bartlett, J. G. 2005. Mother-to-child transmission of HIV infection in the era of highly active antiretroviral therapy. *Clin Infect Dis* 40 (3):458–65.

41. Lindegren, M. L., R. H. Byers, Jr., P. Thomas, S. F. Davis, B. Caldwell, M. Rogers, M. Gwinn, J. W. Ward, and P. L. Fleming. 1999. Trends in perinatal transmission of HIV/AIDS in the United States. *JAMA* 282 (6):531–38.

42. Sherr, L., and N. Barry. 2004. Fatherhood and HIV-positive heterosexual men. *HIV Med* 5 (4):258–63.

43. Panozzo, L., M. Battegay, A. Friedl, and P. L. Vernazza. 2003. High risk behaviour and fertility desires among heterosexual HIV-positive patients with a serodiscordant partner—two challenging issues. *Swiss Med Wkly* 133 (7–8):124–27.

44. Bendikson, K. A., D. Anderson, and M. D. Hornstein. 2002. Fertility options for HIV patients. *Curr Opin Obstet Gynecol* 14 (5):453–57.

45. Sunderland, A. 1990. Influence of human immunodeficiency virus infection on reproductive decisions. *Obstet Gynecol Clin North Am* 17 (3):585–94.

46. Kirshenbaum, S. B., A. E. Hirky, J. Correale, R. B. Goldstein, M. O. Johnson, M. J. Rotheram-Borus, and A. A. Ehrhardt. 2004. "Throwing the dice": pregnancy decision-making among HIV-positive women in four U.S. cities. *Perspect Sex Reprod Health* 36 (3):106–13.

47. Smits, A. K., C. A. Goergen, J. A. Delaney, C. Williamson, L. M. Mundy, and V. J. Fraser. 1999. Contraceptive use and pregnancy decision making among women with HIV. *AIDS Patient Care STDS* 13 (12):739–46.

48. Bernstein, K., C. Trexler, and L. D'Angelo. 2006. "I'm just like anyone else": Risk behaviors and health consequences in perinatally infected HIV-positive adolescents. Annual Meeting of the Society of Adolescent Medicine, Boston, MA.

49. United Nations Population Fund. Supporting Adolescents and Youth. http://www.unfpa.org/about/index/htm.

50. Denenberg, R. 1993. Applying harm reduction to sexual and reproductive counseling. A health provider's guide to supporting the goals of people with HIV / AIDS. *SIECUS Rep* 21:8–12.

51. Grady, C. 1997. Human immunodeficiency disease: Ethical considerations for clinicians. In *AIDS: Etiology, Diagnosis, Treatment, and Prevention*, 4th ed., 633–644, ed. V. T. DeVita, S. Hellman, and S. A. Rosenberg. Philadelphia: Lippincott-Raven.

52. Wiener, L., A. Septimus, and C. Grady. 1998. Psychological support and ethical issues for the child and family. In *Pediatric AIDS: The Challenge of HIV Infection in Infants, Children, and Adolescents*, 3rd ed., ed. P. A. Pizzo and C. M. Wilfert. Baltimore: Williams & Wilkins.

Chapter 8

MENTAL HEALTH ISSUES FOR CHILDREN INFECTED AND AFFECTED BY HIV AND THEIR FAMILIES

Willo Pequegnat, Ph.D.

What Is Depression Anyway?

By Anita, 03/19/2002

I was 11 when things started to change for me.
My attitude started getting bad.
I no longer did as I was told
I became disrespectful
I had little interest in food
I became frustrated easily with my schoolwork
I slept more and didn't want to get out of bed
Things really got on my nerves
I daydreamed more
I really didn't care if I lived or died
So taking my medicine for HIV wasn't important to me.
Of course, that led to more fights at home.
The more fighting there was, the angrier I became.
The more angry I became, the worse I felt about myself

I knew I could do better at home and at school
I knew something was wrong
I felt something was happening in my head
But I wasn't sure what it was
I remembered my mom went through something like this
    after her mom died.
She was yelling a lot
Crying a lot
And generally unhappy

It is hard to accept that you are depressed
It is one thing to have something wrong with your body
You have no control over that
But to have something wrong with your mind is different
You think you should be able to "get over it"

Then I learned about the word "depression"
From someone who knows me well and I can trust
I learned how my brain controls my emotions
And that medicines can help take away some of the feelings that were
    overwhelming to me
The medicine would not be able to bring my mom back
It would not be able to bring my dad back either
And it would not be able to take away the fact that I have HIV
But it could and it did take away the feeling that I couldn't go on
I began to smile again
That was when I realized how long it had been since I had smiled before
    I began to feel hungry again
I learned to swallow pills
Schoolwork became easier
I had enough energy to get out of bed and do fun things
I argued less
I fought less about taking my medicines (I still hated swallowing pills)
I began to make plans about the future

I still think about my mom and my dad all the time
I will always miss them
But now, I can feel them with me
I feel less guilty about being the one to survive
And I am learning to cope with my feelings.
I am able to talk about my mom and dad without crying
And I am making lots of stuff to help me remember them

I know that depression is something that I will always have to watch out
for
It runs in families, just like blue eyes or being short
I know the signs to look for.
I am no longer embarrassed about needing help for depression because I
know I can get better.

If you have any of the signs I described, talk to someone who you trust
Like HIV, there was treatments for depression.
Unlike HIV, it doesn't have to threaten your life!

As a global epidemic, HIV is a major threat to the health of families. Both
the number of children with HIV and the number of families affected by a
parent with HIV continues to increase at an alarming rate.[1-6] Yet, there are not
good data in a population-based sample of the prevalence of mental distress or
disorders in children with HIV disease. The Methodology for Epidemiology
of Mental Disorders in Children and Adolescents Study estimated that almost

21% of U.S. children ages 9 to 17 years had a diagnosable mental or addictive disorder associated with at least minimal impairment.[7] The Surgeon General's Report on Children's Mental Health asserts that one in five children experiences the signs and symptoms of a DSM-IV disorder during the course of a year, but only about 5% of all children experience what professionals term *extreme function impairment.*[8]

This chapter examines the mental health impact of HIV on both infected and affected children and their families. In this chapter, "children" are defined as they are by the National Institutes of Health: an individual under the age of 21. The first section discusses the problems and the second section reviews some of the interventions. The final section outlines future research directions.

MENTAL HEALTH ISSUES ASSOCIATED WITH HIV

Families affected by HIV must meet multiple challenges beyond those of the disease. Whether the infected person is a parent, sibling, or the child, the disease affects the entire family. There is limited research on the longitudinal impact of HIV on parents or siblings and achievement of milestones during critical developmental periods of HIV-infected children. What is known suggests that there are profound long-term effects on the development and later behavior of HIV-infected children.[9,10]

What Are These Problems?

These families are handling problems of HIV within the context of cumulative stressful life events caused by racism, poverty, and few resources.[11] Problems that contribute to psychological distress and exacerbate psychiatric disorders include:

- Concern about treatment failure, side effects of treatment, and recurrent HIV-related illness episodes
- Psychological distress associated with HIV disease (e.g., depression, hopelessness, feelings of loss, confusion, loneliness, fear, and suicidal ideation)
- Difficulty in maintaining "normalcy" or routine in living
- Handling the stigma of HIV disease
- Isolation of families, which depletes the available social support
- Guilt about having infected loved ones
- Overwhelming task of relating to multiple health and mental health providers
- Need for custody planning in the event that treatment does not slow the progression of the disease
- Anxiety related to lack of financial support, sexual involvement, and medical outcomes

- Lack of available and affordable housing and frequent dislocations
- Lack of respite from providing care

Impact of Parental HIV on Family Environment

The severity of the parent's disease can have an impact on the way the family interacts, which in turn determines the family environment. With a severely ill parent in the house, the family environment may be characterized by unpredictability, depression, and an accumulation of stressful events.[12,13]

Women have been the traditional caregivers for children, but many seropositive women have few resources to provide for their infected and affected children. Many are drug abusers, and others have multiple health and mental health problems, lack family or other social support, experience chronic depression, and exhibit poor self-esteem.[14-16] They may have few work-related skills and therefore have limited ways to support themselves and their children.

When mothers are HIV-positive and experiencing these problems, their children are experiencing these problems both directly and indirectly.[17] The mothers may be unable to provide consistent caretaking and physical affection, which contributes to a chaotic family system.[18] Maternal neglect or unavailability during the early years of a child's life can lead to developmental delays and vulnerabilities in later life.[19] Children may be left alone to solve their own problems, be unsupervised, or expected to fulfill inappropriate roles. They may be forced to be absent from school to care for an ill parent or younger children, which results in anger. They often are not able to participate in age-appropriate activities that nurture their psychosocial development.

The consequence of such a situation for a mother is that without another family member to step forward to assume the parental role, children may be shifted from one foster home or institutional setting to another.[20] Having an ill mother, multiple caretakers, and an unstable living arrangement can undermine children's ability to respond to environmental stimuli, to acquire skills, and ultimately to perform well on cognitive tasks.

Whether intentional or not, maltreatment that arises in such situations during childhood can be associated with later risky sexual behaviors (i.e., more partners, less frequent condom use, more frequent intercourse, and less testing for HIV). This is particularly true when other factors (e.g., psychological distress, drug use, general self-efficacy) coexist to mediate the relationship between these earlier experiences and HIV risk behavior in an adolescent.[21] The age and developmental stage of the HIV-affected or infected child also mediate the impact of these unpredictable events.

Children whose mothers carefully monitor their activities within a positive mother-child relationship are most likely to be resilient despite the impact of HIV.[22,23]

A series of research projects have examined the impact of mother's HIV serostatus on their children. What we have learned from these studies is that children whose mothers have HIV/AIDS are more likely to have behavioral and emotional problems, such as aggressive behavior or anxious and depressed mood.[24] Maternal restrictions in activity were more important than illness severity in predicting which children had mental health distress or problems. Furthermore, the greater the maternal psychological distress, the more behavioral problems were observed in children. Although certain factors were hypothesized to be protective (family cohesion, adaptability, parent-child relationship and child-dependency, productivity, cognitive ability), this research has shown that the more cohesive the family was rated by the mother, the more behavioral symptoms were reported in the children. This may be because these families are more enmeshed and the impending loss of a mother causes more distress. Of special concern, this team found that only 35.5% of the children experiencing serious clinical problems were receiving mental health services.

Contributing to the impact on the health of children are a parent's behaviors, as well as their HIV status. If parents were involved in injection drug use (IDU), several investigators have documented that this is associated with more conduct problems and mental health symptoms in children.[25,26] One study assessed the relationship between status of IDU in mothers and their children's psychopathology and social functioning.[27] The children were 6 to 11 years old living in an urban area with the IDU parent. Parental HIV infection was associated with an eightfold increase in the prevalence of disruptive behavior disorder in their children, compared with children of HIV-negative parents. Parental depression was associated with a threefold increase in the prevalence of children's disruptive behavior.

The death of a parent has a special impact on children. The impact of HIV-related parental death was evaluated on 414 adolescents over six years.[28] The adjustment of bereaved adolescents was compared over four time periods relative to the parental death and was also compared with the adjustment of nonbereaved adolescents. Bereaved adolescents had significantly more emotional distress, negative life events, and contact with the criminal justice system than nonbereaved teens. Depressive symptoms, passive problem solving, and sexual risk behaviors increased soon after parental death, but passive problem-solving levels were similar to the levels of nonbereaved peers.

Donna[*]

Donna was diagnosed HIV-positive when she was 16 years old. She had already had 10 sexual partners and she did not know who had infected her. Donna's parents were divorced when she was 12 years old, and her mother had died from HIV when she was only 14 years old. Donna described herself as a "parentified" child who took primary responsibility for the care of her younger brother and sister, before her mother's death. Because her father and other family members were not willing to make a home for Donna and her brother and sister, they lived in a successive number of foster homes. She was not able to form a warm relationship with any "parental figure" and began to stay out late and fail in school. She came to the attention of Child Protective Services who referred her for evaluation, because she appeared to be depressed; however, Donna denied depression on interview and on self-report questionnaires. Despite her initial reaction to learning her diagnosis, she reported that she was hopeful about the future. As she came to trust her therapist, however, she reported suicidal ideation after having forced sexual relations with a person, which the therapist labeled a sexual assault. After being diagnosed with Major Depression, Single Episode without Psychotic Features, and Post-traumatic Stress Disorder, she was hospitalized in a psychiatric hospital on an adolescent unit. Donna was placed on an aggressive treatment regimen, and she was able to be moved to a group home where she was able to successfully return to school.

These results suggest the importance of early family mental health intervention soon after HIV diagnosis and before parental death, which is sustained over time. Some of the themes or constructs that are consistently identified as contributors to positive family environment and good mental health of family members, which could be targets for interventions, are communication, problem-solving skills, warmth-negative affect, social support (both within and outside the family), parenting (supervision, monitoring, parental control), and caregiving and caretaking.[29,30]

Psychological Distress and Psychiatric Disorders

The next question is how these factors in the family environment impact the psychological distress and psychiatric disorders of infected and affected children.[31,32] Although the prevalence of psychological symptoms among children with poor health has been documented, the prevalence of psychiatric symptoms in HIV-infected children has not been clearly established. Nonetheless, it is generally felt that these symptoms occur at a higher rate among HIV-infected children.[33] Some children, particularly younger ones,

---

[*]The details of cases have been changed to protect the identity of individuals.

exhibit symptoms that seem to simulate autism. Some older children have episodes where they have flat affect and appear to be depressed. To illustrate how difficult it is to demonstrate the nature of such symptoms, it has been observed that the latter could be due to problems with facial muscles and not an underlying psychiatric syndrome! At the same time, some preschool and early school-age children with HIV infection seem to show above-average levels of hyperactivity and attentional difficulties that are often disruptive and maladaptive.[34] Even when these children possess average and above average abilities, they have been held back one or two grades.

There has been more acceptance of HIV disease as people learn more about the routes of transmission and treatment methods improve, but children with HIV continue to experience more psychological distress than their uninfected peers, which is manifested as depression, anxiety, and hyperactivity; however, few research projects have identified psychiatric disorders. Frequently there are problems in diagnosing psychiatric disorders in children because the physical manifestations or neurocognitive dysfunction from HIV can mask depression. In one of the few studies that reported disorders of seropositive adolescents using the Structured Clinical Interview for DSM-III-R-Patient Version (SCID-P), 44% were assessed with current major depression, 26% mood disorder ever; 59% substance abuse ever, and only 15% had no diagnosis. However, there were only 34 subjects in the study and it was based in a medical clinic setting.[35]

In another study that was designed to assess psychiatric problems in HIV-positive children and their relationship to central nervous system disorders and the severity of the disease, 47% exhibited major depression and 29% exhibited attention deficit-hyperactivity disorder.[36] Major depression was significantly associated with neuroimaging or clinical neurologic abnormalities, but this was not true of hyperactivity. The study concluded that low CD4 lymphocytes are associated with psychiatric complications and that these indicate that there is severe HIV disease and the depressive disorder may be a clinical form of encephalopathy. Therefore low CD4 should be a trigger to screen for psychiatric problems in seropositive children.

Theories of stress and coping account for a significant amount of variance in HIV-infected children's psychological adjustment.[37] In this study, higher rates of psychological adjustment problems were found in seronegative children than in seropositive children. Children with HIV disease who have not been told their diagnosis and children who endorse more emotion-focused coping strategies tended to exhibit more psychological adjustment problems.

In summary, evidence is growing that children with serious ongoing health conditions and their families are at a heightened risk for mental health problems. The effects of poor physical health may interact with other risk factors for mental health problems such as stress, poor coping strategies, fear of disclosure, and limited social support.

Mental Health Intervention Programs: What Might Make a Difference?

Because HIV is often a multigenerational disease in the family setting, comprehensive mental health service delivery programs need to provide services that are truly family based. Ideally, they will be part of an effort to address psychosocial, psychiatric, and medical problems of all infected and affected individuals in the family. An appropriate goal might be increased treatment adherence (Table 8.1).

Many of these affected families do not have good problem-solving skills.[38] They are often also afflicted by high rates of substance abuse and mental illness. As a result, services provided to them should be provided by multidisciplinary teams to tailor the services to the diverse needs of families and the individuals infected and affected by HIV disease.[39] These patients have multiple problems that may be more likely recognized and diagnosed by service providers with different expertise; for example, a psychologist may identify depression and not disease progression as a problem, whereas the neurologist might realize the patient is experiencing more problems as a result of dementia, not muscular compromise.

Table 8.1
Comprehensive Program for Mentally Healthy Families Infected and Affected by HIV

- A commitment to meeting the broad needs of the family
- Multidisciplinary professional expertise in the treatment of children supported by administrative policies and procedures to facilitate integration of health and mental health care
- Easy access to an array of services tailored to the needs of the family
- Systematic methods of culturally congruent diagnostic assessment of both family systems and individuals
- Crisis intervention and emergency services
- In/outpatient medical and psychiatric services, including substance abuse treatment
- Health education and adherence programs
- Consultation programs to school systems about infected and affected children
- Aggressive outreach for less accessible populations (e.g., the homeless, seriously mentally ill, runaway youth)
- Mobile services for home care and respite care
- Referrals to appropriate research protocols providing the latest treatments

Rick

Rick's primary physician observed depressed mood and psychomotor retardation shortly after telling Rick that his disease had progressed to AIDS. Because he thought that this was due to Rick's realization that poor adherence to his medical regimen had contributed to his disease progression, his doctor made a referral to a psychologist for treatment of depression; however, psychological testing revealed a significant decline in cognitive functioning from the baseline five years ago. Additional evaluations confirmed motor slowing, a decrease in processing speed, decreased constructional ability, and decreased short-term auditory memory. Because this cluster of symptoms can be associated with HIV dementia and depressed mood, Rick was referred to a neurologist for a differential diagnosis. The neurologist confirmed HIV dementia and changed his medications. Rick also received counseling and home visits from the treatment specialist to increase treatment adherence and to enhance his everyday living skills.

Comprehensive programs should use an intensive case management approach to engage and retain these beleaguered families in treatment, care, and prevention services.[40,41] The advantage of this sort of support is twofold: first, as many of these patients have a poor history with medical service providers and do not feel comfortable in these settings, an understanding and supportive case manager may serve as a "champion" who understands their problems and helps ensure they get the right services and don't feel stigmatized in the process of getting care.[42] Of equal importance is the role a case manager may play in getting their clients to accept mental health intervention. They often feel that medical care is necessary, but that engaging in any kind of therapy is a sign of weakness and failure on their part, which they do not want to admit. The case manager, as counselor and friend, can help them overcome these feelings.

Although what has been learned about the psychosocial problems associated with chronic illness of children in families can provide some guidance in meeting the challenge of HIV, there are some significant differences that require more innovative and coordinated responses.[43] With many chronic health problems (e.g., childhood diabetes, leukemia, asthma), only the child is ill, and the parents can attend to the care of their children. As has been noted previously, for many of our families, multiple members may be ill. This is compounded by the fact that HIV is also associated with a number of perennial social problems, including poverty, homelessness, and drug abuse, which means that health is not the only difficult life circumstance.[44-46] These are the very problems that may have been at the heart of the social milieu that helped create the right situation for HIV infection to have occurred and now serve to exacerbate the health and mental health care problems associated with caring for seropositive children and their families.

Psychosocial Interventions

Psychosocial interventions should support rather than usurp the parental role. As much as possible, families should be involved in any decision making and support in raising children. Maintaining the family structure will require adequate support of families through social and community services. It is also important that support be given to children infected and affected by HIV in developing independence, mobility, and self-care, which enhances their sense of self. Special care needs to be given to the socialization of seropositive children, because they may be held to a higher standard of conduct (e.g., no rough-housing, biting, kicking, sharing food and possessions). When true crises arise, such as the death of a parent, it is critical to help children handle this death and develop a way to reminisce about the lost parent.

Families require a comprehensive system of health prevention education, social services, and mental health care to meet the urgent dual demands of prevention and treatment. Health care providers must be prepared to talk with children about their feelings; discuss their relationship with family, friends, neighbors, and strangers; evaluate their suicide potential; and discuss openly their concerns about their parents' death or, if they are positive, about their own death. Similarly, health care providers must be prepared to talk with parents about feelings and relationships, guiding them in their approach to community resources. When foster care parents are involved, their needs must be similarly addressed.

In a study to improve behavioral and mental health outcomes among HIV-positive mothers and their children, an intensive intervention resulted in the children having lower emotional distress, problem behaviors, family-related stressors, and higher levels of self-esteem than in the standard of care condition.[47] In this longitudinal study, a family-based intervention reduced the long-term impact of parents' HIV status on themselves, their children, and even their grandchildren. Outcomes over four years demonstrate that interventions can result in fewer children becoming teenage parents, or having conduct disorders.[48]

Educational Interventions

Educational interventions are necessary, but not sufficient, to ensure good mental health functioning and academic functioning of children infected and affected by HIV.[49] Psychiatric symptoms may influence performance on neuropsychological tests. Therefore the existence of psychiatric symptoms will need to be assessed to specify the causes of the observed performance difficulties. Health and mental health care providers have a special responsibility to ensure school attendance by all children. They often consult on school policy, educate teachers and administrators, and add their voices to the public dialogue.[50] HIV-infected children have cognitive/behavioral disabilities that require special educational services.

The trend toward earlier intervention with disabled, developmentally delayed, and at-risk children is evident in new amendments to PL 94–142 (Education for All Handicapped Children Act) contained in PL 99–457, allowing states to address the needs of disabled and at-risk infants and toddlers and their families and strengthening the incentive for states to serve all handicapped children ages three to five years old. Several educational programs have been developed to provide specialized early intervention for HIV-infected children from birth to five years old. This program has been incorporated in the Individuals with Disabilities Education Act.[51] The efficacy of such programs should be evaluated, and the feasibility of extending such programs into the primary grades should be explored.

Substance Abuse Treatment

The route of transmission of HIV infection for many families is often directly or indirectly associated with substance abuse. Intravenous drug use is directly related to HIV infection through blood contamination of shared injection equipment. In addition, there is also evidence that drug use (intravenous and nonintravenous) is correlated with sexual activities that place persons at risk for HIV infection. The processes by which drug use mediates risk (e.g., disinhibition) are currently undergoing investigation.

Ongoing drug treatment and prevention projects are examining a wide array of services and service delivery models. Areas of attention should include the challenges of identification, outreach, and retention, as well as the multiple needs of the population (e.g., substance abuse education, psychosocial support, prenatal care, safe housing, vocational training, transportation, and child care services). All of these issues may influence participation in, and effectiveness of, a prevention or treatment program.

Although drug-abusing women may be difficult to locate and maintain in traditional therapeutic programs, reports from a number of clinical studies suggest that it would be useful to provide a continuum or care via therapeutic programs along with comprehensive supportive services and extensive community outreach. Among the principles being emphasized in the drug treatment and prevention projects currently underway are: (1) a family orientation for programs, with a broad definition of family; (2) inclusion of child care services in programs; (3) use of a range of services with varying levels of intensity; (4) close coordination among service agencies and systems; (5) use of in-home and center-based program components; and (6) use of multidisciplinary teams.

The Structural Ecological Therapy (SET) program is a tested, ecosystemic, family-based program that targets social interactions with formerly drug-abusing, seropositive women with their families.[52] Results indicate the efficacy of SET in reducing distress and family-related hassles. This program worked better for women with high familial conflict and less well for women who had current psychopathology. This program has the potential to improve the family environment and mental health functioning of the seropositive parent and her infected and affected children.

FUTURE RESEARCH DIRECTIONS

To ensure the delivery of high-quality mental health services for children and their families, it is critical to identify which interventions work for which groups and why, so that successful approaches can be adapted and replicated. Programs should evaluate the efficacy of various types of mental health interventions, as well as compile information on obstacles to successful treatment intervention.

Because of the constellation of problems of children and their families with respect to this disease process, an integrated and coordinated research initiative is required.[53] To plan effective prevention and treatment programs, it is necessary to understand the long-term impact of medical treatment on the disease process, the growth and developmental problems that both HIV infection and drug therapy can cause, and alternative models of psychosocial support programs that may foster the continuum of care, not only for children, but for the parents, siblings, and other care providers. Some of the research priorities in these areas might include:

- Assessing the short-term versus long-term consequences of disclosure of HIV status to the child in terms of psychological distress and development of psychiatric disorders
- Identifying moderating variables that impact the relationship between timing of disclosure, developmental level of child, disease severity, and psychological distress and poor performance
- Evaluating the efficacy of coping styles in maintaining good physical and mental health status of both the mother and children
- Developing improved methods for accurately distinguishing between symptoms of depression and anxiety and symptoms due to treatment and HIV disease progression experienced by young children
- Testing an array of psychological and psychiatric services that can be tailored to the dysfunction of the children and other members of the family to increase mental and physical health outcomes

- Assessing quality of life, an index of overall status, as one outcome measure in treatment protocols and clinical studies

As with all research programs, investigating these areas will take a commitment by our national and international research support agencies to acknowledge the importance of and provide tangible support for this work. Another generation of HIV-infected children and adolescents cannot be allowed to pass by without trying to answer some of these problems.

CONCLUSIONS

A constant review of the emerging knowledge about the nature of HIV disease is critical. Improved treatment options are continuing to be developed, and these have a strong impact on the medical condition and quality of life of HIV-infected and affected families. Because the social context of the epidemic mutates as rapidly as the virus, it is imperative that new prevention and treatment programs are continually developed and implemented to manage the biological, psychological, social, and cultural factors.

The goal of service delivery and systems of care with families coping with HIV disease is to limit the consequences of the illness, so that both the parents and the infected and affected children can live productive lives. As clinical, pharmacologic, and other treatments produce variable health benefits, understanding the impact of these treatments on HIV-infected children's lives and their general development becomes more important. The quality of life construct provides an index of overall life status and can be an initial step toward the combination of nontraditional psychosocial and biobehavioral variables in clinical trials. A coordinated research effort is required to identify the mental health services and psychosocial resources that will support positive mental health outcomes for the child and family.

ACKNOWLEDGMENT

Special thanks to Rayford Kytle, who conducted the literature search and secured the relevant articles cited in this chapter.

REFERENCES

1. UNAIDS. 2004. *Report on the global AIDS epidemic.* New York: UNAIDS.

2. Schuster, M. A., D. E. Kanouse, S. C. Morton, S. A. Bozzette, A. Miu, G. B. Scott, and M. F. Shapiro. 2000. HIV-infected parents and their children in the United States. *Am J Public Health* 90(7):1074–81.

3. Michaels, D., and C. Levine. 2001. Estimates of the number of motherless youth orphaned by AIDS in the United States. *JAMA* 268(24):3462–64.

4. Stein, J. A., M. Riedel, and M. Rotheram-Borus. 1999. Parentification and its impact on adolescent children of parents with AIDS. *Fam Process* 38:193–208.

5. Personal Communication. Jennifer Ruth, Centers for Disease Control and Prevention (CDC). November 2005.

6. National Center for Health Statistics (NCHS). 2005. *Fact Sheet.* Washington, D.C.: NCHS.

7. Shaffer, D., P. Fisher, M. K. Dulcan, M. Davies, J. Piacentini, M. E. Schwab-Stone, B. B. Lahey, K. Bourdon, P. S. Jensen, H. R. Bird, G. Canino, and D. A. Regier. 1996. The NIMH Diagnostic Interview Schedule for Children Version 2.3 (DISC-2.3): Description, acceptability, prevalence rates, and performance in the MECA Study. Methods for the Epidemiology of Child and Adolescent Mental Disorders Study. *J Am Acad Child Adolesc Psychiatry* 35 (7):865–77.

8. U.S. Public Health Service. 2000. *Mental Health: A Report of the Surgeon General.* Washington, D.C.: DHHS.

9. Pequegnat, W. and J. H. Bray. 1997. Families and HIV/AIDS: Introduction to the special series. *J Fam Psychol* 11:3–10.

10. Pequegnat, W., and J. Szapocznik. 2002. The role of families in preventing and adapting to HIV/AIDS; Issues and answers. In *Working with families in the era of AIDS,* ed. W. Pequegnat and J. Szapocznik, 3–16. Thousand Oaks, CA: Sage.

11. Gewirtz, A., and S. Gossart-Walker. 2000. Home-based treatment for children and families affected by HIV and AIDS. *Child Adolesc Psychiatr Clin North Am* 9(2):313–20.

12. Robbins, M. S., J. Szapocznik, J. F. Alexander, and J. Miller. 1998. Family systems therapy with children and adolescents. In *Comprehensive clinical psychology,* ed. M. Hersen, A. S. Bellack and T. H.Ottendick, 149–480. Oxford, UK: Elsevier Science.

13. Toulou-Shams, M. 2005. Mental health and HIV risk in African-American adolescents: The role of maternal depression and parenting. *Diss Abstr Int* 65(7–8):3729.

14. Anderson, G. R. 1984. Children and AIDS: Implications for child welfare. *Child Welfare* 63(1):62–73.

15. Ellenbogen, M. A., and S. Hodgins. 2004. The impact of high neuroticism in parents on children's psychosocial functioning in a population at high risk for major affective disorder: A family-environmental pathway of intergenerational risk. *Dev Psychopathol* 16 (1):113–36.

16. Szapocznik, J., D. J. Feaster, V. B. Mitrani, G. Prado, L. Smith, C. Robinson-Batista, S. J. Schwartz, M. H. Mauer, and M. S. Robbins. 2004. Structural ecosystems therapy for HIV-seropositive African American women: Effects on psychological distress, family hassles, and family support. *J Consult Clin Psychol* 72 (2):288–303.

17. Sander, J. B., and C. A. McCarty. 2005. Youth depression in the family context: Familial risk factors and models of treatment. *Clin Child Fam Psychol Rev* 8(3):203–19.

18. Dubik-Unruh, S., and V. See. 1989. Children of chaos: Planning for the emotional survival of dying children of dying families. *J Palliat Care* 5(2):10–15.

19. Diamond, G. W. 1989. Developmental problems in children with HIV infection. *Ment Retard* 27(4):213–17.

20. Rendon, M., P. Gurdin, J. Bassi, and M. Weston. 1989. Foster care for children with AIDS: A psychosocial perspective. *Child Psychiatry Hum Dev* 19(4):256–69.

21. Newcomb, M. D., T. F. Locke, and R. K. Goodyear. 2003. Childhood experiences and psychosocial influences on HIV risk among adolescent Latinas in southern California. *Cultur Divers Ethnic Minor Psychol* 9(3):219–35.

22. Dutra, R., R. Forehand, L. Armistead, G. Brody, E. Morse, P. S. Morse, and L. Clark. 2000. Child resiliency in inner-city families affected by HIV: the role of family variables. *Behav Res Ther* 38 (5):471–86.

23. Rotheram-Borus, M. J., D. A. Murphy, H. M. Reid, and C. L. Coleman. 1996. Correlates of emotional distress among HIV-positive youth: Health status, stress, and personal resources. *Ann Behav Med* 18(1):16–23.

24. Bauman, L. J., S. Camacho, E. J. Silver, J. Hudis, J., and B. Draimin. 2002. Behavioral problems in school-aged children of mothers with HIV/AIDS. *Clin Child Psychol Psychiatry* 7:39–54.

25. Coatsworth, J. D., H. Pantin, and J. Szapocznik. 2002. Familias Unidas: A family-centered ecodevelopmental intervention to reduce risk for problem behavior among Hispanic adolescents. *Clin Child Fam Psychol Rev* 5(2):113–32.

26. Zayas, L. H. and K. Romano. 1994. Adolescents and parental death from AIDS. In *AIDS and the new orphans,* ed. B. O. Dane and C. Levine, 59–76. Westport: Auburn House.

27. Pilowsky, D. J., P. A. Zybert, P. W. Hsieh, D. Vlahov, and E. Susser. 2003. Children of HIV positive drug-using parents. *J Am Acad Child Adolesc Psychiatry* 42(8):950–56.

28. Rotheram-Borus, M. J., R. Weiss, S. Alber, and P. Lester. 2005. Adolescent adjustment before and after HIV-related parental death. *J Consult Clin Psychol* 73(2):221–28.

29. Bray, J. H. 1995. Family assessment: Current issues in evaluating families. *Fam Relat* 44:469–77.

30. Bray, J. H. 1995. Methodological advances in family psychology. *J Fam Psychol* 9:107–109.

31. Collins-O'Neal, K. 1989. Growing up with AIDS: Preschool and school years: Preschool and school years: Psychosocial concerns. In *Pediatric AIDS.* Columbus, Ohio: Ross Laboratories.

32. Katoff, L. 1994. Psychological study of long-term survivors of AIDS. *HIV/AIDS Clin Insights* 3(1):5–6.

33. Stein, R. E., and D. J. Jessop. 1984. Relationship between health status and psychological adjustment among children with chronic conditions. *Pediatrics* 73(2):169–74.

34. Wolters, P. L., and P. Brouwers. 2006. Neurobehavioral function and assessment of children and adolescents with HIV-1 infection. In *Handbook of Pediatric HIV Care,* ed. S. L. Zeichner and J. S. Read, 309–31. Cambridge University Press.

35. Pao, M., M. Lyon, L. J. D'Angelo, W. B. Schuman, T. Tipnis, and D. A. Mrazek. 2000. Psychiatric diagnoses in adolescents seropositive for the human immunodeficiency virus. *Arch Pediatr Adolesc Med* 154(3):240–44.

36. Misdrahi, D., G. Vila, I. Funk-Brentano, M. Tardieu, S. Blanche, and M. C. Mouren-Simeoni. 2004. DSM-IV mental disorders and neurological complications in children and adolescents with human immunodeficiency virus type 1 infection (HIV-1). *Eur Psychiatry* 19(3):182–84.

37. Bachanas, P. J., K. A. Kullgren, K. S. Schwartz, B. Lanier, J. S. McDaniel, J. Smith, and S. Nesheim. 2001. Predictors of psychological adjustment in school-age children infected with HIV. *J Pediatr Psychol* 26(6):343–52.

38. Rapkin, B. D., J. A. Bennett, P. Murphy, and M. Munoz. 2000. The Family Health Project: Strengthening problem solving in families affected by AIDS to mobilize systems of support and care. In *Working with families in the era of AIDS,* ed. W. Pequegnat and J. Szapocznik. Thousand Oaks, CA: Sage Publications.

39. Rosen, L. D., C. A. Mellins, S. Ryan, and J. F. Havens. 1997. Family therapy with HIV/AIDS-affected families. In *Psychotherapy and AIDS: The Human Dimension,* ed. L. Wicks, 115–41. Washington: Taylor and Francis.

40. Boyd-Franklin, N. 1989. *Black Families in Therapy: A Multisystem Approach.* New York: Guilford Press.

41. Havens, J., C. Mellins, S. Ryan, and A. Locker. 1995. Mental health needs of children and families affected by HIV/AIDS. In *Mental health services for HIV-affected populations in New York City: A program perspective,* ed. G. Goldstein, H.Goodman, and G. Landsberg. New York: The Coalition of Voluntary Mental Health Agencies.

42. Lyon, M. E., and K. Woodward. 2003. Nonstigmatizing ways to engage HIV-positive African-American teens in mental health and support services: A commentary. *J Natl Med Assoc* 95(3):196–200.

43. Cadman, D., P. Rosenbaum, M. Boyle, and D. R. Offord. 1991. Children with chronic illness: Family and parent demographic characteristics and psychosocial adjustment. *Pediatrics* 87(6):884–89.

44. Brown, L.K., K. J. Lourie, and M. Pao. 2000. Children and adolescents living with HIV and AIDS: A review. *J Child Psychol Psychiatry* 41(1):81–96.

45. Hahn, R.A., I.M. Onorato, T.S. Jones, and J. Dougherty. 1989. Prevalence of HIV infection among intravenous drug users in the United States. *JAMA* 261(18):2677–84.

46. Lyon, M. E., T. J. Silber, and L. J. D'Angelo. 1997. Difficult life circumstances in HIV-infected adolescents: cause or effect? *AIDS Patient Care STDS* 11(1):29–33.

47. Rotheram-Borus, M. J., M. B. Lee, M. Gwadz, and B. Draimin. 2001. An intervention for parents with AIDS and their adolescent children. *Am J Public Health* 91(8):1294–302.

48. Rotheram-Borus, M. J., M. Lee, N. Leonard, Y. Y. Lin, L. Franzke, E. Turner, M. Lightfoot, and M. Gwadz. 2003. Four-year behavioral outcomes of an intervention for parents living with HIV and their adolescent children. *AIDS* 17(8):1217–25.

49. Price, J. H. 1986. AIDS, the schools, and policy issues. *J Sch Health* 56(4):137–40.

50. Leviton, L. C., A. M. Hegedus, and A. Kubrin. 2004. Evaluating AIDS prevention: Contributions of multiple disciplines. *New Direc Progr Eval* 1990(46):63–73.

51. http://www.wrightslaw.com/idea/index.htm

52. Szapocznik, J., D. J. Feaster, V. B. Mitrani, G. Prado, L. Smith, C. Robinson-Batista, S. J. Schwartz, M. H. Mauer, and M. S. Robbins. 2004. Structural ecosystems therapy for HIV-seropositive African American women: Effects on psychological distress, family hassles, and family support. *J Consult Clin Psychol* 72(2):288–303.

53. Pequegnat W. and the NIMH Consortium on Family and HIV/AIDS Research. 2002. Research issues with children infected and affected with HIV and their families. *Clin Child Psychol Psych* 7(1):7–154.

Chapter 9

PREVENTING HIV INFECTION IN ADOLESCENTS: WHAT WORKS FOR UNINFECTED TEENS

Ralph J. DiClemente, Ph.D. and Richard A. Crosby, Ph.D.

Eternal Achiever

By Michael A. Dowling

If in my quest
To achieve my goals
I stumble or crumble
And lose my soul
Those that knew me
Would easily co-sign
There was never life
As hard as mine
No father no money
No chance and no guide
I only follow my voice inside
And if it guides me wrong
And I do not win
I'll learn from my mistakes
And try to achieve again

In the United States, adolescents have historically been disproportionately likely to acquire sexually transmitted infections such as gonorrhea and chlamydia.[1-3] Unfortunately, HIV infection also occurs among a substantial number of adolescents. In the era of AIDS and the growing complacency surrounding the HIV epidemic, one of the greatest fears in public health is that increasingly, young people will be faced with this life-threatening illness before their 21st birthday. Although less than 20% of all AIDS cases occur among adolescents, the personal, social, and economic losses incurred by AIDS in adolescence are exacerbated by the fact that a preventable, potentially fatal illness has interrupted an adolescent's life trajectory. Fortunately, a great deal of research has been devoted to helping adolescents adopt the sexual protective behaviors necessary to prevent HIV infection.

This chapter describes the emerging body of HIV prevention research and emphasizes effective intervention strategies. We begin by noting the unique nature of adolescence with respect to sexuality and to HIV-associated sexual risk behavior. Next, we describe the psychosocial antecedents of adolescents' sexual risk behavior. The chapter then emphasizes what is known about effective intervention strategies. Finally, we conclude with a discussion of research and policy-related agendas that could greatly improve prevention programs for adolescents, decreasing their risk of contracting HIV.

ADOLESCENCE AND SEXUALITY

Developmentally, the period of adolescence is fraught with multiple challenges. Paramount among these is the development of identity (who you are) and self-esteem (how you feel about yourself). For better or worse, sexuality is a central aspect of these developmental tasks. Moreover, the newly experienced changes associated with puberty may exacerbate adolescents' perception of the need to translate their sexuality from thought to action. This stage of life can also be characterized by a tendency toward risk taking fueled by illusions of invulnerability to bad consequences and premature death.[4] In essence, the period of transition between childhood and adulthood is likely to be stormy, to say the least!

Although adolescence can be a difficult period for many adolescents to navigate safely through, recent findings from the Youth Behavioral Risk Surveillance System (YRBS) suggest many are not engaging in HIV-associated sexual risk behaviors. For example, less than half of U.S. high school students have ever engaged in sexual intercourse (47.6%) and far fewer (34%) reported having sex recently (last three months). Of those having sex, nearly two-thirds (63%) reported condom use during their most recent act of intercourse, and 14% reported having had sex with four or more partners.[5] These findings suggest that adolescents are not a homogenous group. Quite to the contrary, adolescents are a highly heterogeneous population, with many subgroups, each with diverse developmental, social, and cultural differences. Some may be at risk of sexually transmitted disease (STD)/HIV acquisition, but many others have opted to avoid sex, to limit their number of sex partners, and to use condoms. Naturally, this widespread variation in risk-taking among adolescents makes the task of developing tailored and targeted STD/HIV prevention programs a real challenge.

The challenge, however, must be placed squarely in the context of adolescent sexual development and should not be viewed from a moralistic perspective. That adolescents experience sexual fantasy, desire, and impulses has been well established. Unfortunately, a segment of society has opted to believe that adolescents should not be viewed as sexual beings. This view is antithetical to STD/HIV prevention efforts directed toward adolescents, as it denies the possibility that "healthy" adolescent development includes sexual thinking and, quite possibly, sexual behavior. Labeling all adolescent sexual behavior as "risky behavior" removes this human dimension and replaces it with a public health paradigm that may not acknowledge the realities of sexual identity formation and sexuality as part of adolescents psychological well being. As one author recently noted, "The idea that mutual masturbation or oral sex experiences may be educating, pleasurable, and self-affirming is alien to the risk perspective. Developmentally, however, such experiences are exactly the point of adolescence" (p. 297).[6]

The "thin line" that anyone interested in STD/HIV prevention must walk has bad consequences on either side. On one side is the need to prevent sexually transmitted diseases that adolescents may acquire; on the other side is the need to help foster healthy sexual development. The path through these potentially conflicting needs may best be described by the "promotion" of sexual health, a concept endorsed by the Institutes of Medicine in the widely acclaimed report, *The Hidden Epidemic: Confronting Sexually Transmitted Diseases.*[7] This approach accepts the premise that the developmental period of adolescence includes sexuality. It also acknowledges the diverse nature of adolescent sexual expression including sexual behaviors that pose risk to themselves and others. Consider, for example, the behavioral pattern, or "psychological construct," known as "sexual adventurism." In our research, we have found that sexual adventurism is closely related to sexual risk behavior among teen females.[8] We have also found that teen females report a perceived "lack of sexual sensation" as a reason for choosing not to use condoms.[9,10] In essence, then, efforts to successfully intervene among teens, like those we have sampled in the past, must begin by recognizing what sexuality is for most teens rather than imposing an adult-created reality into the curriculum design to teach these things in school.

Finally, it is important to recognize that adolescents are learning to navigate relationships (which may or may not include sexual relationships). Issues of how teens relate to one another often preoccupy adolescents' time, and these issues may easily become a source of tremendous stress. When one partner (usually a male) becomes aggressive, the possibility for dating violence becomes a reality. Dating violence can take the form of verbal, emotional, or physical assault. In our research with adolescents, we've found that a history of physical dating violence was reported by 18.4% of adolescent females, 14 to 18 years old.[11] This study examines the association between having a history of dating violence and adolescent females' sexual health. Adolescents, with a history of dating violence in the past six months, were almost three times more likely to have an STD, almost three times more likely to have nonmonogamous male partners, and half as likely to use condoms consistently. Further, adolescents with a history of dating violence were almost three times as likely to fear the perceived consequences of negotiating condom use; two and a half times more likely to fear talking with their partner about pregnancy prevention; twice as likely to perceive a higher risk of acquiring an STD; almost two and a half times as likely to perceive less control over their sexuality; more than three times more likely to have peer norms nonsupportive of using condoms; and twice as likely to have norms nonsupportive of having a healthy relationship. In essence, adolescents who experienced dating violence are more likely to exhibit a spectrum of unhealthy sexual behaviors, attitudes, beliefs, and norms. Thus, while physically abusive relationship partners pose a direct threat to an adolescent female's health, they can also indirectly affect adolescents' health by shaping their norms, attitudes, and beliefs about relationships that are associated with HIV/STD acquisition.

PSYCHOSOCIAL ANTECEDENTS OF ADOLESCENTS' HIV-ASSOCIATED SEXUAL RISK BEHAVIOR

The following question has been a challenge confronting public health researchers: Why do adolescents put themselves at risk of acquiring HIV? The task of answering this question is particularly complex because investigation of such a personal, and often nonpublic and nondisclosed behavior, is complicated. Yet, human and financial resources have been mobilized to identify and understand these basic starting points because this process is widely considered essential to the development of programs designed to prevent or reduce adolescents' health risk behaviors.

To make it easy to understand this question, it is useful to organize answers by two categories of theory: individual-level theory and ecological-level theory.

In many respects, individual-level theories have dominated health promotion efforts for decades, including sexual health promotion programs. Examples of important background contributors suggested through individual-level theories include adolescents' depression, impulsivity, self-efficacy for safer sex, HIV-associated risk perceptions, barriers to condom use, knowledge and skill about safer sex practices, and attitudes (motivation level) toward these practices.[3] One likely reason for the widespread use of individual-level theories may be that they propose the individual as the key decision maker responsible for his or her health and, as a corollary; an individual can change to decrease his or her risk behavior. Note, this type of thinking implies that behavior is under willed or volitional control and that outside influences are not critical determinants of risk behavior. On the other hand, scholars have recently questioned the wisdom of relying exclusively on individual-level approaches. Instead, they argue that community and other outside factors may have a pervasive, sustained, and profound effect on risk behavior.[12] This logic naturally implies that intervention strategies should then address multiple spheres of influence, including (but not limited to) family systems; neighborhoods; the community; local, state, and federal policies, as well as cultural norms and values. Table 9.1 displays examples of ecological-level factors that might contribute to an adolescent's HIV-associated sexual risk behavior.

As shown, the five categories each suggest that using an individual-level approach to behavior change (i.e., designing and delivering educational content to teens) may not have an optimal impact on predisposing factors or antecedents. Each antecedent is critically important to creating lasting sexual protective behaviors in teens. Next we review some of the evidence supporting this idea.

Table 9.1
Ecological-Level Antecedents of Adolescents' HIV/STI Associated Risk Behaviors
Antecedent

Antecedent	Summary Comments
Parental monitoring	Emerging evidence strongly suggests that parental monitoring is positively associated with adolescents' STI risk behavior.
Parent-adolescent communication	A substantial body of literature provides evidence that greater frequency of parent-adolescent discussion about sex-related topics increases adolescents' adoption of safer sex behaviors.
Peer and community norms	Adolescents, like adults, tend to engage in risk perceptions and adopt protective behaviors based on their perceptions of whether recommended actions are consistent with local norms. Recent studies support the hypothesis that adolescents residing in locales with close ties between members are more likely to adopt safer sex practices.
Availability of services	Lack of access to "adolescent-friendly" STI screening and treatment services combined with widespread inaccessibility of preventive services fosters increased STI incidence rates.
Gender and power differentials	Available evidence clearly suggests that economic and social environments that favor female reliance on males and male-controlled sexual decision making, respectively, pose barriers to females' adoption of safer sex practices.

Parental Monitoring

Parental monitoring encompasses knowledge of a child's or adolescent's where-abouts, activities, and peer associations. Poorly monitored adolescents tend to engage in more risk behaviors such as delinquency[13]; drugs, alcohol, and tobacco use[14,15]; and sexual risk behaviors.[16] Indeed, a growing number of studies have investigated associations between parental monitoring and adolescents sexual risk behavior.[17] Findings from several key studies include the following:

- As parental monitoring increases teens are more likely to use condoms.
- More frequent parental monitoring may help teens delay sexual initiation.
- Teens who report infrequent parental monitoring are more likely to become pregnant and to acquire an STD

Of interest, several studies have investigated the influence of parental monitoring on a grouping of behaviors generally termed, *adolescent deviance*, and some of these studies included ever having sex under this classification of deviant behavior. It is noteworthy that more frequent parental monitoring has been significantly associated with a lower likelihood of delinquency (including reports of ever having sex).[16] Also noteworthy is that a substantial body of research has supported the general hypothesis that parental monitoring may buffer negative peer influences and prevent adolescent substance abuse.[17]

Parent-Adolescent Communication

Studies assessing the relationship of parent-adolescent communication about sex and sex-related issues to adolescents' sexual risk behavior have produced some interesting findings. At the outset, however, it should be noted that this kind of communication has often been measured without the necessary attention to the specific content and nature of the communication process.[18] Nonetheless, studies generally support the idea that parent-adolescent communication about sex and sex-related topics can help protect adolescents from sexual risk behaviors.[19]

Findings from multiple studies suggest that mothers are the primary parent who communicate with teens about sex. This may be especially true for girls. Indeed, research has typically focused on specific aspects of mother-daughter communication about sex and sexuality-related issues. Overall, the evidence suggests that mother-daughter communication can be an important determinant of female adolescents' sexual risk-taking behavior.[19] Adolescents who talk about sex-related topics with their mothers are:

- Less likely to report being sexually experienced.
- Likely to report less frequent penile-vaginal sex.
- More likely to report using condoms and other contraceptives.

- Less likely to become pregnant.
- Likely to report fewer lifetime sex partners.

At least three reasons may explain these outcomes. First, the communication may foster a pattern of candid and honest discussion about sex that teens then apply in the context of their dating relationships. Second, the content of the communication may protect teens from unhealthy peer influences on sexual behavior. In this case, the information and attitudes acquired from parent-adolescent communication may act much like a vaccine—inoculating teens from outside influences for example, negative peer pressure. Third, the communication may involve expressed disapproval from a parent about sex, and this expression may translate into delaying sexual initiation. For example, expressed maternal disapproval of premarital sex has been related to increased abstinence from sex and decreased frequency of sex among sexually active female adolescents.[20] In an analysis of data from the National Longitudinal Study of Adolescent Health (Add Health), female adolescents who reported that their mothers had not expressed disapproval of the daughters' having sex were significantly more likely (than those who reported that some degree of maternal disapproval had been expressed) to be infected by a sexually transmitted disease in the ensuing year.[21]

Peer and Community Norms

Peer norms surrounding sexual behaviors and condom use are robust influences on risky sexual behavior.[3] Perceiving that friends and similar-age teens are engaging in risky sex may foster the same behaviors. In contrast, perceived peer norms supportive of sexual-protective behaviors may influence the adoption and maintenance of safer sex practices.[22] In a nutshell, adolescents' friends and acquaintances may exert a profound influence on their sexual behaviors. Thus, for example, religiosity has been associated with sexual protective behaviors among teens, probably as a result of their affiliations with church-attending peers rather than a direct influence of religious beliefs. The same type of positive peer influence on sexual protective behaviors has been found for social organizations that serve young people. At the other extreme, adolescents belonging to street gangs may exert undue influence on one another to engage in diverse health risk behaviors, including sexual risk behaviors. For example, one study found that African American adolescent females involved in a gang, relative to those who were not gang-involved, were more likely to test positive for common sexually transmitted diseases such as *Trichomonas vaginalis* and *Neisseria gonorrhoeae*.[23]

In many respects, community norms regarding safer sex may be thought of as an extension of peer norms. Such norms may translate into policy practices that allow for comprehensive sex education programs to be taught in middle schools and high schools. Norms that support open and honest communication about the topic of sex may also foster adolescents' communication with trusted adults about specific sexual issues. Evidence from at least one study suggests that such communication may be protective against behaviors that impact STD acquisition.[21]

Community norms may positively influence adolescents in multiple ways. For example, the sexual values held by adults in a community may have a profound influence in shaping the sexual attitudes and corresponding behavior of adolescents residing in the same community. Related to this is the idea of "social capital" of a community, or the willingness of people in the community to trust and work with others in the community.[24] More and more, this is being seen as an important factor that may be amenable to change. Social capital has been associated with public health measures such as violence behavior, child welfare, mortality, and health status. In general, as social capital increases communities become less likely to experience risk behavior and their adverse health outcomes. Unfortunately, the process of building social capital has not been well established. However, it is reasonable to speculate that the organization of community coalitions (designed to bring various subpopulations within a community together) could be a useful starting point. Planned community events could also be designed to bring parents of adolescents together. Every exchange between parents has the potential to build their level of trust, cooperation, and reciprocity with one another, thereby increasing social capital. The same principle applies to adolescents, thereby supporting the value of organized community activities that bring young people together for positive exchanges.

A recent study illustrates the potential role of social capital in shaping adolescents' sexual behavior. A state-level analysis using data from the YRBS found that social capital was protective against teen pregnancy. The correlation was strong ($r = -.58$) for females and somewhat lower ($r = -.42$) with respect to males causing a pregnancy.[25] The same study found that social capital was protective against ever having sex, early sexual initiation, current sexual activity, having multiple sex partners (this effect was found only for males), and having sex without the use of contraceptives. Given this evidence, it is reasonable to speculate that social capital may be a protective factor reducing adolescents' risk for acquisition of STDs, including HIV.

Availability of Services

STDs are often asymptomatic and therefore screening programs that target at-risk adolescent populations are warranted. Indeed, evidence suggests that screening programs, combined with prompt and directly observed treatment, may be an effective means of lowering STD rates among adolescents.[26] Unfortunately, widespread STD screening of adolescents is not currently practiced. In the absence of screening and treatment, STDs can easily thrive in the small-knit groups created by adolescents as a furthering of their sexual relationships.

Although availability of services is largely an economic and policy-associated pubic health issue, it is also important to think about perceived barriers that may prevent adolescents from seeking diagnosis and care for an STD, including HIV. Thus it is perhaps beneficial to consider adolescents' psychosocial and behavioral reactions to the potential diagnosis of STD or HIV. Indeed, a few studies have examined this issue. For example, a multisite study of persons greater than 13 years of age found that about one-third of the sample delayed care seeking by at least seven days. Delay did not vary by age for females; however, males younger than 34 years were more likely to delay care than their older counterparts. For both genders, the most common reason for delay (provided by nearly 50% of both males and females) was "hoping symptoms would go away."[27]

Other influences of care-seeking behavior have also been identified. Recent studies of persons 12 years and older found that STD-related stigma and low literacy may be important barriers to seeking care for STD symptoms.[28,29] In a sample of younger adolescents (ages 13–20 years), evidence indicated that greater perceived barriers to care seeking, lower ability to deal with an acquired STD, stigma, and increased perceived seriousness were related to delays in care seeking.[30] Symptomatic females, relative to males, were especially likely to delay care seeking. This observation suggests that adolescent females may experience levels of anxiety and fear related to an STD diagnosis that may delay care seeking (of interest, history of STDs was not associated with delay in care seeking).

Gender and Power Differentials

Ample evidence indicates that adolescent females may experience a tremendous disadvantage with respect to sexual decision making. This is probably true for two reasons: (1) paternalistic cultural values favor male over female decision making regarding sex, and (2) adolescent females are likely to date older males, thereby creating a power differential based on age.[3] As we will show in the next section of this chapter, a promising intervention strategy for adolescent females is to help them recognize these power imbalances and their impact on sexual risk behavior and provide the training and skills necessary to overcome these gender and power differences.[31]

Male control of sexual decision making has been studied as a contributing factor for risky sexual behaviors for adolescent females. Of interest, data from the YRBS, over more than 10 years, have shown that adolescent males are more likely than their female counterparts to report condom use during the most recent act of sex. This observation suggests that adolescent females may have difficulty negotiating condom use, especially with older partners. Indeed, the evidence suggests that perceived male partner barriers to refusing sex or negotiating condom use may be powerful determinants of STD-risk behavior for adolescent females.[34] Consistent with this proposition, other studies have shown that more assertive women are more likely to practice safer sex. For example, a recent study of young adult females found that assertive communication skills, self-control over condom use, and perceived control over their partner's use of condoms each, independently, predicted consistent condom use by females (Table 9.2).[35]

WHAT IS KNOWN ABOUT EFFECTIVE PREVENTION STRATEGIES?

This section is not designed to simply provide you with an exhaustive review of the research literature. Instead, we use examples from the research literature to illustrate central issues related to the prevention of HIV/STD among adolescents. You are invited to learn more about the programs included here by taking advantage of the reference list found at the end of the chapter.

First, it is important to acknowledge that HIV-prevention education tactics designed specifically for adolescents originated in schools. As these programs became progressively more skill-based, similar programs became available through community locations. Presently, school- and community-based programs continue to evolve and some have recently added "community-change" components to an otherwise individual-level approach. This section of the chapter reviews programs that exemplify state-of-the-art approaches to promoting safer sex among adolescents. The term *safer sex* is used here to denote any program than includes a comprehensive range of options to help adolescents protect themselves from HIV infection, as well as infections with other sexually transmitted diseases. Programs providing adolescents with no options—that is, "abstinence only programs"—are not classified as safer sex education. Evidence to date does not support the efficacy of abstinence only approaches.[36] Moreover, an abstinence only program fails to acknowledge that even those who chose to remain abstinent during their teen years will someday benefit from skills related to HIV and STD prevention. Conversely, safer sex programs encourage a broad range of options including abstinence, long-term monogamy, condom use, and alternate forms of sexual expression between couples (Table 9.3).

Safer sex programs have been developed for use in three distinct settings: schools, clinics, and community-based organizations. Unfortunately, schools have been understudied, thereby creating a dearth of evidence regarding safer sex programs in the one place that best "captures" adolescents. One notable exception is a project funded by the Centers for Disease Control and Prevention known as Safer Choices.[38] This program acknowledged the important

Table 9.2
Do Adolescents Use Condoms Correctly?

Evidence from studies of college students implies that it is quite possible that adolescents (like college students) do not use condoms correctly. A recent study of college men found that 43% reported recently putting a condom on after starting sex, and 15% recently reported taking a condom off before sex was over.[32] It is possible that this "incomplete use" of condoms is based on the event of ejaculation. That is, the condom may be used only immediately before and during ejaculation. Given the potential for sperm and semen (carrying pathogens) to be emitted from the male urethra well before ejaculation, however, the former finding alone is quite telling.

Indeed, a broad spectrum of user errors may exist in relation to condom use. *Consider, for example*:

Not checking the condom for visible damage before use
Not checking the expiration date
Putting the condom on after starting sex
Not holding the tip and leaving space for the ejaculate
Putting the condom on the wrong side up (having to flip it over)
Using a condom without lubricant
Taking a condom off before sex is over
Starting sex before condom was unrolled to base of penis
Using a condom that was stored in a wallet
Letting ejaculate drip onto partner's mouth, genitals, or anus
Using oil-based lubricant on condom
Not storing condom in a cool and dry location
Unrolling the condom and then trying to put it on the penis
Letting the condom contact sharp objects (teeth, jewelry, fingernails)
Knowingly using an expired condom
Using a condom again during same sexual session
Knowingly using a damaged condom
Needing additional water-based lubricant, but having none available
Having a condom break
Having a condom slip off during sex
Having a condom slip off while withdrawing penis

One study found that most men reported experiencing one or more of the items shown in a 90-day period. Nearly one-third reported that the condom had broken or had slipped off at least once in the past 90 days. The average number of errors reported was 4.5. A subsequent study showed that college women experienced similar rates of errors.[33]

role of ecological supports and thus included attention to the school environment, as well as the creation of a sex education curriculum. The study involved nearly 4,000 ninth-graders and found that a school-based safer sex intervention positively impacted a broad range of social and cognitive factors and

Table 9.3
Do Condoms Really Work?

Condoms work but only when used correctly (see Table 9.2). The real question is how well do they work? Like any other device intended to protect health, condoms do not provide a blanket guarantee against HIV or STD infection. For example, even the correct and consistent use of condoms cannot always protect against the acquisition or transmission of genital herpes because the fluid that spreads this virus comes from vesicles that may not be located on the penis (e.g., vesicles could be on the scrotum). The same is true for human papillomavirus. However, the sexual transmission of HIV is dependent upon a discharge from the male urethra (ending at the tip of the penis) or from the vagina to a microabrasion on the penis. In either case, the correct and consistent use of a latex condom is protective. A summary of the evidence follows:

- In June 2000, the Department of Health and Human Services (DHHS) convened four federal agencies. A panel of experts assembled by these agencies evaluated 138 published studies and concluded that ample evidence supports the value of condoms to prevent HIV infection.
- Although the panel concluded that condoms do prevent female-to-male transmission of gonorrhea, they noted that evidence was insufficient to judge the adequacy or inadequacy of condoms for the prevention of other STDs.
- Subsequent to the DHHS report further studies suggested that condoms have a strong protective value against chlamydia and male-to-female transmission of gonorrhea. At least one study provided evidence suggesting that condoms are protective against trichomoniasis.

Again, however, the degree of protection is not perfect and varies based on the quality of condom use. Unfortunately, several methodologic limitations (inherent in studies of sexual behavior) each contribute to an underestimate of condom effectiveness. Consider, for example, a study of adolescent females. The study collected data on condom use behaviors and assessed teens for three types of STDs (chlamydia, gonorrhea, and trichomoniasis). Of the 380 teens studied, 90 acquired an STD during the observation period. For those reporting 100% condom use, 17.8% acquired an STD. By comparison, 30.0% of those reporting less than consistent condom uses tested positive. This difference was significant ($p = .005$), but the question became— why did more than one of every six who reported consistent use acquire an STD?[37] The question has three answers.

1. Adolescents may have exaggerated their level of condom use.
2. Adolescents may have used condoms consistently but not correctly.
3. Adolescents may not have used condoms from start to finish of penetrative sex.

This study, like others that may follow, was not able to eliminate these three forms of bias. Consequently, we can only conclude that condoms provide a reasonably high (but unknown) level of protection against STDs.

increased parent-adolescent communication about sexual issues. Compared to control subjects, adolescents receiving the intervention reported less frequent intercourse over a three-month recall period and were more likely to report using a condom during last intercourse. A similar approach designed for middle school students was also developed. This program (known as Draw the Line/Respect the Line) was tested in 19 northern California schools using a cohort of nearly 3,000 sixth graders tracked for three years. The intervention was effective in delaying sexual initiation for boys, but not for girls. Some of the potential reasons why the intervention was more successful for boys were that (1) boys may have perceived less peer support for having sex, (2) they may have had more favorable attitudes toward abstinence, and (3) they may have been less likely to place themselves in situations where sex might occur.[39]

Without question, schools are a potentially invaluable place for the promotion of safer sex to U.S. adolescents. The problem, however, is that school districts are typically faced with political pressure (often from a vocal minority of community members) that precludes an innovative approach to safer sex education. Nonetheless, some schools have managed to implement programs such as (1) condom distribution through a school based clinic, (2) STD screening and treatment through school-based clinics, and (3) comprehensive sex education programs. The challenge currently facing the majority of U.S. schools, however, is to focus less on teaching "knowledge" (e.g., facts about HIV and AIDS) and focus more on teaching skills that will help teens navigate relationships, delay sexual initiation, respect sex, use condoms when sexual initiation occurs, and talk openly with their parents about sexual issues.

Unlike schools, many community-based organizations are not bound by a vocal faction of community members who oppose sex education for adolescents. Therefore it is not surprising that some of the best evidence to date for the effectiveness of safer sex programs for teens comes from community-based settings. For example, a recent study demonstrated that a community-based safer sex program designed for low-income African American adolescent females worked well.[40] Adolescents who received the training, when compared to those who did not, were nearly twice as likely to report using condoms consistently in the past 30 days and were more than twice as likely to report using condoms consistently in the past six months. Also, they were less likely to acquire *Chlamydia* or *Trichomonas* infection. They were also less likely to report having sex with a new sex partner, they more frequently applied condoms to sex partners, and they had better condom application skills. A large number of psychosocial factors related to safer sex were also favorably impacted by the intervention. Given the success of this program, it is important to take a look at its content (Table 9.4).

The program content is primarily aimed at the individual level, with an emphasis on relationships and skill building. At this point, it is important to

Table 9.4
Content of an HIV Intervention Program Designed for African American
Adolescent Females

Session 1: Emphasized ethnic and gender pride by discussing the joys and challenges of being a young African American female, acknowledging the accomplishments of African American women, reading poetry written by African American women, and framing artwork created by African American female artists.

Session 2: Enhanced awareness of HIV risk-reduction strategies such as abstaining from sex, using condoms consistently, and having fewer sexual partners.

Session 3: Enhanced adolescents' confidence in initiating safer sex conversations, negotiating safer sex, and refusing unsafe sexual encounters through role-play and cognitive rehearsal. Also, peer educators discussed the importance of abstinence, described proper and consistent condom use, and modeled condom skills.

Session 4: Emphasized the importance of having healthy relationships. Health educators described how an unhealthy relationship can make it difficult to avoid or practice safer sex.

---

look back at Table 9.1 and again consider the factors that may influence adolescents' HIV risk and protective behaviors. After a second look at Table 9.1, imagine a program that combined the elements of Table 9.4 with the elements of Table 9.1. The resulting vision would be a program that combined individual-level approaches with the clear advantages of community and social change. This combination would perhaps have a greater positive impact, one that is sustained over time, thereby substantially reducing their risk of HIV/STD. Of course, one could easily argue that such an elaborate approach would be expensive. In the era of AIDS, however, such concerns are less valid given the lifetime costs associated with the medical treatment of HIV-infected adolescents. In fact, recent reports from the Institutes of Medicine document the cost-effectiveness of prevention programs for HIV and other STDs such as chlamydia.[7,41]

Numerous programs designed for implementation in community settings have been rigorously tested and found to be effective in the promotion of safer sexual behaviors for adolescents.[42–44] Although each program uses a slightly different approach to promoting safer sex, they all follow these basic principles:

- Use a wide variety of learning techniques and emphasize interactive learning.
- Use a theoretical framework to guide the intervention program.
- Use peer facilitators when appropriate.
- Develop effective strategies to foster peer norms supportive of safer sex.

- Create gender-specific methodologies.
- Design culturally specific methodologies.

Clinical settings are also a key place to reach adolescents at risk of HIV/ STDs. In particular, STD clinics provide an opportunity to intervene with adolescents at high risk of HIV infection. This is true for at least two reasons. First, having an STD serves as a biological risk factor for HIV by making it easier to acquire the virus from an infected person. More important, however, STDs are common among teens,[7] and thus, the odds of being infected by microorganisms such as *Chlamydia trachomatis, Trichomonas vaginalis, Neisseria gonorrhoeae,* and various strains (many of which are carcinogenic) of the human papillomavirus are far greater than the odds of encountering and being infected by HIV. Therefore STDs may best be thought of as a "sentinel event"—having one is then a type of early warning system that an adolescent's sexual behaviors may be conducive to acquiring HIV.

A recent review of clinic-based STD/HIV interventions for adolescents identified nine rigorously evaluated programs that appear to work.[45] (It should be noted that some of these programs could also be considered community-based, as the intervention program was not provided concurrently with clinical care.) Overall, the review concluded that the effect of these programs was relatively modest. Thus, an important question becomes, "can modest effects make a difference when magnified by widespread adoption of the program into STD clinics throughout the United States?" Unfortunately, the answer to this question depends on whether the behavior change was sufficient to confer any protective value against STD/HIV for adolescents. This determination, however, is difficult unless the newly adopted behavior is 100% condom use (without errors). If, for example, a program can be said to increase condom use by twofold, this could mean that teen boys (as a group) go from using condoms about 4 of every 10 times to 8 of every 10 times. Is that protective? The answer depends on the seroprevalence of STD/HIV within the community. In communities with high rates of STD/HIV, even high levels of condom use may not be sufficient to afford protection from infection as the odds of encountering an infected sex partner are extremely high. Conversely, when seroprevalence is low, 80% condom use is far more likely to be protective. Of course even then, the protective value of condoms depends on how infectious the sex partner is.

Another key issue is how to maintain or keep the positive effects of a program over time. A primary shortcoming of the psychological interventions that target the sexual risk behavior of adolescents has been the failure to achieve long-term positive effects. In fact, maintenance of effects may best be characterized as the "current frontier" in the science of averting STD/HIV acquisition and transmission among U.S. adolescents. Again, this challenge is precisely why we included Table 9.1 in the early portion of this chapter and devoted a considerable amount of text to elaborating on the ecological-level influences. In brief, the gains in positive, health-protective, individual-level approaches tend to disappear over time. This decrease in the effects occurs because adolescents return to an essentially unchanged environment that may have negative peer influences and behaviors. If the community had been favorably changed through broader intervention approaches, however, then these ongoing influences (e.g., parental monitoring, parent-adolescent communication, supportive norms, ample services, and lack of gender and power differentials) could become a continued source of reinforcement for the HIV prevention program. This form of prevention becomes the intervention that never ends, thus moving beyond the shortcomings of a one-time "program dose."

CONCLUSION

Prevention of HIV and STDs among U.S. adolescents is an urgent public health priority that comes with a large number of critically important challenges. One challenge is to accept responsibility for potentially shaping how adolescents view sex and sexuality, thereby having a profound influence on their development as they make the transition from childhood to adolescence and from adolescence to adulthood. Another challenge is to synthesize individual-level antecedents of risk and protective behaviors with ecological influences. The results of this synthesis will lead to improved ways to build ecological influences into prevention programs. Doing so may increase adolescents' adoption of safer sex behaviors and simultaneously promote long-term maintenance of health-protective behaviors.

REFERENCES

1.   Berman, S. M., and K. Hein.1999. Adolescents and STDs. In *Sexually Transmitted Diseases,* eds. K. K. Holmes, P. F. Sparling, P. Mardh, et al., 129–42. New York: McGraw Hill.

2.   DiClemente, R. J., G. M. Wingood, and R. A. Crosby. 2003. A contextual perspective for understanding and preventing STD/HIV among adolescents. In *Reducing Adolescent Risk: Toward an Integrated Approach,* ed. D. Romer, 366–73. Thousand Oaks, CA: Sage Publications.

3.   DiClemente, R. J., and R. A. Crosby. 2003. Sexually transmitted diseases among adolescents: Risk factors, antecedents, and prevention strategies. In *Blackwell Handbook of Adolescence,* eds. G. R. Adams, and M. Berzonsky, 573–605. Oxford, UK:Blackwell Publishers Ltd.

4.   Lapsley, D. K. 2003. The two faces of adolescent invulnerability. In *Reducing adolescent risk: Toward an integrated approach,* ed. D. Romer, 25–32. Thousand Oaks,CA: Sage Publications.

5.   CDC. 2003. Youth Risk Behavioral Surveillance. Available on-line at http://www.cdc.gov/mmwr/preview/mmwrhtml/ss5302a1.htm. Accessed August 2, 2005.

6.   Fortenberry, J. D. 2003. Adolescent sex and the rhetoric of risk. In *Reducing Adolescent Risk: Toward an Integrated Approach,* ed. D. Romer, 293–300. Thousand Oaks, CA: Sage Publications.

7.   Eng, T. R., and W. T. Butler. Eds. 1997. *The Hidden Epidemic: Confronting Sexually Transmitted Diseases.* Washington, D.C.: National Academy Press.

8.   DiClemente, R. J., R.Milhausen, J. Spitalnick, et al. (unpublished). *Validation of the Sexual Adventurism Scale for Adolescents (SASA) for Use in HIV/AIDS Prevention Research.*

9.   Crosby, R. A., L. F. Salazar, R. J. DiClemente, and W. L. Yarber. (in press). Correlates of having unprotected vaginal sex among detained adolescent females: An exploratory study of sex factors. *Sex Health.*

10.   Crosby, R. A., R. J. DiClemente, G. M. Wingood, C. Sionean, B.Cobb, and Harrington, K. 2000. Correlates of unprotected vaginal sex among African American female teens: The importance of relationship dynamics. *Arch Pediatr Adolesc Med* 154(9):893–99.

11.   Wingood, G. M., R. J. DiClemente, D. Hubbard-McCree, et al. 2001. Dating violence and African-American adolescent females' sexual health. *Pediatrics* 107(5):E1-E4.

12.   Green, L. W., and M. W. Kreuter. 2005. *Health Program Planning: An Educational and Ecological Approach,* 4th ed. Boston: McGraw Hill.

13.   Sampson, R. J., and J. H. Laub. 1994. Urban poverty and the family context of delinquency: A new look at structure and process in a classic study. *Child Dev* 65(2 Spec No):523–40.

14.   Flannery, D. J., A. T. Vazsonyi, J.Torquati, and A. Fridrich. 1994. Ethnic and gender differences risk for early adolescent substance use. *J Youth Adolesc* 23:195–213.

15.   Biglan, A., T. E. Duncan, D. B. Ary, and K. Smolkowski. 1995. Peer and parental influences on adolescent tobacco use. *J Behav Med* 18(4):315–30.

16.   Romer, D., M. Black, I. Ricardo, et al. 1994. Social influences on the sexual behavior of youth at risk for HIV exposure. *Am J Public Health* 84:977–85.

17.   DiClemente, R. J., R. A. Crosby, and G. M. Wingood. 2002. Enhancing HIV/STD prevention among adolescents: The importance of parental monitoring. *Minerva Pediatr* 54:171-77.

18.   Dittus, P. J., J. Jaccard, and V. V. Gordon. 1999. Direct and nondirect communication of maternal beliefs to adolescents: Adolescent motivations for premarital sexual activity. *J Appl Soc Psychol* 29:1927–963.

19.   Crosby, R. A. and K. S. Miller. 2002. The pivotal role of the family on adolescent females' sexual health. In *Handbook of Women's Sexual and Reproductive Health,* eds. G. M. Wingood, and R. J. DiClemente, 113–128. New York: Kluwer Academic/Plenum Publishers.

20.   Jaccard, J., P. J. Dittus, and V. V. Gordon, 1996. Maternal correlates of adolescent sexual and contraceptive behavior. *Fam Plann Perspect* 28(4):159–65, 185.

21.   Crosby, R. A., Leichliter, J. S., and Brackbill, R. 2000. Longitudinal prediction of STDs among sexually experienced adolescents: Results from a national survey. *Am J Prev Med* 18:367–72.

22.   Crosby, R. A., R. J. DiClemente, G. M. Wingood, C. Sionean, B. Cobb, and K. Harrington. 2000. Correlates of unprotected vaginal sex among African American female teens: The importance of relationship dynamics. *Arch Pediatr Adolesc Med* 154(9):893–99.

23.   Wingood, G. M., R. J. DiClemente, R. A. Crosby, et al. 2002. Gang involvement and the health of African-American female adolescents. *Pediatrics* 110(5):e57–e61.

24. Putnam, R. D. 2000. *Bowling Alone: The Collapse and Revival of American Community*. New York: Touchstone.

25. Crosby, R. A., D. R. Holtgrave, R. J. DiClemente, G. M. Wingood, and J. Gayle. 2003. Social capital as a predictor of adolescents' sexual risk behavior: A state-level exploratory study. *AIDS Behav* 7(3):245–52.

26. Cohen, D. A., M. Nsuami, D. H. Martin, and T. A. Farley. 1999. Repeated school-based screening for sexually transmitted diseases: A feasible strategy for reaching adolescents. *Pediatrics* 104(6):1281–85.

27. Hook, E. W. III, C. M. Richey, P. Leone, G. Bolan, C. Spalding, and K. Henry. 1997. Delayed presentation to clinics for sexually transmitted diseases by symptomatic patients: A potential contributor to continuing STD morbidity. *Sex Transm Dis* 24(8):443–48.

28. Fortenberry, J. D., M. McFarlane, A. Bleakley, S. Bull, M. Fishbein, D. M. Grimley. 2002. Relationships of stigma and shame to gonorrhea and HIV screening. *Am J Public Health* 92(3):378–81.

29. Fortenberry, J. D., M. M. McFarlane, M. Hennessy, S. S. Bull, D. M. Grimley, and J. St Lawrence. 2001. Relation of health literacy to gonorrhea related care. *Sex Trans Infect* 77(3):206–11.

30. Fortenberry, J. D. 1997. Health care seeking behaviors related to sexually transmitted diseases among adolescents. *Am J Public Health* 87(3):417–20.

31. DiClemente, R. J., G. M. Wingood, K. F. Harrington, D. L. Lang, S. L. Davies, E. W. Hook 3rd, M. K. Oh, R. A. Crosby, et al. 2004. Efficacy of an HIV prevention intervention for African American adolescent females: A randomized controlled trial. *JAMA* 292(2):171–79.

32. Crosby, R. A., S. Sanders, W. L. Yarber, C. A. Graham, and B. Dodge. 2002. Condom use errors and problems among college men. *Sex Transm Dis* 29(9):552–57.

33. Crosby, R. A., S. A. Sanders, W. L. Yarber, and C. A. Graham. 2003. Condom use errors and problems: A neglected aspect of studies assessing condom effectiveness. *Am J Prev Med* 24(4):367–70.

34. Sionean, C., R. J. DiClemente, G. M. Wingood, R. A. Crosby, B. K. Cobb, K. Harrington, S. L. Davies, E. W. Hook 3rd, and M. K. Oh. 2002. Psychosocial correlates of refusing unwanted intercourse among African American female adolescents. *J Adolesc Health* 30(1):55–63.

35. Wingood, G. M., and R. J. DiClemente, 1998. Partner influences and gender-related factors associated with noncondom use among young adult African American women. *Am J Community Psychol* 26(1):29–51.

36. Robin, L., P. Dittus, D. Whitaker, R. A. Crosby, K. Ethier, J. Mezoff, K. Miller, and K. Pappas-Deluca. 2004. Behavioral interventions to reduce incidence of HIV, STD, and pregnancy among adolescents: A decade in review. *J Adolesc Health* 34:3–26.

37. Crosby, R. A., R. J., DiClemente, G. M., Wingood, et al. 2003. The value of consistent condom use: A study of STI prevention among African American adolescent females. *Am J Public Health* 93:901–902.

38. Coyle, K., K. Basen-Engquist, D. Kirby, G. Parcel, S. Banspach, R. Harrist, E. Baumler, and M. Weil. 1999. Short-term impact of Safer Choices: A multicomponent, school-based HIV, other STD, and pregnancy prevention program. *J Sch Health* 69(5):181–88.

39. Coyle, K., D. B. Kirby, B. V. Marin, C. A. Gomez, and S. E. Gregorich. 2004. Draw the Line/Respect the Line: A randomized trial of a middle school intervention to reduce sexual risk behaviors. *Am J Public Health* 94(5):843–51.

40. DiClemente, R. J., G. M. Wingood, K. F. Harrington, D. L. Lang, S. L. Davies, E. W. Hook 3rd, M. K. Oh, R. A. Crosby, et al. 2004. Efficacy of an HIV prevention

intervention for African American adolescent females: A randomized controlled trial. *JAMA* 292(2):171-79.

41.   Ruiz, M. S., A. R. Gable, E. H. Kaplan, M. A. Soto, H. V. Fienberg, and J. Russell. 2001. *No Time to Lose: Getting More from HIV Prevention.* Institutes of Medicine. Washington, D.C.: National Academy Press.

42.   Jemmott, J. B. 3rd, L. S. Jemmott, and G. T. Fong. 1998. Abstinence and safer sex HIV risk-reduction interventions for African American adolescents: A randomized controlled trial. *JAMA,* 279(19):1529–36.

43.   St. Lawrence, J. S., T. L. Brasfield, K. W. Jefferson, J. Galbraith, S. Feigelman, and L. Kaljee. 1995. Cognitive behavioral intervention to reduce African American adolescents' risk for HIV infection. *J Consult Clin Psychol* 63(2):221–37.

44.   Stanton, B. F., X. Li, I. Ricardo, J. Galbraith, S. Feigelman, L. Kaljee. 1996. A randomized, controlled effectiveness trial of an AIDS prevention program for low-income African-American youths. *Arch Pediatr Adolesc Med* 150(4):363–72.

45.   DiClemente, R. J., R. Milhausen, J. M. Sales, L. F. Salazar, R. H. Crosby. 2005. A programmatic and methodological review and synthesis of clinic-based risk reduction interventions for sexually transmitted infections: Research and practice implications. *Semin Pediatr Infect Dis* 16:199–218.

Chapter 10

PROGRAMS THAT WORK: PREVENTION FOR POSITIVES

Heather D. Tevendale, Ph.D. and Marguerita Lightfoot, Ph.D.

Teenager, Almost Seen 13

By Tia

Sweet, crazy, wild
Almost 13
Loves boys and Lil' Bow Wow
Being heard and seen
Middle school, parties, dancing
Skating and class clown
Making people laugh
Can't sleep, always wound
Brown, short and beautiful
A doctor I will be
Pediatrician is the goal
Making kids laugh, that's me!
Camps, hyper, and dreamer
Television, friends and PE
I like a boy named Shay
How dare he, he doesn't like me.
I asked him for his 6th period class
He said PE,
I know this isn't true
I have 2nd period PE and so does he!
I live a normal life
Filled with drama and fun
Little time for homework
And the battle I have won

You see, I have a virus that lives with me
That needs to be destroyed every day
It crashed my body without warning
But I won't let it take away
My love for life or my dignity
My desire to live
Or my hopes for a future that will be free
Of life with HIV.

Reducing the transmission of HIV from infected to noninfected individuals is a top public health priority within the United States.[1] From a public health perspective, secondary prevention programs that successfully help youth living with HIV (YLH) reduce their HIV transmission-related risk behaviors are needed. The young people themselves face two other major challenges that can be addressed by secondary prevention programs: (1) initiating and maintaining health care regimens and (2) maintaining or improving their mental health and quality of life.[2–4] Intervention programs must support YLH and help them meet all three challenges for both their own well-being and that of others. This focus on improving the well-being of YLH, in addition to protecting potential partners, provides a personal motivation for YLH to actively participate in such interventions.

Michael and Crystal

Michael and Crystal are two young people living with HIV. At the time that Michael began to participate in a secondary prevention program for YLH, he was 20 years old. He had left his home two and a half years earlier. His father forced him to leave when Michael disclosed to his family that he was gay. He had not spoken to his parents since he left. He did occasionally speak with his sister, with whom he had always been close; however, she avoided the topic of his sexuality. Michael found the situation with his family to be quite painful given that he wanted them to accept and understand him. Michael also struggled with his own issues about being gay. Furthermore, he experimented with respect to both sex and drugs. He lived with his boyfriend and worked part-time. He indicated that he and his partner often had unprotected sex.

Crystal was 18 years old. Like Michael, she had little positive social support in her life. She had no contact with her family. She lived with her boyfriend. She used substances regularly, as did her boyfriend. All of their friends were also heavy substance users. Crystal was open to the idea of using condoms. Although her partner was HIV-negative, he refused to use them. Crystal indicated that she had no one in her life that supported either her desire to reduce her risky behaviors or to pursue her life goals.

As illustrated by Michael and Crystal, YLH face many challenges beyond being HIV-positive. Many of these young people have difficult relationships with their families, lack other social support, have limited financial resources, and are members of already disenfranchised groups (i.e., youth of color, gay or bisexual youth). In addition to these many issues, YLH also struggle with normative developmental tasks such as making education and career choices, and forming and maintaining romantic attachments.

In this chapter, we examine the need to identify and intervene early with young people who are HIV-positive. Intervention targets for prevention programming for YLH that meet the needs of these youth, as well as public health needs associated with reducing HIV transmission, are described. Two programs that have been found to effectively reduce HIV transmission risk behavior among young people are then described, as well as research findings indicating the extent of their effectiveness. The impact of these programs are illustrated through the experiences of Michael and Crystal. Finally, implications for secondary prevention with YLH are discussed.

IMPORTANCE OF IDENTIFYING AND INTERVENING WITH YLH

Being able to intervene with YLH while they are still young requires that they become aware of their HIV status. Thus, the first step in preventing HIV transmission is early testing. For testing to occur, young people at risk must be made aware of the value of being tested and be willing to be tested. Health care providers are in a particularly good position to promote HIV testing among young people.[5] Youth have indicated that they prefer to talk about HIV with their physician rather than their parents or teachers,[6] and such conversations can easily lead to a discussion of the need for testing. Social marketing campaigns are another means to encourage high-risk youth to be tested. Recently, a six-city campaign was implemented in which a variety of methods were used to advertise the importance of youth being aware of their HIV status. This campaign resulted in increases in the number of young people who were tested in those cities.[7]

Advances in HIV testing also show promise for increasing the proportion of youth who find out that they are HIV-positive. When HIV testing and counseling are conducted over two visits, approximately one-third of those tested do not return for the second visit and thus do not become aware of their status.[8,9] However, 98% to 99% of patients who received a rapid HIV test in research conducted with adult samples obtained their results, and the vast majority who tested HIV positive entered medical care.[9–11] As with adults, youth have reported a strong preference for tests with a rapid result time.[12,13] Thus, rapid testing has the potential to lead both to more youth finding out that they are HIV-positive and more youth who are seropositive being linked to health care and prevention services.

Providing prevention services to YLH, while they are still in adolescence or young adulthood, is important for a number of reasons. Young people in general are more willing to take risks and not consider the consequences of their behavior.[14] Youth also are more likely to have multiple partners than are older adults.[15] Findings from a review of thousands of medical records of HIV-positive individuals indicated that both male and female HIV-positive youth under 25 years old were more than twice as likely as HIV-positive adults to engage in high-risk behaviors such as unsafe sex and needle sharing. Youth in the study also were significantly more likely to be diagnosed with an STD.[16] These findings indicate the importance of intervening with individuals with HIV during the developmental period in which they are most likely to engage in behaviors that could infect others and/or lead to STDs that could further compromise their health.

The advent of highly active antiretroviral therapies has resulted in substantial improvements in the treatment of HIV over the last decade. HIV-infected youth are living longer and are experiencing greater feelings of health. These improvements, however, mean that YLH have more time and opportunities to engage in behaviors that may transmit HIV to others and may feel a decreased sense of risk if their viral load is suppressed. Recent findings from a study comparing high-risk sexual behaviors of YLH before highly active antiretroviral therapy (HAART) to that of YLH after the advent of HAART indicate that engaging in unprotected sex and the likelihood of having many partners have increased among YLH.[17] These apparent increases in risk behavior among YLH further heighten the need for prevention activities.

INTERVENTION TARGETS

As is the case with adults, once youth find out that they are HIV-positive, many will reduce the sex risk and substance use behaviors that could lead to transmission of HIV.[18–20] A substantial proportion, however, continue to engage in these high-risk behaviors, suggesting the need for programmatic interventions that target reduction in unprotected sex and substance use.[20,21] For example, in a multisite study of 323 YLH, 65% of the youth were sexually active and, of those youth, approximately 43% reported having unprotected sex at last intercourse at each of six assessments across 15 months.[21] Also, though rates of injection drug use seem to be fairly low among YLH who know their status,[16,19] relatively high rates of other types of substance use and abuse among YLH are of concern given the link between substance use and continued high-risk sexual behavior.[21,22]

In addition, given the benefits with respect to health outcomes and reduced transmission risk, interventions for YLH must target outcomes related to successful management of HIV disease. YLH need to have high rates of adherence to antiretroviral medications, good communication and assertiveness skills when interacting with medical providers, and help adapting to a chronic and life-threatening disease.[23] To improve disease management, interventions for YLH need to not only directly address methods for improving health care behaviors, but also address other difficulties that may interfere with enacting such behaviors. In particular, problems with taking medication as prescribed have been linked to both substance abuse and depression.[24–27] Both problems are common among YLH.[21,22,28] Furthermore, physicians may be reluctant to prescribe antiretrovirals to substance abusing youth due to fears that the young person will not be adherent.[29,30] Thus interventions that address both substance use and mental health issues seem more likely to result in YLH having access to antiretroviral medication and being able to obtain the greatest health benefits from the medication.

With respect to the physical health needs of YLH, preventive interventions also must include current information on HIV disease and its treatment. For example, a belief that an undetectable viral load means that HIV cannot be transmitted would lead to an increased risk of unprotected sex. Information regarding viral loads, medications, and monitoring viral load should all be included in secondary prevention programs for YLH.

Finally, broader quality of life and mental health also must be addressed. Quality of life includes feelings of physical and emotional health and well-being. The need to reduce mental health problems of YLH as well as improve health care behaviors, and thus physical health, has already been discussed. Changes in these areas are likely to lead to improvements in quality of life. However, quality of life also includes aspects of positive mental health, such as experiencing positive emotions, self-worth, a sense of control over one's own life, and overall feelings of well-being. It is these positive experiences that seem to lead individuals to value their lives and take actions to care for themselves.[31] Thus interventions that help YLH find the means to experience a sense of well-being and recognize the value of their lives provide motivation for these young people to sustain healthy behaviors over time.[32]

EFFECTIVE PREVENTION PROGRAMS FOR HIV-POSITIVE YOUTH

Two programs have been developed for YLH that have been indicated to effectively reduce high-risk sexual behavior. One is Teens Linked to Care (TLC). This is a 31-session intervention that is provided to YLH in small groups. The second effective program for reducing high-risk sexual behavior is called Choosing Life: Empowerment, Action, Results (CLEAR). This program was adapted from TLC. It is 18 sessions long and was designed to be delivered by program facilitators working one on one with YLH. In these interventions, the targets for change are (1) reducing unsafe sexual behavior, needle use, and alcohol/drug use to protect others from HIV; (2) improving physical health and adherence to medical regimens; and (3) improving quality of life for YLH. Manuals for both programs can be found online at chipts@ucla.edu.

TLC and CLEAR are both based conceptually on Social Action Theory.[33] This model theorizes that health protective behaviors, such as reducing high-risk sexual or substance use behaviors, are influenced by (1) self-regulation skills (i.e., skills associated with being able to manage one's own behavior and emotions), (2) the extent to which a person's environment supports or does not support the use of those skills, and (3) the degree to which affective and arousal states (e.g., depression, anger) influence the use of self-regulation skills. TLC and CLEAR provide education, modeling, and repeated practice of self-regulation skills that are important for reducing behaviors that may transmit HIV, as well as for health-related behaviors. These skills are general, including problem solving and emotion management, as well as specific to reducing HIV-transmission risk and improving health, including putting on a condom correctly, avoiding triggers for injection drug use, and communicating assertively with medical professionals.

With respect to providing environmental support for using these new skills, group facilitators provide consistent and ongoing support and reinforcement. Also, facilitators encourage group members to provide support and reinforcement to one another and supportive interactions quickly become a standard part of each group (e.g., praising one another for meeting personal goals). Furthermore, because many of the health behaviors targeted in the intervention are interpersonal in nature (e.g., not sharing needles, practicing safer sex), participants are taught skills (e.g., negotiating condom use with a partner) that increase positive support for healthy behaviors. Simultaneously, the interventions seek to help participants decrease contact with those who do not support healthier behaviors and may encourage continued risky behaviors (e.g., avoiding others with whom the YLH previously injected drugs).

The influence of affect and arousal on implementing new skills and behaviors also is addressed throughout the interventions. YLH learn to recognize the degree of emotional arousal or distress in multiple situations. They are taught and practice techniques (e.g., relaxation) for managing emotions such as depression or anxiety, particularly with respect to situations related to risky or health care behaviors. Being able to manage negative emotions is necessary to act in a healthy manner in high-risk situations.

YLH must experience sufficient motivation to apply self-regulation skills when they find themselves in risky situations. For HIV-negative individuals, the motivation to reduce high-risk behaviors is associated with taking care of one's own health. YLH can be motivated in a similar way to take medicine as prescribed, attend health care appointments, and reduce substance abuse, as well as to protect themselves from more virulent strains of HIV and from other STDs that could compromise their health. Motivation for YLH to change behaviors that may transmit HIV also comes out of a sense of altruism and concern for others. Recognition of a discrepancy between an individual's values and how that individual behaves on a day-to-day basis can provide motivation to change such behaviors.[34] For example, motivation to use condoms is enhanced for a young person who recognizes that engaging in unprotected sex with an HIV-negative partner is inconsistent with his concern for his sexual partner's well-being. Both CLEAR and TLC include regular discussion of values relevant to reducing risk behaviors and enhancing self-care. The interventions then assist YLH in practicing new behavior patterns regarding risk situations (e.g., using condoms) and self-care (e.g., adhering to medication schedules) that are consistent with their values.

Every session of TLC and CLEAR follows the same pattern. Each session begins with a review of participants' attempts to meet goals set at the end of the previous session. Facilitators and group members provide support and reinforcement for successfully meeting goals, and problem solving is used to address any difficulties. Participants then learn about new behavior patterns that will help them engage in less risky behavior and assist them in better meeting their health-related needs. These new behaviors are practiced in session via role play and then, at the end of each session, participants identify goals for the next week that will allow them to practice these new behavior patterns during the course of their day-to-day lives.

Teens Linked to Care (TLC)

TLC is made up of three modules. The first is "Stay Healthy." In the 12 sessions that make up this module, participants first explore their goals for the future to develop additional motivation for a lifestyle that is healthy and free of substance use. They then begin to address barriers to staying healthy, including attitudes about being HIV-positive, issues related to disclosing serostatus to others, and coping with HIV-related stigma. YLH then learn to monitor feelings, thoughts, and actions relating to substance use and set personal goals for reducing use. The final three sessions of this module focus on improving the ability to participate in medical care decisions. For example, YLH problem solve barriers to attending health care appointments and role play communicating with their physician in an assertive manner.

The second module is "Act Safe" and consists of 11 sessions. The focus of this module is on reducing HIV risk behaviors. The sessions regarding sex risk behavior seek to motivate safer behaviors by using discussions and role-plays to help youth articulate their own values and by considering ethical issues regarding protecting partners and disclosing HIV status. These sessions also provide information on the relative risk of sex acts, provide opportunities to learn to counter anticondom beliefs, and teach male and female condom use skills. YLH also are taught and provided practice in assertiveness skills specific to negotiating with partners for safer sex and refusing unprotected sex.

The sessions regarding substance use are based on the trigger-thought-crave-use pattern of alcohol/drug abuse.[35–37] Triggers are environmental cues (e.g., a friend with whom the YLH often gets high) and internal cues (e.g., feeling anxious) that lead to thoughts about drug use that, in turn, lead to cravings and eventually use. The intervention seeks to prevent substance use from occurring by teaching YLH to identify and avoid external triggers that are specific to each youth (e.g., limit time spent with drug using friends),[38,39] manage internal triggers (e.g., use relaxation techniques to reduce anxiety), as well as reframe and challenge thoughts and beliefs that may lead to continued substance abuse.[40] Participants also are provided with information about substance abuse treatment resources. This module ends with an examination of the negative consequences of mixing sex and drugs and practice at applying assertiveness skills to resist high-risk behaviors in situations where sex and drugs may be mixed.

The third module of TLC is "Being Together" and it consists of eight sessions. The intention of this module is to improve the quality of life of YLH and increase the emotional resiliency of participants as a means to maintain improvements in health risk and health care behavior. The sessions seek to improve life satisfaction and emotional well-being by (1) identifying a set of personal values that includes taking care of oneself and not being self-destructive; (2) helping YLH accept their serostatus while reducing feelings of pain, loss, and discontent; (3) increasing participants' sense that they have control over their lives; (4) decreasing motivation for self-destructive behavior, particularly substance use; and (5) living fully and joyously in the present moment. These goals are met by exploring issues related to life satisfaction through discussion, role play, and opportunities to consider and share personal guidelines for living. YLH also are taught meditation to increase awareness of themselves and their day-to-day life.

When Michael first attended TLC groups, he was very vocal and always contributed to the conversation. He was very opinionated in the group, but very respectful of the other group members. He was particularly vocal during problem-solving exercises and thrived on helping the other group members. When asked to argue against negative beliefs, he was often able to give the "right" answer. He always had a suggestion for options in problem-solving exercises. Many of the providers that worked with Michael viewed him as "having it all together." However, Michael was very guarded about his own problems. During the course of the TLC groups, he became more open and forthcoming about his struggles. He expressed that he felt like a hypocrite, being able to tell others how to live their lives but not "practicing what he preached."

Michael often had unprotected sex with his partner. During sessions that addressed sexual decision making, Michael reluctantly disclosed that his partner hit him. Through discussion with the group, Michael examined why he allowed himself to be treated that way and how he felt about himself. He used the assertive communication skills he learned in group to not only talk to his partner about the need for using condoms regularly, but to assert his other needs in the relationship. When discussing triggers for unsafe sex, Michael was able to identify his own depression and low self-worth as triggers for his passive response to using condoms. He explained that he felt unlovable and that he had been willing to accept a bad relationship, because he felt that no one else would want to be in a relationship with him.

After the experience of disclosing his HIV status to his family, he had not disclosed his status to anyone else for fear of their reaction. As a result he felt unable to connect in a "real" way with friends because he always had a secret he was hiding. During the session on disclosure, Michael was able to identify who he wanted to disclose to, what he wanted from that person, and how he was going to disclose. With this preparation, he was able to successfully disclose to a friend who provided Michael with ongoing and invaluable social support.

By the end of TLC, Michael had left his abusive relationship and seemed to have accepted being alone. He wanted to be in a relationship, but said that he was waiting for the right one. Although Michael had not yet fully reconciled with his family, he had developed and nurtured a number of deep and satisfying friendships. During the last group, Michael indicated that he could not remember the last time he was happy and felt okay in his own skin. He thanked the facilitators of TLC and the rest of the group for helping him.

Just as TLC seemed to help Michael, findings from the randomized controlled trial of TLC indicated that it was effective at meeting many of the goals relating to preventing HIV transmission for YLH.[41,42] Participants in the trial were more than two-thirds male, with approximately 90% of these youth identifying as gay or bisexual. The majority belonged to ethnic minority groups. For those attending Stay Healthy (Module 1), significant increases were found in reports of social support and, for young women, in reports of positive lifestyle changes and positive coping. Among those attending Act Safe (Module 2), there was a significant decrease in substance use based on a weighted index of frequency of use and severity of drug. Results from those participating in this module also indicated significant reductions in the number of unprotected sexual acts, overall number of sexual partners, and number of seronegative sexual partners. Youth who participated in Being Together (Module 3) reported significantly less emotional distress on multiple indices.

Choosing Life: Empowerment, Action, Results

As noted, CLEAR was developed from TLC. The experience with TLC illustrated the value of a small group intervention for many YLH. TLC, however, also demonstrated three challenges to implementing such groups. First, it can be challenging to engage youth in an extensive program. Therefore CLEAR was designed to be implemented more quickly than TLC. CLEAR is 18 sessions of 1.5 hours each, whereas TLC is 31 sessions of 2 hours each. Second, approximately 30% of YLH who agreed to receive the intervention did not participate in the group sessions,[41] raising questions about this delivery strategy for some youth. HIV is highly stigmatized and attendance at a group session for YLH equated to publicly acknowledging one's serostatus to others. Given the life circumstances of some YLH, the fear of stigmatization was high, and so some YLH were reluctant to attend groups. Third, it sometimes took several months to accrue enough YLH to form a sufficiently sized group. Given that TLC was implemented in large cities with relatively high rates of HIV infection, small group interventions would likely not be possible in cities and rural communities with low seroincidence among youth. As a result, CLEAR was designed to be delivered individually and thus address concerns associated with group interventions with YLH. The adaptations also allow for the intervention to be delivered in a manner consistent with current case management models that are being implemented nationally with funding from Ryan White and the Centers for Disease Control and Prevention.[42] Finally, CLEAR was designed to address medical breakthroughs, particularly HAART, which occurred after TLC was designed. Therefore with these two interventions, providers are able to provide services that are best suited for the individual YLH's preferences and life circumstances. Although some YLH would prefer and benefit most from a small group program, other YLH would prefer and benefit most from a one-on-one individualized program.

The topics covered in CLEAR are organized in a somewhat different manner than they were for TLC. The modules for CLEAR are "Act Safe-Substance Use" (Module 1), "Act Safe-Sexual Behaviors" (Module 2), and "Stay Well: Self-Care and Health-Care Behaviors" (Module 3). Because substance abuse heightens risk for unsafe sexual behavior and lessens compliance with medical regimens, substance use was addressed in the first module of the intervention. As with TLC, initial sessions of the CLEAR intervention focus on enhancing motivation for behavior change by exploring long-term goals, helping YLH identify the youth's ideal self, and examining how thoughts and attitudes about being HIV-positive can be a barrier to change. Reductions in substance abuse are targeted by having participants (1) monitor their own substance use and set goals for reducing use, (2) examine connection between reducing substance use and being able to meet long-term goals, and (3) learn to interrupt the substance use cycle by avoiding triggers and preventing thoughts from leading to a perceived need for alcohol or drugs. Participants also are provided with treatment referrals for substance abuse problems.

Module 2 focuses on decreasing sex risk behaviors with the ultimate goal of reducing HIV transmission. Intervention activities are quite similar to those found in TLC. Participants first examine ethical dilemmas regarding sexual activity and protecting sexual partners and themselves to motivate safer sex behaviors. Participants are then provided with knowledge and skills necessary to stay safe sexually including: (1) identifying triggers for unsafe sex, (2) learning the relative risk of different sex acts, (3) practicing arguments against anticondom beliefs, (4) learning and practicing male and female condom use, and (5) learning and practicing skills to negotiate condom use with a sexual partner and to refuse unprotected sex.

Module 3 of the CLEAR intervention focuses on self-care and health-care behaviors that, if enacted, will lead to a greater quality of life for participants. The first three sessions are quite comparable to ones offered in the first module of TLC. Participants explore reasons to stay healthy as part of motivating behavior change and the maintenance of such change. They then examine their own thoughts and behaviors regarding attending medical appointments, and youth are engaged in developing counterarguments against negative thoughts that decrease attendance at medical appointments. Assertiveness skills with respect to communicating with health providers are reviewed and practiced. The next two sessions in the module address medication adherence with respect to HAART. Participants first review information on HIV replication and antiretroviral therapies as a rationale for improving medication adherence. They then learn to reframe cognitions that may interfere with adherence to medication regimens. Youth also are taught five behavioral strategies to improve medication adherence: (1) determine ways that taking medication can be worked into habits of daily living, (2) create simple reminder strategies, (3) build in rewards for adhering to medication schedule, (4) plan to have extra medication in case of unexpected situations, and (5) develop an overall adherence plan. In the last session of the module and the intervention, YLH examine the improvements that they have made with respect to substance use, sex risk, and self-care/health-care behaviors. They then focus on setting overall life goals and selecting ongoing goals in each of the three areas addressed by the CLEAR intervention.

Crystal identified three main goals through the course of her sessions in CLEAR. The first was to decrease her weekly use of substances. Crystal realized that her life was not going to improve until she stopped using. She found that identifying her triggers for using and then applying the problem-solving steps to avoid or lessen exposure to triggers was most helpful in her attempts to stop using.

Crystal's second goal was to decrease risky sexual behavior. Through her discussions with the facilitator, Crystal recognized that the biggest factor in her unsafe sexual practices was her boyfriend. Although he was HIV-negative, he did not want to use condoms. Crystal was uncomfortable not using condoms because she worried about infecting her partner, but she felt she did not have the power to make him use condoms. Crystal had success in using the assertiveness skills she learned in CLEAR to talk with her boyfriend about her concerns. He was initially resistant, saying that he did not like to use condoms and if he had not gotten HIV from her by now, chances were he was not going to get it. However, Crystal was committed to asserting her feelings and reasons for wanting to have safer sex. Crystal was able to convince her boyfriend to use condoms.

Crystal's final goal was to receive more positive social support for her attempts to be healthier in her life and for her efforts to reduce risky behaviors associated with drugs and sex. During the course of CLEAR, Crystal relied heavily on the facilitator to provide support for her positive behavior changes. Over time, Crystal also decreased her contact with substance using friends, who provided no support in Crystal's efforts to reduce her risk.

Crystal also indicated that she found CLEAR's focus on long-term goals particularly helpful and motivating. She often did not consider the future and her bleak outlook was fueled by her lack of faith in herself and feeling like her life would never get any better. Crystal decided that she wanted to go to college to become a teacher. She continually used these long-term goals as her motivation for reducing her involvement in high-risk behaviors. By the end of the intervention, Crystal had reduced both her sex risk behavior and her substance use.

Behavior change also was found among other YLH who participated in CLEAR. CLEAR was evaluated in a randomized controlled trial.[43] Participants were 16 to 29 years old and were 78% male. Three-quarters of male participants identified as gay or bisexual. The majority of the participants were young people of color. In an attempt to intervene with higher risk YLH, participants had to have used drugs at least five times in the prior three months to be eligible to participate in the trial.

Those YLH that received CLEAR significantly increased the number of sex acts protected by condoms overall and with HIV-seronegative partners. Although a decrease in substance use was seen for those participating in the intervention relative to those in the comparison group, the differences did not reach statistical significance despite moderate effect sizes. The fairly small sample size (approximately 60 participants in each condition) may have made it more difficult to detect significant differences. No change was found with regard to medication adherence or attendance at medical appointments.

CONCLUSION

Evaluations of both TLC and CLEAR indicate that high-risk sexual behavior can be reduced among YLH through programmatic interventions. These interventions, therefore, can play an important role in meeting public health goals of reducing transmission of HIV. The positive effects of these interventions on sexual transmission risk are seen if the intervention is offered in a small group format or via in-person one-on-one sessions. This allows for greater flexibility depending on the setting in which the intervention is being offered. In a setting where there are a number of YLH in need of service simultaneously, groups provide a cost-efficient means to intervene. In a setting or locale where there are fewer YLH, an intervention that can be delivered to individuals one –on one may be the only means by which to provide services. Of interest, a recently developed intervention that seeks to reduce sexual transmission risk and increase medication adherence among YLH is attempting to use the strengths of both individual and group formats by providing an intervention with seven group sessions and five individually tailored sessions.[44, 45] This intervention, known as Adolescent Impact, is currently being evaluated in a randomized controlled trial.

Evidence of reduced substance use among YLH was found in the trial of TLC, but not in the evaluation of CLEAR. This outcome reduces risk for HIV transmission by reducing the context (i.e., being high) in which many high-risk sexual acts occur. The lack of significant findings for substance use change in the CLEAR trial may have been due to an insufficiently large sample size. Alternatively, a greater intervention dose (e.g., more sessions) may be required to make changes in these behaviors.

TLC and CLEAR had a limited impact on health-care behaviors. Effectively changing such behaviors may require more intervention sessions spread out over a longer period. Involving significant others such as family members or romantic partners in intervention sessions that target improvements in health-related behaviors provides an option to create ongoing support for behaviors such as attending medical appointments and taking medications as prescribed. This type of approach has been effective in improving medication adherence among adults living with HIV.[46]

Given the number of youth in the United States who are currently infected with HIV and the ongoing high-risk behaviors found among YLH, the importance of working with these young people to reduce transmission risk cannot be underestimated. Furthermore, YLH face a range of other issues that also need to be addressed as soon after diagnosis as possible. TLC and CLEAR are the type of intensive interventions that can meet these needs. These programs, however, do not offer a quick fix. Rather, they provide an approach that can be revisited on an ongoing basis to help individuals living with HIV as they strive to maintain a long, healthy, and happy life.

REFERENCES

1. CDC. 2003. Advancing HIV prevention: New strategies for a changing epidemic—United States *MMWR* 52(15):329–32.

2. Luna, G. C., and M. Rotheram-Borus. Youth living with HIV as peer leaders. 1999. *Am J Community Psychol* 27(1):1–23.

3. Luna, G. C. 1997. *Young People Living with HIV: Self-evident Truths.* New York: Hayworth Press.

4. Rotheram-Borus, M. J., D. A. Murphy, C. L. Coleman, M . Kennedy, H. M. Reid, T. R. Cline, et al. 1997. Risk acts, health care, and medical adherence among HIV+youths in care over time. *AIDS Behav* 1:43–52.

5. Rotheram-Borus M. J., and D. A. Futterman. 2000. Promoting early detection of human immunodeficiency virus infection among adolescents. *Arch Pediatr Adolesc Med* 154(5):435–39.

6. Rawitscher L. A., R. Saitz, and L. S. Friedman. 1995 Adolescents' preferences regarding human immunodeficiency virus (HIV)-related physician counseling and HIV testing. *Pediatrics* 96:52–58.

7. Futterman D. C., L. Peralta, B. J. Rudy, S. Wolfson, S. Guttmacher, A. S. Rogers, Project ACCESSS Team of the Adolescent Medicine HIV/AIDS Research Network. (2001). The ACCESS (Adolescents Connected to Care, Evaluation, and Special Services) project: Social marketing to promote HIV testing to adolescents, methods and first year results from a six city campaign. *J Adolesc Health;* 29S:19–29.

8. Ekwueme D. U., S. D. Pinkerton, D. R. Holtgrave, and B. M. Branson. 2003. Cost comparison of three HIV counseling and testing technologies. *Am J Prev Med;* 25:112–21.

9. Metcalf C. A., J. M. Douglas Jr., C. K. Malotte, H. Cross, B. A. Dillon, S. M. Paul, S. M. Padilla, L. C. Brookes, C. A. Lindsey, R. H. Byers, and T. A. Peterman, RESPECT-2 Study Group. 2005. Relative efficacy of prevention counseling with rapid and standard HIV testing: A randomized, controlled trial (RESPECT-2). *Sex Transm Dis* 32:130–38.

10. Kendrick S. R., K. A. Kroc, E. Couture, and R. A. Weinstein. 2004. Comparison of point-of-care rapid HIV testing in three clinical venues. *AIDS* 18(16):2208–10.

11. Kendrick S. R., K. A. Kroc, D.Withum, R. J. Rydman, B. M. Branson, and R. A. Weinstein. 2005. Outcomes of offering rapid point-of-care HIV testing in a sexually transmitted disease clinic. *J Acquir Immune Defic Syndr* 38:142–46.

12. Peralta L., N. Constantine, B. Griffin Deeds, L. Martin, and K. Ghalib. 2001. Evaluation of youth preferences for rapid and innovative human immunodeficiency virus antibody tests. *Arch Pediatr Adolesc Med* 155(7):838–43.

13. Spielberg F., A. Kurth, P. M. Gorbach, and G. Goldbaum. 2001. Moving from apprehension to action: HIV counseling and testing preferences in three at-risk populations. *AIDS Educ Prev* 13(16):524–40.

14. France, A. 2000. Towards a sociological understanding of youth and their risk-taking. *J Youth Studies* 3:317–31.

15. Santelli J. S., N. D. Brener, R. Lowry, A. Bhatt, and L. S. Zabin. 1998. Multiple sexual partners among U.S. adolescents and young adults. *Fam Plann Perspect* 30(6):271-75.

16. Diamond C., and S. Bushkin. 2000. Continued risky behavior in HIV-infected youth. *Am J Public Health* 90:115–18.

17. Lightfoot M. L., D. Swendeman, M. J. Rotheram Borus, S. Comulada, and R.Weiss. 2005. Risk behaviors of youth living with HIV: Pre- and post-HAART. *Am J Health Behav* 29:162–71.

18. Crepaz, N, and G. Marks. 2002. Towards an understanding of sexual risk behavior in people living with HIV: A review of social, psychological, and medical findings. *AIDS* 16(2):135–49.

19. Rotheram-Borus, M. J., M. Lee, S. Zhou, P. O'Hara, J. M. Birnbaum, and D. Swendeman, Teens Linked to Care Consortium. 2001. Variation in health and risk behavior among youth living with HIV. *AIDS Educ Prev* 13(1):42–54.

20. Sturdevant, M. S., M. Belzer, G. Weissman, L. B. Friedman, M. Sarr, L. R. Muenz, et al. 2001. The relationship of unsafe sexual behavior and the characteristics of sexual partners of HIV infected and HIV uninfected adolescent females. *J Adolesc Health* 29: S64–S71.

21. Murphy D. A., S. J. Durako, A. B. Moscicki, S. H Vermund, Y. Ma, D. F. Schwarz, et al. 2001. No change in health risk behaviors over time among HIV infected adolescents in care: Role of psychological distress. *J Adolesc Health* 29:S57–S63.

22. Pao M., M. Lyon, L. J. D'Angelo., W. B. Schuman, T. Tipnis, and D. A. Mrazek. 2000. Psychiatric diagnosis in adolescents seropositve for the human immunodeficiency virus. *Arch Pediatr Adolesc Med* 154(3):240–44.

23. Rotheram-Borus M. J., and D. A. Futterman. 2000. Promoting early detection of human immunodeficiency virus infection among adolescents. *Arch Pediatr Adolesc Med* 154(5):435–39.

24. Finney J. W., R. J. Hook, P. C. Friman, M. A. Rapoff, and E. R. Christophersen. 1993. The overestimation of adherence to pediatric medical regimens. *Children's Health Care* 22(4):297–304.

25. Hosek S. G., G. W. Harper, and R. Domanico 2005. Predictors of medication adherence among HIV-infected youth. *Psychol Health Med* 10:166–79.

26. Murphy D. A., M. Belzer, S. J Durako, M. Sarr, C. M. Wilson, and L. R. Muenz. Adolescent Medicine HIV/AIDS Research Network. 2005. Longitudinal antirctroviral adherence among adolescents infected with human immunodeficiency virus. *Arch Pediatr Adolesc Med* 159(8):764–70.

27. Rotheram-Borus M. J., D. A. Murphy, C. L. Coleman, M. Kennedy, H. M. Reid, T. R. Cline, et al. 1997. Risk acts, health care, and medical adherence among HIV+ youths in care over time. *AIDS Behav* 1:43–52.

28. Rotheram-Borus M. J., D. A. Murphy, D. Swendeman, B. Chao, B. Chabon, S. Zhou, J. Birnbaum, and P. O'Hara. 1999. Substance use and its relationship to depression, anxiety, and isolation among youth living with HIV. *Int J Behav Med* 6(4):293–311.

29. Ferrando S. J., T. L. Wall, S. L. Batki, and J. L. Sorensen. 1996. Psychiatric morbidity, illicit drug use and adherence to zidovudine (AZT) among injection drug users with HIV disease. *Am J Drug Alcohol Abuse* 22(4):475–87.

30. Sontag D., and L. Richardson. 1997. Doctors withhold H.I.V. pill regimen from some; failure to follow rigid schedule could hurt others, they fear (human immunodeficiency virus; treatment complicated by ability of patients stay on schedule). *New York Times* 146: sec1:1(N), 1(L), col 3.

31. Lawton M. P. 1999. Quality of life in chronic illness. *Gerontology* 45(4):181–83.

32. Rotheram-Borus M. J., Murphy D. A., Wright R. G., Lee M. B., Lightfoot M., Swendeman D., et al. 2001. Improving the quality of life among young people living with HIV. *Evaluation and Program Planning* 24:227–37.

33.   Ewart, C. K. 1991. Social action theory for a public health psychology. *American Psychologist* 46(9):931–46.

34.   Higgins, E. T. 1987. Self-discrepancy: A theory relating self and affect. *Psychol Rev* 94:319–40.

35.   Beck A. T., F. D. Wright, L. Newman, and B. Liese. 1993. *Cognitive Therapy of Substance Abuse.* New York: Guilford Press.

36.   Rawson R. A., J. L. Obert, M. J. McCann, and W. Ling. 1991. Psychological approaches for the treatment of cocaine dependence: A neurobehavioral approach. *J Addict Dis* 11:97–119.

37.   Shoptaw S., R. A. Rawson, M. J. McCann, and J. L. Obert. 1994. The Matrix model of outpatient stimulant abuse treatment: Evidence of efficacy. *J Addict Dis* 13:129–41.

38.   Rotheram-Borus M. J., M. Rosario, and C. Koopman. 1991. Minority youths at high risk: Gay males and runaways. In *Adolescent Stress: Causes and Consequences,* eds. S. Gore and M. E. Colten, 181–200. New York: Aldine de Gruyter.

39.   Shulman, G. D. 1989. Experience with the cocaine trigger inventory. *Adv Alcohol Substance Abuse* 8(2):71–85.

40.   Sarason I. G., G. R. Pierce, and B. R. Sarason. 1996. *Cognitive Interference: Theories, Methods, and Findings.* Mahwah, NJ: Lawrence Erlbaum.

41.   Rotheram-Borus M. J., M. B. Lee, D. A. Murphy, D. Futterman, N. Duan, J. M. Birnbaum, M. Lightfoot, Teens Linked to Care Consortium. 2001. Efficacy of a preventive intervention for youths living with HIV. *Am J Public Health* 91(3):400–405.

42.   CDC, National Center for HIV, STD and TB prevention. 1997. *HIV Prevention Case Management. Guidance. September.* Available at: http://www.cdc.gov/hiv/pubs/hivp-cmg.htm. Accessed on May 10, 2005.

43.   Rotheram-Borus M. J., D. Swendeman, S. Comulada, R. E. Weiss, M. Lee, and M. Lightfoot. 2004. Prevention for substance-using HIV-positive young people: Telephone and in-person delivery. *J Acquir Immune Defic Syndr* 37:S68-S77.

44.   Koenig L. J., C. Sulachni, L. Peralta, R. Stein, and W. Barnes. 2005. Adolescent impact: Conceptual basis for a developmentally-targeted intervention to minimize sexual transmission risk and promote adherence to treatment and care among adolescents living with HIV/AIDS. Atlanta: National HIV Prevention Conference.

45.   Lyon M., W. Barnes, J. Trexler, S. Abramowitz, D. Moschul, J. Lewis, S. Chandwani, et al. 2004. Adolescent Impact: Improving Adherence and Reducing Risk in HIV Infected Teens. Symposium on Adolescent Impact: Improving Adherence & Reducing Risk in HIV-Infected Teens. Paper presented at the Annual Meeting of the American Psychological Association, Honolulu, Hawaii.

46.   Remien R. H., M. J. Stirratt, C. Dolezal, J. S. Dognin, G. J. Wagner, A. Carballo-Dieguez, N. El-Bassel, and T. M. Jung. 2005. Couple-focused support to improve HIV medication adherence: A randomized controlled trial. *AIDS* 19(8):807–14.

Part III

PROVIDING SUPPORT

Chapter 11

THE VOICES OF TEENS LIVING WITH HIV: HOW YOU CAN SUPPORT US

Latoya C. Conner, Ph.D., Arnita M. Wilson, and Maureen E. Lyon, Ph.D., A.B.P.P.

The Gift of Love

By Michael A. Dowling

Love is a gift
That enables us to care
A feeling that we give to those we hold dear
Without love there can be no peace of mind
Love is a force that releases the bind
Love is a feeling that captures the soul
A special feeling that never lets go
Love is an emotion that you should let grow
And share with others
Even those you don't know
For giving love under any light
Purely shows that your heart shines bright

The Burgess Clinic is an HIV/AIDS specialty clinic that operates within the Division of Adolescent Medicine at Children's National Medical Center in the District of Columbia. One of the oldest, largest, and most comprehensive care clinics in the United States of America, the Burgess Clinic is a model of integrated multidisciplinary care. The integrated HIV services include medical care and treatment, psychological evaluation and psychotherapy, case management, risk reduction education and counseling, nutritional assessment and care, and research opportunities. The Burgess Clinic is dedicated to educating and treating adolescents to prevent the spread of HIV/AIDS.

To give a human voice to our work, we invited a group of adolescents from the Burgess Clinic to share their personal and psychosocial experiences of living with HIV. Focus groups and semistructured interviews were conducted, which resulted in the following themes: social support, disclosure, HIV-related needs and challenges, and the role of spirituality and religion in coping. As a result, youth-specific suggestions for peers and others who have been recently diagnosed with HIV are offered along with advice for family, peers, teachers, health care providers, and clergy, with regard to how they can support teens living with HIV/AIDS. We review the youth's experiences with HIV-related research, and close the chapter with recommendations for advocacy, empowerment, and education.

SOCIAL SUPPORT

HIV/AIDS is associated with social, psychological, and behavioral stressors that significantly affect coping patterns, psychosocial factors, and overall health status. Youth living with HIV identified the significance of social support in their survival, coping, and general livelihood. The presence of informed, nonjudgmental understanding and reliable support systems has resulted in positive outcomes for many HIV-infected youth. Conversely, the lack of understanding, acceptance, and positive social support has also been correlated to deleterious social and emotional effects.

Who Do You Look to in Your Life to Give You Support with Your HIV Status?

"My mom, mainly because she is pretty much the only one that knows."
"I would say my mom because she is the only one in my family that is infected and she is the only one in my family who accepts me."
"My sister because she understands me and my best friend because I have known her 11 years."
"My mom, because she is the only one who knows and she has been there since the beginning, when I first found out."
"I haven't told my parents. The only person I told was my best friend, because he told me he was HIV-positive. We got into a conversation about that. I have a great support network, which includes the advocates here at Children's."
"I would really say myself because I don't have a lot of support systems in my family."
"My family."
"Myself. Since I have been told, I have basically been on my own. I can't depend on my family. I don't use drugs or drink a whole lot."
"Nobody, because I really don't have anyone. But, there is this one lady at church that I can talk to or ask questions because she is positive and works in the field now."
"Honestly, I might go to my mom or brother for some things, the church for other things. I might go to God for some things I really need, but not all the time the way I am supposed to—so I'm learning how to go to Him. But

there is no one person I go to for everything, support with financial, spiritual, emotional things."

Since Receiving Your HIV Diagnosis, Who in Your Life Has Been *Most* Supportive?

"My boyfriend, he's very supportive. He listens. He asks me what do I think I should do. He doesn't tell me what to do."

"My Mom. I can't explain it, because she always supported me in whatever I did. "Mainly she gave me the 'your life is not over' speech, 'you can still live on,' 'you have a lot to look forward to.' I knew a lot of that before, but she reinforced that."

"My Mom. She has common sense. I've never been hospitalized. I've always been healthy. She says, "I've been blessed." I've never missed school. I can get up in the morning and do what I want to do."

"At one point in time it was my Mom, but me and her had a falling out. Now, it's more my sister or my boyfriend. They bring sunshine into my life. They'll be like, "You're blessed you don't get as sick as your other friends. If you are in the hospital, it's just for normal things.' I shouldn't take it for granted."

"The two most important people have been my best friend and [my care advocate]. He just came up to me and told me. '[I'm] there to listen. We can talk.' And the care advocate here, he makes sure I do what I need to be doing and just taking care that I am a balanced person. They've been real supportive in that way. My best friend's whole approach is not judgmental and not coming to you in a negative way. 'You need to take care of yourself. This is what you need to do.' I was real upset and he helped me keep a positive attitude. It crossed my mind to tell my family, but it crossed real quickly. I was having a hard time dealing with it myself so I wasn't about to put a burden on them. So when my friend told me, I didn't feel like I was putting a burden on him."

"My best friend's aunt was very supportive of me. Even though I didn't tell my best friend, I told her aunt, because she was in the same situation as me. She was in a nursing home before she died [of AIDS]. She told me about her situation. She told me that she didn't think that she could live with it. That's why she let herself go and didn't take her medicine. She told me that I could do better for myself. I was there when she passed."

"I would really say the staff at Children's. I am always in their face. I know I can come to anybody and they help me."

"People who aren't in the same situation can be helpful too."

"Me—I just feel like I have to worry about being healthy and doing what I need to do to survive and stuff."

"Myself. My first social worker was good, but I didn't come here. I come a lot more now than I did because my advocate is always calling and nagging me. I don't want to hear her mouth so I come in and take care of my business."

"For me, I don't think that there is one person. I meet people in life that are supportive along the way that have been encouraging. Some people might have been there for one year or two to three years that have said positive things that have been encouraging to me."

DISCLOSURE

Disclosure of one's HIV diagnosis may be one of the most challenging experiences for HIV-positive teens to negotiate. It is common for adolescents to experience feelings of shame and guilt regarding their infection, which may result in a downward spiral of isolation, fear, discrimination, and depression. The decision to disclose to family members, friends, and sexual partners is a complex issue that requires sensitivity, support, and understanding. The individuals, who help facilitate the disclosure of the youth's HIV status to important people in the youth's social and personal networks, must consider the benefits and potential detriments of such disclosure. Barriers to disclosure and social support strategies need to be identified in advance.

What Was Your Best Experience When You Shared Your Diagnosis with a Family Member or Friend?

"I was just relieved. Before I told anyone I felt like I was in a box. I couldn't sleep. I was like, 'Who can I tell?' I wanted to tell my grandmother, but when I called her she wasn't home. I went to my mom's house. My mom just got back from work. My little brothers and sisters were out with their father. We went down and had dinner. We talked about it. I think my mother about passed out, once she heard the words coming out of my mouth. She got up and walked out of the room. She went to the basement. I thought she was going to get a bat. I had to go by the front door, so I could run you know (laughing). She came back. She hugged me for about two hours. She was hurting me. She was suffocating me. Her bosoms are big, you know."

"Well it was when I was talking to my best friend. It was definitely relieving. To me, it definitely made a difference that he could relate. It was a real big shock. We had known each other for 11 years. We had worked together. He would have been on my short list of people to tell. He just told me [he had HIV]. I thought there ain't no better time than now. It made me feel better about the whole situation myself, too. Other people are living with it and are normal and living their everyday life. They are not letting it run them. It can have a positive impact on your life."

"Mine was when I told my first love. It was because I really liked him. We both had the same feelings for each other. He really did care about me. Our relationship grew more. He had a damn good response."

"The best experience I had was telling the whole school. I came into it thinking it was going to be a negative experience. They were treating me well. And it was high school students and they were helpful and supportive at the same time. I am just saying that I am very surprised that high school students took it in a mature manner. It was more so [that the] teachers who were ignorant than students. There were a lot of teachers who said, 'What gave me the right to go on their morning announcements and tell the whole school?' They even complained to the principal and hounded the guidance counselors. It was still a positive thing, because a lot of people who were not educated about the subject became educated about it."

"I have not had any good experiences. My aunt tried to be there, but she was too nosy. She would always ask me about what I was doing and if this boy knew that I was positive."

"For me, a lot of people were more accepting than rejecting. However, I do wonder to this day, I can hear my aunt say, 'Y'all better stop hanging out there with those girls before you catch that stuff.' I've had more good experiences than bad."

HIV-RELATED NEEDS AND CHALLENGES

With respect to treatment and care, HIV/AIDS-related needs for infected individuals are similar to those of other individuals living with chronic illnesses. An expressed need of young people living with HIV/AIDS is that of a supportive help system, for example family and peer acceptance, healthy emotional attachments, basic living necessities, spiritual and psychosocial outlets. Some challenges of living with HIV/AIDS can be directly connected to the disease itself, such as adherence to antiretroviral therapy, resistance to medical treatment, and the mental ability to deal with the illness itself. Challenges also include stigma, which can prevent adolescents from obtaining proper care. Once adolescents are diagnosed with HIV, education and treatment may encourage them to use programs.

What Are Some of the Issues That Teens with HIV Need Help With?

"Keeping doctor's appointments. There's so many of them. Run these tests. Take this assessment. You really don't have a clue what's going on. It took me a long time to understand about my T cells. Instead of just saying it in doctors' terms, say it in regular terms."

"One, I say is that they need to know exactly what this disease does to your immune system . . . bones, muscles what organs are affected. They need a support group, some other peers that are experiencing it too, that can help them. They need help with taking medication and have a person that will help them understand the medication and what it does and just send them home with a bottle of pills to take. Also, they need reminders of doctor's appointments and just encouragement."

How Can Health Care Providers Help?

"Make sure [the] family understands, too. It goes back to having a support network. I might forget about my doctor's appointment. Or a care advocate [may say], 'You know you have an appointment in a month? You know you have an appointment in three weeks? You know you have an appointment in two weeks? You know you have an appointment tomorrow?' Call us and remind us about our appointments."

"Just be there for them and don't always try to give answers. Because you can't always answer every question. Sometimes you just got to be there and listen."

"Let me decide when I want to come in and make my own appointments."

"Hire more peer support, more youth. Just because they are talking to their social worker or doctor don't make the assumption that they feel comfortable or mentally related to the social workers. Bring more youth on to the team or HIV-positive youth, not to say that just because they are positive or youth that they will be able to relate but they may feel more open to communicate than adults. Will they do that? I don't know. But that's my suggestion."

THE ROLE OF SPIRITUALITY AND RELIGION IN COPING WITH HIV-RELATED ISSUES

It is characteristic for people faced with a life-threatening illness to search for meaning, understanding, and coping mechanisms to deal with their circumstances. The search for meaning often leads some to search for spiritual and religious answers. For some, their spirituality or religiosity serves as a protective factor and contributes to their ability to cope effectively with their HIV status. However, others have questioned, 'Why me?' with regard to their infection, which they associate with punishment. Individuals' attributions and faith may have an impact on their mental health, disease progression, and long-term survival. Therefore we believe that it is imperative to comprehend and begin query into the youth's spiritual and religious coping styles.

How Does Spirituality or Religion Impact Your Life and Coping?

"[I] pray and read the Bible."

"That's my reason behind everything. I can't explain everything. I just go to God and say, 'You know the reason, the reason behind everything.' Otherwise, I would be all stressed out so I just take it to God."

"I believe in God. But I am not sure if this is right. I mean, how come I have to have a disease, you know?"

"Sometimes I throw spirituality up. I believe that I am going to live a long life, I believe I have a purpose and the purpose is to help youth do something . . . HIV can be a mind boggler, it can bring fear, low self-esteem and depression based on the things you hear. I know I'm not going anywhere and am going to be here for a long time so I just brush it off. I believe that God's got something better for me."

"Honestly, sometimes with me, I question whether I am going to be healed, 'Okay God you are a healer and why can't you heal me?' Now I view healing differently. I see other people living with cancer and other things. God can heal the body at the same time there are different forms of healing, physical, mental or spiritual healing, and it is knowing what God has done for you. I know that God is a healer and I believe that I will be healed, that I have a purpose. I may have difficulty taking medication and wonder about whether I will be resistant or something. But, I am not leaving this world until God has finished the purpose that he put me here to do."

ADVICE FOR FAMILY, PEERS, TEACHERS, HEALTH CARE PROVIDERS, AND CLERGY

Adolescents living with HIV/AIDS express the need for their support systems to be more active in their lives. This need was most pronounced at the time of diagnosis. Youth are also concerned that their support systems try to understand the difficulties of managing a chronic illness. This includes finding a doctor with whom they are comfortable, someone to help them schedule medical appointments, and having a professional explain HIV/AIDS to them in terms that are practical and easily understood. It is important for support systems to inform young people of their options and invite them to collaborate in their treatment planning. For teens diagnosed with HIV/AIDS to maintain medical care, it is essential that adolescents have consistency, feel supported, and are given positive reinforcement and encouragement by those in their support system.

What Advice Would You Give to Parents When Attempting to Be There for Someone They Care about Who Was Recently Diagnosed with HIV?

"First is definitely just listening and being more educated about it. While I haven't shared it with my parents, part of it is [that] I don't want to put an emotional burden on them. The other part is, I don't want to tell them something and they are going to base their reaction on a lot of ignorant facts they just heard or assumptions. I would be damned if I would eat off of a paper plate or get treated a certain way because of a health condition, because they aren't educated about it. The best thing is to get as much education about it as you can. Keep an open mind and don't judge. How it happened is irrelevant. The important thing is that it did happen and how are you all going to work with it as a family and that the person gets the best care possible."

"I think if a parent doesn't understand what is going on with a child, they should research it on their own, before trying to deal with it with their child. They might come off bad or the child [may] be offended. Of course their reaction might be, huh! Or in denial. I think they should go to the doctor's with them and get their questions answered."

"I was going to say the best source of information is the doctors and case managers and also listening to their child, because most parents don't know much about it."

"I think parents should ask their child if it is alright if they disclose their status to someone else, even someone else in the family. I don't think the parent should disclose about their sickness or any other sickness."

"When I told my aunt she told me, 'Don't tell anybody.' And then I found out that she told other people in the family. Why is she telling? Why can't I be the one to tell them? She didn't even check to see if I was ready for them to know."

"I think they should have a conversation with their child and their doctor."

"I think it needs to be a partnership. I think it is important that some family member or someone you are close to is involved. So someone can check in on you and encourage you. One of the most important things for a parent to do is to seek professional help. It's just as traumatic for the parent as it is for the child. [They both may think], 'Why is it happening to me?' They should sit on the couch or talk to their clergyperson."

"You may have younger sibs who are sexually active. This is an opportunity to educate other family members."

"I love my mother to be involved. She stays on top of them, because doctors will get you to do studies or new medicine and the parent is there to say 'Wooo, what's going on?' If it wasn't for her I wouldn't be here today."

"If you don't have a support system, you have to reach inside yourself. I brought my late significant other with me. I had to be my own mother, my own father. To push myself to go down that road."

"The fact that I don't have someone to hold me accountable is a positive thing. To be honest, [my parents] are ignorant about HIV. That's why I don't want to tell them. Certain members of my family are insensitive. It's already a bad situation and they could make it worse. I don't want to burden my mother. It will hit her hard. If it gets to a point that I do need to tell them, I will. Right now I want to work on educating them, in little bits. So that if I do decide to discuss it, they won't say, 'Oh you been shooting up heroin.' Certain of my family members aren't going to be supportive. I think my parents will be supportive; it's a matter of preparing them for it and not just hitting them with it. Test the waters before I jump in."

"Don't judge; No type of judgment."

"Continue to care, support and give advice. Comfort them and listen. Just be there."

What Advice Would You Give to a Brother, Sister, or Friend Who Has Recently Been Diagnosed?

"It depends on how close that friend is to you. Say you had a friend since third grade and you had HIV since you were born. You didn't really know what it was, because you were so young. I think if it is a long-term friend and you want to have that friend for a long time, you should disclose to them. I would research where she is coming from and what is going on with her. I would have a conversation like we are. So they won't get so emotional or depressed about it."

"Some of the same guidelines as with family as a friend. It's just like if you have a friend who is paralyzed, you can't run track with them, but the mentality of how you treat them doesn't change. I think the consistency is important. Treat them the same way as before. You may not ever go to the doctor with them. Just check on them, 'how are you feeling today?' If they know you have an appointment with your doctor on a Friday, after say' how did it go?' Let them know that someone else cares. Don't make it the center of your friendship. Don't make it a big deal: 'Oh this is my friend Tony with AIDS.' (Laughter). Like you are only still their friend because you have HIV or with any kind of disease or whatever."

"It's really simple. Just be a friend. I still have school. Don't ask them everyday, 'How is your life with HIV today?' Like if they have a doctor's appointment and you think they should come, ask them to come."

"How would they feel about being friends with someone who is HIV-positive? I would like for a person to tell me. I don't want you being my friend just to give me sympathy. That's why I don't have friends; I hang by myself and my significant other. I be chillin' in my room and partying."

"Tell them it's going to be okay."

"I don't have friends, but I would want them to treat me the same."

"Listen, be there and comfort them. Don't down them if they are homosexual or something. Just be there to support them with whatever like going to doctor's appointments. Love them no matter what decisions they have made and let them know that no matter what happened there is still life on the other side and that it doesn't have to kill you."

If There Is a Teacher That Finds Out a Student Is HIV-Positive, Is There Any Advice You Would Give That Teacher about Being Supportive?

"Ask the student to be the teacher now. The teacher is now going to be the student."

"This is one I can talk about. I told the whole school on World AIDS Day. A lot of teachers wanted me to teach a class about it. It was really interesting to sit there and see them taking notes and asking questions. It was high school students. And there was no snickering or ignorance. Teach the teacher and the class, because that's real."

"Well I did notice one thing I didn't like is that some teachers wanted to be around me more. Trying to be extra nice and extra sympathetic. One teacher in chemistry passed me because she felt bad. I don't want to be treated differently. Don't give me no A."

"I went to school and no one wanted to learn anything. It was, 'She's got AIDS, don't touch her.' I would go to the pool with my mother and everyone would get out of the pool. My mother cried. I was the first student with HIV to be in a regular school. If a student was sick, they could call and say she shouldn't come to school. Sometimes you can't teach people."

"There is a saying, 'The road to hell is paved with good intentions.' With teachers you may mean the best for the student, they should definitely understand that confidentiality is the key. Don't go talking to others without the person's permission. Let the student guide how to deal with the issue. I may feel differently about my English teacher knowing and my chemistry teacher knowing. I don't want it to infringe on my relationship in class."

"First of all if the teacher don't know much about it I think she should research it and get the facts [about HIV/AIDS] before she approaches you so she won't be afraid and will know what's going on."

"Don't treat the student any differently. Don't give out sympathy grades. Keep it to yourself."

"Just know your place and when to keep things confidential and not to spread their business. Not to treat them different than the rest of the youth. Be sensitive to their needs and at the same time don't give them too many privileges because they are different."

What Have Front Desk Staff/Reception Done to Make Being HIV-Positive Easier?

"One is always friendly and very real with me. We joke. It's not like I'm the patient, but like we are friends."

"I think the health care staff are really good. They refer to you by name. How are you doing? Are you still working there? It's a personal touch. You should take vitamins. Just small stuff. They not going to diagnose you or anything."

"I've been coming to Children's since I was 3. I'm 19 now. They greet you. They even buy you lunch. They treat me like I am one of their children."

"I don't know—they be nice, but I'm assuming being nice is a part of their job."

"Be nice and polite."

"They're just friendly, that's all. Kept a smile on their face."

What Have Your Doctors Done to Make Being HIV-Positive Easier?

"My old doctor, he got to know me. He usually asked me what's going on in my life. He would ask if there are any questions about my status or if I needed advice about anything. He made me feel like I was an equal. I don't think he was just doing it because it was his job. My new doctor I don't know yet."

"All of my doctors since I was a baby [lists all of her doctors] they are all wonderful. They treat you like they are your mother, 'You know if you don't do this, this is the consequence.' Even while they are in there giving you an exam, they have a conversation with you like, 'How is your day?' Like you are a family member."

"It doesn't seem like I'm a dying patient; doesn't seem like I'm dying from anything. It's just like come on in for your check up and do what I got to do."

"She asks personal questions. She is nice to me no matter what. She asks my opinions about treatments and gives me time to decide what I want."

"Just open. To me they seem caring to me, some of them."

What Have Social Workers, Case Managers, and Care Advocates Done to Make Being HIV-Positive Easier?

"My old social worker, she's no longer on the team. I miss her very much. They are like a buddy system. 'Do you want to participate in this outing or do you want me to schedule your appointments?' If there is something going on in the hospital that they think would be good for you, they let you know."

"The atmosphere is good. They actually do care about you. They want to guide you and support you in any way they can. They don't always ask first about our HIV status. They ask about other things, like school and work and how you are feeling in general."

"The one thing I love about coming to the clinic is dealing with the case managers and care advocates. They make me feel like one big family. Even though I pick on them, I love them to death. We're going to spend a lot of time with each other."

"My care advocate talks to me every time I come here. I can talk to her like the big sister I don't have. She's really nice to me."

"I think I have the best care advocate here. He didn't just drag me in here. I about passed out when they told me I was HIV-positive. My care advocate took me home. He made sure I was all right. I was going to go to work, but he suggested taking the day off, which I did. It's gone from a professional relationship to a kind of like a brother relationship. I don't know how I would have handled it. He made sure I was okay, because I had a whole lot on my mind."

"They just give me type of resources that I can use to my advantage to help."

"Remind me of appointments. Sign me up for groups that I can make money for coming to. Buy cards for my birthday. Help me with stuff like finding apartments and jobs."

"Well, I can say one social worker for me, she showed me different avenues for doing things, that I have never seen, like getting us involved in activities. She opened my eyes to things that I was not used to doing, even at home with my own family."

What Have Mental Health Professionals, Like Psychologists or Therapists, Done to Make Being HIV-Positive Easier?

"They can be supportive. I had a nice one. Sometimes they make you think you are crazy, but really you are not. They don't just sit there and say you got this diagnosis, like bipolar disorder or postpartum depression. They listen to you. They listen to your emotions. They ask you what you think is wrong with you and what do you think it's coming from and why. It was helpful. I don't have to see a psychiatrist no more."

"My psychologist helps me when I get a chance to see her. We put everything out on the table. When the session is over I think, 'Damn, I want to keep talking.' She makes me feel that everything is okay. She makes me feel motivated. She's very open. She's not quick to tell me what to do. I'm mostly controlling the whole conversation. To have someone actually listening, I don't get that where I am now. She helps me to see things clearly."

What Can the Church or Other Spiritual Organizations Do to Help Persons Living with HIV/AIDS?

"I would tell them to put more information about it for their young people. Because in church they are like, 'young people are not supposed to have sex until married.' But not everybody waits; so they're not teaching them anything because they're assuming they're going to wait until marriage."

"Be more accepting of everyone."

"Don't be judgmental, like, 'they sinners.' Open some kind of ministry, do something with them. Help the people."

THE ROLE OF RESEARCH

There is currently no known cure for HIV/AIDS, but clinical, community, and behavioral research agendas are focusing on prevention, treatment, health promotion medication adherence, and risk reduction among adolescents. Research targeted towards HIV-infected youth provides opportunities for the participants to: (1) learn information about HIV and how it works,

(2) increase adherence to therapy, (3) reduce transmission risk behaviors, (4) promote healthy lifestyles, and (5) explore end-of-life decision making, to name a few. Many youth stated that research gives them the opportunity to help other teenagers who have HIV/AIDS, as well as those who are not infected, whereas others discussed the burden research places on them and offered suggestions to balance the cost-benefit equation for both the researchers and participants.

What Has Research Done to Make Being HIV-Positive Easier?

"During research studies they help you a lot and educate you about HIV. It's not just like you are sitting around asking questions and they give you answers. It's part of a gathering. It's actually fun, like a party, a gathering. You learn and you have fun at the same time and you get to know more people that are very understanding."

"I think that research definitely helps with the education part, and the monetary assistance they provide is really helpful for the financially strapped and broke patients like myself. (Laughter). But it's definitely helpful in coming up for a cure for HIV. It may not work for you but it may change someone else's life. Being a partner in change for someone else's life too. I think that's the great work that they are doing."

"It really helped me to learn more about my diagnosis with HIV. The research projects, the research assistants, and nurses can also help me to help someone else also. It's a two-way street."

"It gives you information about it if you go to a research group and didn't know about HIV—it gives you more information about it. They also bring the fact that you are not the only person going through this; you might be with other people going through this."

"It pays me to come in and learn."

"It just taught me different stuff that I didn't know about HIV."

ADVOCACY, EMPOWERMENT, AND EDUCATION

Advocacy is an important part of prevention, care, and treatment for young people living with HIV/AIDS. Advocacy is what revolutionizes policies. Policies and practices can increase or reduce the availability of prevention education or access to effective treatment therapy. Adolescents believe that HIV/AIDS advocacy can be more effective through review processes that include those who are infected or affected combating this epidemic. Also, young people have identified that working with someone who has been diagnosed with HIV/AIDS is helpful. The basic needs of HIV/AIDS advocacy for youth are advocates who are open-minded, listen, make the young person feel comfortable, and most important, are informative.

Advocacy also works hand in hand with empowerment. Empowerment includes education and skills building. Youth infected with HIV/AIDS would benefit from educational workshops that create awareness and prevention methods that can reduce the transmission and acquisition of HIV/AIDS. Education dispels myths and counters misinformation about HIV/AIDS. Youth would like HIV/AIDS education to be easily accessible to all populations to increase its effectiveness. Educational materials should also be straightforward, culturally relevant, inoffensive, and nonjudgmental. Advocacy, empowerment, and education can help sustain proper use of information regarding HIV/AIDS. These are powerful tools for adolescents who are infected and affected by this epidemic. These tools can help them make better choices.

What Can Health Care Providers, Advocates, or Social Workers Do to Help to Get Young People Who Have Just Been Diagnosed More Engaged in Care or Keep You Engaged in Care?

"Phone calls, just like reminders. Letting you know 'Okay come in.' Sometimes the care advocate will just have you come in and just check in and that physical contact. See you in person and keep you informed about what's going on and open you up to different experiences and other educational opportunities, like a trip that's coming up or a research project."

"I would say making it feel like it's one big happy family, because it really helps me too. Helps me to be on time and keep my appointments. That's what really makes it helpful. Interact, laid back. It's relaxed, not so professional all of the time, not that you are not professional."

"Try to talk them into coming without forcing them to come in. Let them deal with everything the way they want. Comfort and be nice to them."

"They need to have more activities involving the youth and one thing that I know, for a person like me that wants to go into this field, they don't have too many opportunities. Have more peer-to-peer or youth functions. Give them a little stipend or incentive to work somewhere or learn something. Give out some money for some youth jobs in HIV."

What Should We Do to Help Teens Who Have Received Their Diagnosis, but Are not Coming Back in for Care? How Can We Get Them Engaged in Care? Should We Leave Them Alone? Become More Aggressive?

"I think you should be very persistent and stay on top of the person, but not to the extent that you are badgering them, more like let's go out and talk for lunch and talk. So it's not so much surrounded around HIV status."

"That's the only way. I got dragged in here. I got tricked. (Laughter). By the time I realized I was coming in, I was here. Once you see someone else who doesn't have to care [but] goes out on their own time [and] not because they are afraid you are going to die. It goes back to training. Certain language, manners, make it easier. They have a flow, if they do it right. General expectations can make it easier and comfortable, outgoing and aggressive approach, if you do it right, is the most beneficial approach. Use an aggressive direct approach. When I look back I am definitely glad. The case manager thought about the situation. I could tell he planned it out. He only went at it one time. He put it out there. I did a Friday group. It blew my whole weekend, but by Monday I came in here. If I hadn't come in, in hindsight, I could have not cared and said it is not that serious and put others at risk, too. I think it was definitely a positive thing. He reached out to me."

"It may take some time for people, just call and talk to them about how it would be better to come in. Call to see how they are doing. Not something you need to do everyday and not something you have to talk with everybody. A person doesn't want to explain what's going on with themselves, because they think it is going to get out. They are afraid someone else is going to find out. That's why I didn't want to come in [after diagnosis]."

"Not totally leave them alone because you don't know what's going on in their head. I would check up with them. You got to let them make the decision to come back in for care. 'What they say in MI [motivational interviewing]?' Roll with the resistance."

"Find a way to make coming here fun. Don't be negative. Tell the truth no matter what."

"First they need to give more information up front when they are doing the counseling and testing. Organizations need to make sure they are giving information, getting information from people during the counseling and testing session, and have people willing to go out and find those that came to get tested, but did not get their results or are not following up with care."

What Can We Do to Encourage More Young People to Be Tested and Learn about Their HIV Status?

"Show them that it's not as hard as it may seem and it's not the end of the world. It's a new beginning, by not making it look so scary and complicated. You're sick. It's a blood disorder, just like any other sickness. It's a sickness—more terminal, more severe than others. I don't think that people should look at it the way they look at it. I think they should look at it like cancer, just another way of getting it."

"A lot of times, the people providing the tests are doctors who make it more complicated and scary than it needs to be. Don't walk in and find out if you have AIDS. Just make it as simple and as less threatening as possible. You are going to have people staying away and not come in, if they feel threatened. People look at HIV/AIDS as a death sentence. If I go out and say something to somebody about getting tested for syphilis or gonorrhea or other STD, they may come in because there is a cure for those diseases. Because of the perceived death image and no cure and the stigma attached to HIV/AIDS, people don't come in. You need to let them know it is not a death sentence and also that nothing can be wrong with you. Also there is a stigma. You can learn something and then you can protect yourself and others, so that it won't happen to you."

"You could come in and nothing could be wrong with you. It's beneficial because it can protect you and others."

"Some people might see it as a death sentence or something, let them know it doesn't mean that they will die."

"Use nonoffensive ads. Be honest and ask for what you want. Slogans are annoying. Don't use one mode of transmission as focus for the whole commercial."

"Proper advertisement. You got to do something exciting that's going to bring the youth out, like some kind of party with a go-go band. Entice them, and when they get out have people with flyers or something. Offer them an incentive to come in and get tested."

Is There Anything You Feel Other People Can Do to Make Life Easier for Young People Who Are HIV-Positive?

"Try to educate themselves more about the situation. Don't criticize a person about what's going on with them, without knowing what's going on with them. When people think about HIV they think, 'You got it from having sex.' One way or the other it was your fault. That's what my mother told me, but I also told her you really need to look into this disease before you blame me for the situation."

"Give them unconditional love."

"Just learn more about it!"

"Be supportive no matter what. Never betray that person. Never give up on them."

"Just watch what they say out of their mouth, get educated because it may be someone in your family. Be a support system and just love them. Try to be there for them." [For those who are HIV-positive] Try not to stress themselves out. Try to work on your thinking patterns. Because for me, I used to have negative thoughts, growing up so long in the street, trying to get over on people. But I can't go into a job interview with that same mentality. So basically changing their outlook on life, not viewing the situation as a negative like they are going to die."

In this chapter, we presented the vital voices of teens living with HIV and presented their suggestions for medical, mental health, and psychosocial support. The impact of social support has far-reaching implications for the development of culturally sensitive and contextually informed health promotion strategies, positive coping, and resilience among HIV-infected adolescents. Although the HIV/AIDS pandemic is having a disproportionate impact on adolescents, especially those of African American heritage, it is our hope that pathways to prevention, treatment, and care are moved from the margins of community, interpersonal, social, and political discourse to the center stage of our mental health and medical priorities.

NOTES

We express gratitude to the youth who contributed to this chapter by sharing their personal information, feelings, and suggestions about how others can support teens living with HIV/AIDS. The entire Burgess Clinic and Adolescent Health Center staff at Children's National Medical Center is essential to the care and treatment of the youth living with HIV. Mr. A. Keith Selden is gratefully acknowledged for his assistance in conducting the focus group.

This transcript has been edited to reduce repetition and to protect the privacy of the participants. Although the names used in this transcript have been removed, the integrity of their messages is maintained. The messages of our predominantly African American adolescents from the Burgess Clinic, like those of Jesus and the Dalai Lama, are simple yet powerful.

Chapter 12

TEEN TALK: LIVING WITH HIV

Lori Wiener, Ph.D. and Lauren V. Wood, M.D.

The Swan of Passion

By Travis C.

The other swans laugh and call me names
for I have HIV
Inside me it hurts to see my friends laughing
at me
I want to tell them to stop
I want to tell them it is OK
I want to tell them to see beyond the horizon
But they will not listen
They will not hear but their own voices
They think that they might get it just by
floating by me
They think that they are better than I
They think that I am a threat to them,
their well-being, and to all other swans
What they don't know is that I too can feel
I too can hurt,
I too can heal
I too can fly
So while I appear alone
I know that my heart is filled
with passion
with faith
with acceptance

with desire
I hope that they never have names call upon
them
And if they do
that they realize
that wings can take you anywhere

There is an old expression that "growing up is hard to do." Adolescence and young adulthood are also very exciting times, when more opportunities, choices, and free time are available. You don't always have someone watching over you or telling you what to do. You can make your own decisions. You can choose to do things that feel right to you, like where to go, who to hang out with, what to do after high school, or even if and when you want to become sexually active.

All of this can feel overwhelming to some teens because there are so many choices to make and a lot of different kinds of pressures. This is especially true for teens with HIV, as they have the concerns that all teenagers have in addition to the HIV diagnosis to contend with. Because these concerns are different from those of other teens, we have created a booklet just for teens. It is our hope that the information that is provided here will help teens make informed, intentional decisions, and will also provide useful information about whom to talk to or contact for additional information.

LET'S TALK ABOUT SEX

Part of growing up is reaching sexual maturity and deciding if, when, and with whom you want to be sexually active. It is also thinking about what type of sexual activity you want to engage in. Every teenager must make these decisions, but because you have HIV, your decision has many more implications for your own health and critical implications for the person you are involved with. The first decision all teenagers must consider is whether they are emotionally ready to have sex. To do this, one must weigh the risk of pregnancy and HIV and other sexually transmitted diseases (STDs) in the decision. The following section addresses questions that many teens with HIV have asked us over the years.

How Do I Tell a Boyfriend/Girlfriend/Partner about My Disease?

Telling someone you care about that you are infected with HIV is not easy. Still, it is important that someone you are involved with physically and romantically knows of your diagnosis. It's the right thing to do. You might be scared that he or she won't want to be with you anymore or will be angry that you have kept it a secret. It is hard to know how a person will react.

If you trust the person enough to be with him or her, then you have to trust the person with the truth. If the person reacts negatively, then at least you have protected your own health and theirs by being honest. Having to lie to someone you are close with can be depressing and exhausting. If the person does accept your diagnosis and wants to continue the relationship, you will probably feel relieved and closer with the person. Also, sharing the responsibility for protecting yourselves can make it a lot easier.

Working up the nerve to talk about your diagnosis can be the hardest part. If you think it will help you, you may ask your social worker or other health care provider to be present during the discussion. Think about what you want to say and how you want to say it. Tell your partner that you need to talk to him or her about a subject that isn't easy for you. Explain how important it is for you to be honest with him or her.

You may want to consider saying something like: "This is incredibly hard for me to do, but before our relationship goes any further, there's something about me I think you should know. I am HIV-positive, and I am working hard to stay healthy. I am telling you because I want you to stay healthy, too."

The person may react with a lot of questions about how you got the disease, medical information, and whom you have told. You should answer these questions to the extent that you feel comfortable. You don't have to tell any more than you want to. A good idea would be to give information about how you can and can't transmit HIV. Your partner may have very little information about what having HIV means.

The person may need some time to think about it. Encourage your partner to try to find out information on his or her own, or give your partner printed information if you have it. Be willing to give your partner space and be open to further communication. It is *not good* to say, "I have HIV. Now you know, and I don't want to talk about it anymore."

On the other hand, your relationship does not have to turn completely serious and does not have to be centered on HIV. HIV is important, but it is not the only thing or the main thing about you. You still have interests and ideas. Remind the person that you are still the same person you were before you told him or her of your diagnosis.

Let the person into your world as much as both of you feel comfortable with. Keep things light some of the time. Tell a funny hospital story if you have one. Talk about your feelings and how frightening it was for you to share this information. Let the person try to understand what you are going through.

You may also want to ask the person not to tell anyone else about your diagnosis. Remind the person that you trusted him or her with this information.

If your partner is at risk for having HIV, you should encourage him or her to get tested. If you begin or continue to have sexual relations with your partner, protection needs to be discussed, specifically and completely.

It may feel funny to plan out having sex so thoroughly, and it may be embarrassing to discuss condom use, but remember you are protecting your health and your partner's.

You may fear that your partner will react violently to your disclosure. If he or she has been violent in the past, you should have someone else present who can protect you when you tell your partner, or at least tell the person in a relatively public place. Telling the person over the phone may also be an option; it gives the person time to digest the information before you meet face to face.

How Can I Prevent Myself from Contracting Other Diseases?

It is perfectly normal and healthy to worry about giving your disease to someone else. But protecting your own body also has to be a priority. If you choose to have sex, you need to protect yourself for many reasons.

You are at risk for contracting other diseases that are passed through sex. There are other STDs that can make you very sick. These include chlamydia, gonorrhea, hepatitis B, hepatitis C, herpes, syphilis, tricomonas, genital warts, and other problems caused by human papilloma virus. Some STDs have no cure. They can be passed through semen, blood, vaginal fluids, or skin contact with genital warts or sores.

If you are infected with an STD in addition to HIV, you are three to five times more likely than other HIV-infected persons to transmit HIV through sexual contact. That means that if you get an STD from having sex with someone who does not have HIV, you become more likely to give him or her HIV. And, you can get very sick. So please, protect yourself.

How Can I Prevent Myself from Spreading HIV?

This is a refresher on how HIV is transmitted. HIV transmission can occur when blood (including menstrual blood), vaginal fluid, semen (including preseminal fluid, or "precum"), or breast milk from a person with HIV enters the body of an uninfected person. These fluids can enter the body in several ways.

One way that HIV can enter the body is through a vein, such as occurs when injection drug users share contaminated needles. HIV can also enter through the vagina, the penis, the anus or rectum, the mouth, other mucous membranes (e.g., eyes or inside of the nose), or cuts and sores. Keeping your skin as healthy and intact as possible is a great way to both protect yourself from viruses and bacteria and help you prevent the spread of HIV.

These are the most common ways that HIV is transmitted from one person to another:

- By having sexual intercourse (anal, vaginal, or oral sex)

- By sharing needles or injection equipment
- From HIV-infected women to babies before or during birth, or through breastfeeding after birth

The messages here are:

- If you choose to have sex, protect yourself and your partner correctly.
- Don't do drugs. If you choose to do drugs, *don't share needles.*
- And, again, use protection. This also helps prevent you or your partner from getting pregnant too young and possibly infecting your child.

What If I Transmit HIV to Someone Else?

Knowing that you have transmitted HIV to someone else can be difficult to deal with. You should do everything you can to *prevent* this from happening. If this does happen, you may feel a sense of shock and guilt, which are perfectly normal feelings in this situation. The best thing to do is to seek assistance from a mental health counselor, who can help you and your partner deal with your feelings and take steps to find appropriate medical care.

How Do I Use a Condom Correctly?

Remember, there is no 100% way to avoid passing HIV or other STDs during sex. Not having sex is always the *safest* choice you can make. If you choose to have sex, be sure to use a latex condom *every time*. Make sure that is says "latex" on the condom box and check the expiration date. If you or your partner is allergic to latex, buy Avanti—a more expensive, plastic (polyurethane) condom. Natural membrane (lamb skin) condoms may have tiny pores that can leak viruses, and should *never* be used.

Use a water-based lubricant with the condom for vaginal and anal sex. Look for "use with condoms" on the package. K-Y brand jelly is one kind of water-based lubricant. Nonoxynol-9 helps protect from pregnancy, but it *does not protect* against HIV infection. In fact, it has been found to irritate some people's skin and cause open sores. If this happens, it becomes easier to get or give HIV or other STDs. For this reason, you should avoid using condoms with nonoxynol-9. Never use oil-based lubricants such as Vaseline or petroleum jelly, lotion, hand cream, cold cream, Crisco, or any other oil. These products make latex condoms leak or break.

The other important thing that you need to know is that for condoms to work, they must be used properly. Here is how to do it:

- Use a new latex condom each time you have vaginal, anal, or oral sex.
- Be careful opening the package. Make sure you don't tear the condom. Don't use your teeth or fingernails.

Put the condom on as soon as the penis is hard. Put it on before any vaginal, anal, or oral contact.

- Pinch the tip of the condom. Squeeze out any air, and make sure it is completely unrolled on the penis.
- If you want to use a lubricant, spread it on the outside after the condom is on.
- Hold the rim of the condom and pull out slowly right after coming. Pull the penis out while it's still hard. Be sure to hold on to the rim at the base. Don't let it spill or slip off!
- Take the condom off. Flush it or throw it away.
- Never use the same condom twice.

You can buy latex condoms and water-based lubricants at drug and grocery stores. You don't need a note or prescription from your doctor, health care provider, or parent. You don't have to be a certain age to buy condoms, like you do to buy alcohol or cigarettes. Free condoms are often available at local health departments or school-based clinics.

Keep condoms handy. You partner may not have any. Store them away from sunlight in a safe, cool, dry place. Don't keep condoms in glove compartments, in direct sun, or in a wallet. Heat destroys latex. Don't use alcohol or other drugs. It can make you more careless about using a condom and using it properly. Talk to your partner and agree about protection before you have sex.

When Is It Okay to Kiss Someone?

When you feel close and attracted to someone, a normal feeling is to want to kiss the person. HIV is not casually transmitted, so kissing on the cheek is very safe. Once again, skin is a great barrier. No one has spread HIV through ordinary social contact like dry kisses, hugs, and handshakes. Open-mouth kissing is a little bit different. It is considered a very low-risk activity for transmitting HIV. Still, you do need to be careful. If you kiss with mouths open for a long time, kissing could damage the mouth or lips and allow HIV to pass and enter the body through cuts or sores in the mouth. If you know you are going to kiss someone, or be seeing a boyfriend/girlfriend, don't brush your teeth or floss two hours before, because you could damage or tear gums, creating an easy entry point for HIV and other STDs. If your partner knows that you are HIV-positive, give him or her the same advice.

How Do I Know If I Have Cuts or Sores in My Mouth?

If you know for sure that you have cuts or sores in your mouth, try to avoid kissing until they are healed. If you're not sure, take a look. Inspect your mouth or drink some orange juice—if you see a mark or feel burning when you drink the OJ, there is a good chance there are cuts or sores there.

What Other Forms of Birth Control Are There?

The best and only 100% effective and totally safe method of birth control is abstinence. Abstinence means not having intercourse, so there is no chance of pregnancy or contracting a sexually transmitted disease. If someone pressures you for sex, remember that it is your body and you have the right to say no.

You should talk to your health care provider about what method of protection is best for you. Again, condoms are the most widely used male birth control method. Latex condoms are best for protecting either partner against sexually transmitted diseases, including HIV/AIDS, especially if used with a water-based lubricant. Condoms are 88% to 97% effective as a method of birth control when used properly. However, there is a risk of the condom breaking or slipping off during intercourse.

The female condom is a polyurethane sheath with a flexible ring at each end. The female condom can be inserted into the vagina up to eight hours before intercourse and is 79% to 95% effective at preventing pregnancy. It is available without a prescription. *The female condom should not be used with the male condom.*

Other methods listed are less effective than condoms in preventing the spread of HIV and other STDs.

How Do I Protect Myself during Oral Sex?

It is possible to spread STDs by *performing and receiving* oral sex. If you are *receiving* oral sex from someone else, you are only being exposed to saliva. The concentrations of HIV in saliva are so low that nobody has ever been infected from saliva. Keep in mind, however, that you can get other sexually transmitted diseases (e.g., herpes) by receiving oral sex. As far as HIV is concerned, however, receiving oral sex is extremely low risk. Still, it is important to be very careful.

Just like with kissing, don't brush or floss two hours before engaging in oral sex; you could damage or tear gums, creating an easy entry point for HIV and other STDs. Blood, semen, preseminal fluid (precum), and vaginal fluid may all contain the virus. Cells in the mucous lining of the mouth may carry HIV into the lymph nodes or the bloodstream. The risk increases:

- If you or your partner has cuts or sores around or in your mouth
- If your partner ejaculates in your mouth
- If your partner has another STD

If you choose to have oral sex, and you or your partner is male, *use a latex condom on the penis.* There are nonlubricated and flavored condoms available just for this purpose. Research has shown that using a latex condom on the penis is effective in preventing the transmission of HIV. Condoms are not risk-free, but they greatly reduce the risk of transmitting HIV to a partner.

If you choose to have oral sex, and you or your partner is female, *use a latex barrier (such as a dental dam or a cut-open, nonlubricated condom that makes a square) between your mouth and the vagina.* The barrier reduces the risk of blood or vaginal fluids entering the mouth.

How Do I Use a Dental Dam?

A dental dam is a square piece of thin latex. It can be found in dental and medical supply stores. You can also make a homemade dental dam by cutting a rolled condom in the center and opening it up. Don't use plastic wrap; it is not an acceptable substitute. Only one brand, Sheer Glyde Dams, has been tested and proven effective by the U.S. Food and Drug Administration as a barrier against transmission of STDs during oral sex. *Important:* The dam should be held at both edges and should cover the entire vulva. Be careful not to turn the dam inside-out during oral sex because this will totally defeat the purpose. Just like condoms, dental dams should be used *once* and then thrown away.

- Step 1: Rinse the powdery talc from the dental dam, pat dry with a towel or let air-dry.
- Step 2: Place water-based lubricant on the side that faces either the female genitals (vulva) or the anus.
- Step 3: Place barrier on the genitals or the anus. Do not move the barrier back and forth between the vagina and anus, as this can cause infection.
- Step 4: Throw away the barrier after using. Don't share or reuse dental dams.

Can I Spread HIV through Anal Sex?

Yes. It is possible for either sex partner to become infected with HIV during anal sex, whether they are *male or female.* In fact, *anal sex carries the highest risk for transmission of HIV and other STDS* because of small tears that can occur in the lining of the rectum. HIV can be found in the blood, semen, preseminal fluid, or vaginal fluid of a person infected with the virus. In general, the person receiving the semen is at greater risk of getting HIV because the lining of the rectum is thin and may allow the virus to enter the body during anal sex. However, a person who inserts his penis into an infected partner also is at risk because HIV can enter through the urethra (the opening at the tip of the penis) or through small cuts, abrasions, or open sores on the penis.

Having unprotected (without a condom) anal sex is *extremely* risky behavior. If people choose to have anal sex, they should use a latex condom. Most of the time, condoms work well, but they are more likely to break during anal sex than during vaginal sex. Thus even with a condom, anal sex can be risky.

A person should use a water-based lubricant in addition to the condom to reduce the chances of the condom breaking.

If I Choose Not to Have Sex, How Do I Deal with "Hormones"?

If you are not ready for sex or you feel that it is too much of a risk, there are things you can do. If you are with someone and attracted to her or him, just holding and touching the person can be exciting. People like different things. Some people can spend hours touching each other's hands or faces. Other people like to have their boyfriends or girlfriends kiss their neck or hug them. Other people like to just lie next to each other cuddling and talking. There are many things you can do together besides sex that can feel good. And, it gives you an opportunity to get to know your partner better before you decide to have sex.

How Do I Protect Myself If I Think I Am Gay?

Teenagers are often confused about their sexuality. Some choose to experiment to find out what they really want, and some sense at a young age that they may be gay, lesbian, bisexual, transgendered, or something different. It can be very hard to deal with knowing or feeling that you are "different" from other kids. The risk of giving HIV to someone you are intimate with has to do with the *type of sex that you have and the type of protection you use* during sex. Whether you are gay or straight does not affect your risk of spreading HIV: *only your behavior affects that risk.* You can get help and information by calling toll free the National Gay and Lesbian Youth Hotline at 1–888-THE-GLNH [843–4564], or the Lyric Youth Talk Line at 1–800–347–TEEN [347–8336].

If I Have Sex with Another HIV-Infected Person, Do I Still Need to Use Protection?

You *definitely* need to protect yourself with condoms if you have sex with another person who is already infected with HIV. Your partner may have different strains of the disease than you do, and if you transmit new strains to each other, you may make each other more sick.

Repeated infection with new or different strains of HIV or other STDs can make the illness progress further. You need to keep your health and your partner's health in mind even if you are both infected.

Do I Still Need to Worry about Infecting Others If My Viral Load Is Undetectable?

We know that lower HIV viral loads are associated with a lower risk of transmitting HIV. The problem is, we have no way of knowing for whom this is true and for whom it is not! Another problem is that viral loads in semen and vaginal secretions are different and *often higher* from viral levels measured in the blood. Sexual behaviors still matters most when it comes to the risk of transmission. Aside from not having sex at all, using protection is the only way to ensure the lowest risk of transmission.

For Women: Is It Okay to Have Sex during My Period?

HIV is transmitted during sex by semen or vaginal secretions. Because HIV is also transmitted through blood, having sex during your period may increase the risk for transmitting HIV, but no one really knows how much greater the risk is. Because of this, many women are reluctant to expose their partner to any type of increased risk and so they avoid having sex during their periods. If you do decide to have sex during your period, you should make sure your partner is wearing a condom, and you may want to consider using a diaphragm as well.

When Do I Need to Start Going to a Gynecologist?

Changes in cervical cells are common in HIV-infected females and often without symptoms. In fact, gynecological (gyn) problems are some of the most common complications experienced by women living with HIV. Therefore *seeing a gynecologist is important*. Gyn problems range from irregular periods to vaginal infections that just won't go away. More serious complications can include cancers or painful warts on the vagina, labia (vaginal lips), and the anal area.

If you are sexually active or have an unusual or odorous vaginal discharge, cramping, irregular periods, genital warts, pain and itching around the vagina, painful lesions or sores, or burning or pain when urinating, see your doctor.

LET'S TALK ABOUT EMOTIONS

Where Can I Go to Talk to or Be around Other Kids/Teens with HIV?

A lot of teens with HIV find it helpful to be around other teens who also have HIV. A good place to meet other teens is at the clinic where you are receiving treatment. If the teens who attend the clinic all live in different places, however, it may be hard to keep in touch. If you have email, that is a great way to talk, and the phone can also be good if the bills don't get too high.

If you want to meet other teens with HIV on the Internet, one place to look is www.youthHIV.org. This Web site has links to POZYouth, where you can learn about and subscribe to the Positive Youth email list. This is a support and discussion email list that caters to the unique needs of youth with HIV. It gives you a chance to talk to other young people with similar situations and experiences.

What Should I Do When I Feel Depressed?

Sometimes it is okay to let yourself feel sad or to have a good cry. These emotions are inside of you, and they are going to come to the surface every now and then. Some things that might help you feel better if you are feeling depressed are:

- *Listening* to your favorite music or listening to music that expresses what you are feeling.
- *Writing* in a journal or on a piece of paper about how you are feeling. Writing a poem or a song about your feelings can also help you express yourself. Writing letters to a friend, a parent or family member, someone who has died, someone you haven't talked to in a long time, or God may help you feel better. Even if you can't or don't want to send the letter when it is finished, it usually helps to get your thoughts down on paper.
- *Reading* a book, magazine, newspaper, or something else to take your mind off your problems.
- *Watching* your favorite movie or TV show.
- *Surfing* the Internet if you have access, going to chatrooms for people with HIV, or just going to your favorite sites or emailing or instant messaging with a friend.
- *Drawing, painting, or creating any artwork* to help you to express yourself. Even if you don't think you are a great artist, as long as what you create is coming from you and your feelings, it can be helpful. Even just painting streaks of color that remind you how you are feeling can help. Or, you can make a collage by cutting out pictures and words from magazines that describe you and how you are feeling. Anything that you like to do or make, whether it be bracelets or sculptures, can help you feel better.
- *Exercising.*
- *Meditating or praying.*
- *Talking* to someone you feel close with about what you are feeling, or just about anything that's on your mind. This can either help you understand your feelings or take your mind off your problems.

Depression can be a serious but treatable illness. If nothing seems to be working, you may be depressed and need help. If you are thinking of suicide, or how you might kill yourself, you need treatment. Talking to a social worker, psychologist, or other counselor can often help. There are also medicines that have been shown to help depression, but they must be taken as your health care provider directs. It is important that the provider know what medicines you are taking for HIV and any other medicines you are taking to make sure they don't interfere with each other.

Depression is a common illness that can be cured if it is treated. If it is not treated, however, it is much more likely to get worse and to come back in the future. Untreated depression may also make you turn to alcohol and drugs, and that makes people feel worse.

What Should I Do If I Start Thinking about Suicide?

If you are feeling like you might harm yourself, you should call a crisis line *immediately*. You can check the phone book under "mental health" for numbers or hotlines to call, or call 1–800–999–9999, the Covenant House "nineline" for troubled teens and families. Other numbers are the National Youth Crisis Hotline (1–800-HIT-HOME [448–4663]) or 1–800-SUICIDE [784–2433], a hotline service of the National Hopeline Network.

If you are feeling suicidal, you should talk to someone right away. Don't let embarrassment stand in the way. You can talk to someone that you trust, such as a friend (or friend's parent), a teacher or school counselor, a health care provider or clergy member, or a parent or relative. Remember that you are not alone and that there are people who can help. Suicidal thoughts *can* be treated. *Don't give up on yourself or your life.*

How Can I Deal with Missing Parents or Siblings Who Have Died from AIDS?

When a parent or sibling dies, it changes your life forever. It is important to express the grief that you feel and to try to keep the memory of your loved ones alive. You can start rituals to remember your loved ones in a way that makes you feel close to them. You can write letters, telling your loved ones things that you wanted them to know before they died, or things that you want them to know about your life and what you are doing. You can talk about your memories and experiences with your loved ones. You can make a book of photographs or a collage of your most precious memories with them. It is important to realize that you are still alive and you have to go on with your life. This may take time to understand. Realize that these people will always be with you if you incorporate their memory into your life.

How Can I Deal with Missing Friends Who Have Died from AIDS?

Once again, it is important to decide how you will remember your friends, whether by writing something about them, thinking of special memories, photographs, or something else. Sometimes it helps to send a card to the family of your friend describing fond memories like time spent together at camp, or just your thoughts about your friend. This will be good for both you and the grieving family. Try to think of the contribution that your friends made to your life and the lives of other people, and the things that made them happy.

If you think about your friends' joys and accomplishments, it will help you understand and remember how their lives were, just as yours is.

How Can I Value Myself/My Life?

It is important to set goals for yourself. Think about things that you want for yourself in terms of education, social relationships, work, romance, or whatever is important to you personally. The next step is to figure out realistic ways that you can meet those goals. You should also set short-term goals for yourself, which can be something as simple as saying something nice to your sibling or as complicated as quitting using alcohol or drugs.

Reward yourself when you achieve a goal, whether it's a long-term or short-term goal, or if you do something or make a change that makes you feel proud.

It is also important to live in the moment, and to feel as much joy as possible in your life. Make a list of the good things in your life. This may help you realize that your life has incredible value and that you should enjoy it as much as possible.

What If My Parents/Caregivers Do Not Want Me to Disclose My Disease to Anyone?

Some families make the decision to keep HIV a secret. You may not agree with this decision, but there are reasons why that decision is made. They might be worried about others discriminating against you or them. They may be scared to lose the support of other family members or friends. They may worry about losing jobs or social rejection. However, it can be stressful, burdensome, and lonely to keep this secret, especially as you get older.

The best thing you can do is to try to communicate with your family about what you want. If there is a certain person you want to tell, like a friend or teacher, explain to them that you believe that this person will keep your secret and why you would feel better if they knew about your disease. If they still do not want you to reveal the secret, then it is still important to have open and honest discussions within the family. This can help you cope with keeping the disease a secret from other people and ensure that you have someone to talk to about your feelings concerning your disease.

LET'S TALK ABOUT FRIENDS AND ABOUT BEING SOCIAL

As children grow up and become teenagers, they begin to develop a need to have private thoughts and a desire to keep parts of their lives to themselves. For example, some teens decide to tell only certain friends about personal family information or about how they are doing in school. HIV is another issue that is very personal, and teens with HIV must decide with whom they want and don't want to share this information.

What Should I Do If I Am Offered Alcohol or Drugs? How Will This Affect Me Differently than Other Teens because of My Disease?

Using alcohol and drugs can have many negative effects, and it can cause problems related to HIV. First of all, using drugs and alcohol may mess with the medicines that are working inside your body and cause major health problems. You should talk to your doctor about your individual medical regimen and discuss how alcohol and drugs can affect your body.

Also, drinking alcohol and using drugs can affect your judgment and make you more likely to have unprotected sex. Once again, unprotected sex can be dangerous for you and your partner's health.

If you use drugs that are injected with needles, you are at risk for contracting diseases, and for spreading or being reinfected with HIV by sharing needles. Blood gets into the needles and syringes, and when another person reuses a blood-contaminated needle, it carries a high risk of spreading diseases because infected blood can be injected directly into the bloodstream. Sharing other drug equipment can also be a risk. Blood can get into drug equipment by:

- Using blood-contaminated syringes to prepare drugs
- Reusing water
- Reusing bottle caps, spoons, or other containers used to dissolve drugs in water and to heat drug solutions
- Reusing small pieces of cotton or cigarette filters to keep out particles that could block the needle

People who choose to use drugs need to be careful about where they get their needles. "Street sellers" of syringes may repackage used syringes and sell them as sterile syringes. People who continue to inject drugs should get their syringes from pharmacies or needle exchange programs (programs that replace dirty needles with clean needles). Remember, sharing a needle or syringe for any reason can be a major health risk.

If I Want to Get Tattoos or Piercing, How Can I Do that Without Infecting Others? Should I Be Worried about Blood Loss?

Everyone needs to think seriously before deciding to get a tattoo or piercing. First, ask yourself whether this is something you want to have on your body forever. Tattoos can be removed, but the process can be long, expensive, and painful. It also may leave a mark or scar. Body piercing holes usually close up eventually on their own if you take the piercing out, and you can also have surgery done to fix the hole. But again, this is expensive and it may leave a mark or scar. If you decide to get a tattoo, seriously consider that the design you choose will be permanent and difficult and painful to remove if you change your mind. Also, make sure that you go to a reputable place that uses sterile techniques if you decide to get a tattoo.

Tattooing and body piercing can also cause general infections. This is especially true of tongue piercing, which, if not properly cared for (washing your mouth with hydrogen peroxide and water several times a day), can lead to a potentially life-threatening infection.

A risk of HIV transmission does exist if instruments contaminated with blood are not sterilized or disinfected, or are used inappropriately between clients. Instruments intended to pierce the skin should be used only once, then disposed of or thoroughly cleaned and sterilized.

If you are considering getting a tattoo or having your body pierced, ask staff at the establishment what procedures they use to prevent the spread of HIV and other blood-borne infections, such as hepatitis B and C (liver diseases). When you get to the tattoo parlor or piercing place, make sure that the needles are brand new and disposed of after you use them. Talk to your doctor about your CD4+ cell count, and make sure there are no dangers for healing after blood loss.

How Do I React If a Partner Tries to Hurt Me Physically?

No one has the right to hurt you in any way. No one has the right to hit you or even touch you in a way that makes you uncomfortable. And no one has the right to force you to have sex or to do anything you don't want to do. Remember, your life is precious. If someone is hurting you, you need to get help and get away from that person. That person needs help, too. Without it, the violence will get worse.

There is no one type of person that becomes violent; however, there are some warning signs you may see that indicate a violent tendency. A person with these qualities may not become violent, but is more likely to than other people are. Here are some characteristics of someone who is more likely than others to become violent:

- Jealous and possessive
- Tries to keep you from your friends and family

- Tries to control you
- Uses alcohol or other drugs; the more drunk a person is, the more likely it is for serious injuries and violence to occur during dating
- Has a bad temper, or loses his/her temper often
- Has a family history of seeing or experiencing abuse
- Frequent physical fighting, or a history of violent behavior
- Significant vandalism or property damage
- Gang membership or strong desire to be in a gang
- Announces threats or plans for hurting others

Don't spend time alone with people who show warning signs. If you are in a violent situation, try to *remove yourself first*. If that's not an option, try to remove the person from the situation that's setting him or her off, without putting yourself in more danger. You can ask for help and protection. Ending a violent relationship can be difficult and dangerous. It is not something that you should go through alone. Tell someone you trust and respect, and ask for help. This could be a family member, teacher, guidance counselor, social worker, clergy member, or friend. Crisis centers, shelters, hotlines, and the police can also help. Look for their numbers in the front of the phone book.

Or, call the National Domestic Violence Hotline at: 1–800–799-SAFE (1–800–799–7233) for TDD, call 1–800–787–3224.

LET'S TALK ABOUT THE FUTURE

Will I Ever Be Able to Have Children?

Although there is always a risk of transmitting HIV to your partner and child, new methods are being developed to lessen the risk for adults with HIV who want to become parents. Making the decision to have a child should never be taken lightly. It is something that you need to discuss at length with your health care provider and partner before taking any steps. The following are some options and facts to consider if you choose to try to have a child.

Fathers

Sperm washing may be an option for fathers. *Sperm* is present in *semen*. Semen contains *seminal fluid*, sperm cells, and white blood cells, any of which could contain or transmit HIV. Sperm washing is a procedure for separating sperm from seminal fluid. Once separated, the sperm is washed twice in a chemical solution to try and kill any HIV or other viruses that may be clinging to the outside of the sperm cells. It is a complicated process, but once it is finished the sample is tested for HIV. If there is no trace of it, the sperm is combined with an artificial semen solution and is ready to be used for fertilization.

Sperm washing is an alternative that needs further research and *must be discussed with your health care provider*.

Mothers

Again, the decision to have a child *must* be discussed with your health care provider and partner. The decision cannot be taken lightly, and you must prepare for every possibility before getting pregnant. There are no guarantees that the child will be HIV-negative. Most transmission of HIV from mother to baby happens near or during delivery.

- Women who take an HIV medicine called AZT during pregnancy can lower the risk of perinatal transmission (passing the virus from mother to baby near or during birth).
- Some women may be taking HIV medicines for their own health and become pregnant. If this happens, they should talk extensively with their doctor or health care provider.
- HIV-positive mothers should *not* breastfeed. There is a risk that the baby could become infected with the virus through drinking breast milk.
- The risk of transmission near or during birth is significantly increased if the mother has advanced HIV disease, increased levels of HIV in her bloodstream, or fewer numbers of the immune system cells—CD4+ T-cells—the main targets of HIV.
- If the mother uses recreational drugs while she is pregnant, this also may increase the risk of transmission near or during birth.
- A cesarean section may reduce the chance of transmission, but there may also be more health risks involved for the mother.

Will I Ever Be Able to Get a Job or Go on to College?

Absolutely. Follow your dreams. It is important to do what you want to and what you dream of doing with your life. It is important to set goals for yourself. If it is your personal goal to get a job or attend college, then there is no reason not to. As long as you are in a place where you can receive quality, ongoing medical care, there should be no problem. You should plan a meaningful future for yourself.

How Should I Face Each Day Ahead?

- Laugh every day. It is the best medicine.
- Try to do one thing each day that you haven't done before. If you can't, think of two things to do the next day.
- Treat yourself to one nice thing every day. It can be an extra long shower or nap, or calling a friend you haven't talked to in a while. Something that makes you feel good.

- Do something nice for someone else every day. Tell someone you love them. Come home on time. Tell a friend something you like about them.
- Keep living and learning.
- Never give up hope.

NOTES

The authors wish to note special appreciation to Karen D'Angelo, Special Volunteer, Bethesda, Maryland.

This chapter was originally published by S.P. Hersh, M.D. and the Medical Illness Counseling Center. Printed by EU Services, May 2004. There are no copyright restrictions regarding the duplication and distribution of information contained in this booklet. This is an abridged version. The full version of this electronic PDF booklet with references and resources can be viewed for free and downloaded in English or Spanish at: www.womenchildrenhiv.org.

Chapter 13

WHEN ALL ELSE FAILS: END-OF-LIFE CARE FOR ADOLESCENTS

Maureen E. Lyon, Ph.D., A.B.P.P. and Maryland Pao, M.D.

Another Friend

In Memory of All The Friends We've Loved and Lost
By Joey DiPaolo, age 16, and Rick Harrington, age 15

Another person, another friend
This disease must come to an end
The same illness how hard it can be
To live, to fight, and remember he
Who played and laughed and joked with us
Who ranted and raved and made a fuss
So many faces that begin to fade
So many friends that have died of AIDS
Who will be next, when will I die?
When do we stop asking "why"?
When will this disease come to an end
They will always be remembered as our friend.

HIV/AIDS remains a disease without a cure, despite a steep decline in the death rate due to medical advances.[1,2] Medical crisis, such as renal failure or an overwhelming infection, may be in the future for adolescents, particularly for those who were diagnosed at birth.[3–6] Other HIV-positive adolescents are at risk for premature death because of difficulty adhering to complex treatment regimens,[7] drug toxicities,[8] late entry into treatment,[9] and or dropping out of treatment altogether.[10]

Little is known about the timing and pace of conversations about *Advance Care Planning** or *End-of-life Care*** between adolescents and their families. Their preferences and perspectives are rarely studied. The Institute of Medicine[11] has recommended that *Palliative Care**** conversations commence at the time of diagnosis. This chapter begins with what we do know about HIV-positive adolescents' and families' preferences and perspectives.[12] Next, the discrepancies between existing policy[13] and practice are examined followed by an exploration of what is at stake. We conclude with what clinical experience, psychological theory, and research teach us about having these conversations; how talking about preferences and perspectives has the potential to change the perception of HIV/AIDS from a death threat to a challenge with opportunities for enhancing mastery, effectiveness, and control when all else fails.

COPING WITH DEATH AND DYING: A FAMILY-CENTERED APPROACH

Adolescents want to talk about death and dying. In a survey[14] of healthy and chronically ill adolescents (HIV, cancer, sickle cell, asthma), chronically ill adolescents said that they wanted to share in decision making about end-of-life care and that they wanted to have these conversations before they were hospitalized or dying. Their healthy peers also reported that if they were to have a life-threatening illness they would want to share in decision making about their end-of-life care and that they would want to have these conversations earlier in the course of an illness rather than later. Thus, the willingness to make decisions about their end-of-life care exists.

As part of the same study, youth living with AIDS reported[14] that they gave consideration to end-of-life issues (extent of care, after-death plans for children/belongings), but the formality of writing it down was overwhelming. Some had spoken to relatives about their wishes. Research suggests that

---

*Discussing attitudes and values about death and dying or the process of preparing for an anticipated death.[11]

**Discussing in advance the use of life-support technologies in case of cardiac arrest or other crises, pain management, arranging a last family trip.[11]

***The terminology used in the field of palliative care has become confusing as it has broadened its mission to begin at the time of diagnosis. Originally conceived as the study and management of patients with aggressive, advanced disease with poor prognosis and the focus of care is quality of life,[12] palliative care was always paired with the concepts of hospice. Most recently, palliative care has been defined as care that prevents, relieves, reduces, or soothes symptoms caused by life-threatening illnesses or their treatment and to enhance quality of life.[12,13]

adolescents *do* want to be involved in decision making about their medical treatment,[15] but defer to parental influence, until the seriousness of the decision increases.[16]

In an unpublished study, the Adolescent Clinic of Children's National Medical Center conducted a focus group with families who had lost an adolescent to HIV/AIDS. We asked for their help in developing a program to make it easier for families to talk about advance care planning. The following themes emerged:

- Parents wanted to support their HIV positive adolescents but needed help, "breaking the ice." Parents felt the strain of trying to talk to their adolescents about HIV/AIDS and were afraid that everyone would panic, "because you don't know which way to go and when to talk about it."
- Parents reported that it would have been beneficial if they had had someone to help them sit down and talk with their children. One participant admitted that, "It's hard to talk about and sometimes you find young people who might want to talk about it; some might not, but it's always right there in the back of their heads." Parents felt that their children did not want to burden them. For those parents whose children told them what they wanted, they found it helpful, albeit painful.
- Parents felt that adolescent and family preferences should be respected. One parent related that she had to endure tube feedings for her grandchild over her objections.

COPING WITH DEATH AND DYING: THE VOICE OF YOUTH

In 2004, 15 HIV-positive teens who were participating in the Adolescent Trials Network (ATN/National Institute of Child and Human Development [NICHD]) met to discuss their thoughts about Family-Centered Advance Care Planning. Most of the youth were eager to talk. One young woman with AIDS who had only one effective medication remaining excused herself. She was distressed and received support from a senior ATN nurse. One youth completed an advance directive very quietly during the focus group and asked someone to witness his signature at the end. This range of responses speaks to the need to be sensitive to individual preferences.

What would make the ATN youth not participate in an advance care planning program? Fear of thinking about death and dying, fear of parents' reactions, and fear of letting a parent know their diagnosis. There was sensitivity to the harm adolescents who were depressed, suicidal, or homicidal might experience, and to the need to ensure that the adolescent is competent to make decisions.

Overall, ATN adolescents thought that advance care planning was worthwhile (1) to be aware of the choices they have; (2) to help others, including their families and their health care providers; (3) to have input into the process of decision making; and (4) to have control over the future. They thought their family would want to help them cope with death and to learn to communicate about death and dying. "Then a person can be carefree." "It lifts a burden." "It clears up your wishes."

A Family-Centered Advance Care Planning Program is now being piloted[17] with HIV-positive adolescents and their families. It includes key elements of successful adult programs: a facilitated process, documentation, proactive staged timing, and the development of systems and processes to ensure that planning occurs.[18] The "Five Wishes®"[19] (www.agingwithdignity.org/5wishes. pdf) and "Respecting Choices"[20,21] (www.gundersenlutheran.com/eolpro-grams) are incorporated into this individualized plan.

HIV-positive adolescents' preference to discuss their wishes for end-of-life care earlier rather than later in the course of their illness is a wise one. For with AIDS, as with many diseases, there is a risk of dementia,[22,23] which impairs the ability to make decisions because of memory loss or other impaired mental functioning. Not waiting also gives time to process conflicts among family members or the medical team. The following case illustrates the use of an ethics committee for consultation, as well as the complexities of these conversations.

Daniel[****]

Daniel transferred to the Adolescent Clinic from Florida when he was 16 years old. When asked during the course of a psychological evaluation how he would describe his own personality, Daniel responded matter-of-factly, "I have courage." When Daniel was 12 years old, a Do Not Resuscitate (DNR) order was put in place during a severe illness. Daniel had suffered life-threatening side effects from toxicities to his antiretroviral medications. His grandmother, who had already buried her daughter, had agreed to a DNR; however, Daniel survived. Daniel knew that his CD4 count was zero and that this meant that his immune system was seriously depleted and that any infection could become overwhelming and cause his death. Daniel's HIV was resistant to all available antiretroviral medications. He had been unable to tolerate a new drug because he simply could not sustain the effort to inject his belly twice a day. Furthermore, side effects left his belly swollen and painful.

SHARED DECISION MAKING: WHO AND WHEN?

Daniel's physician and his social worker began to talk with Daniel's grandmother and Daniel about his wishes for his end-of-life care. Daniel's grandmother was his legal guardian, and, as such, his Durable Power of Attorney for Health Care. The latter allows a designated person to make decisions about medical care if the

---

[****] The details of cases and names have been changed to protect identities.

patient is not able to communicate. Daniel's grandmother would be responsible for decision making about his end-of-life care since he was under the age of 18. Nevertheless, Daniel wanted to participate in his advance care planning.

Daniel's social worker scheduled a meeting to facilitate a conversation about advance care planning. Daniel was silent while his grandmother and his physician spoke. When invited to express his wishes, Daniel gave a brief assent to their recommendations, but refused to elaborate despite encouragement from everyone. Later, Daniel let it be known to his social worker that if it were just up to him, he would stop fighting. His love for his grandmother and his desire not to see her suffer made him willing to continue treatment, even if there was little hope. One month later, Daniel was in the Intensive Care Unit (ICU) with renal and hepatic failure, again precipitated by an adverse reaction to medication. He had fought long enough and he was ready to die. When he was encouraged to tell his doctor and his grandmother his wishes for stopping all of the medical interventions, Daniel said he was afraid that if he should tell them what he really wanted, they would be angry that he was "giving up." Daniel understood that his grandmother's actions stemmed from a deep religious commitment to the value of life and that his doctor's actions stemmed from his hope that medical science might give him a few more good months. A family meeting was scheduled to discuss these differences, but before they could meet, Daniel became unconscious.

WHEN ALL ELSE FAILS: POLICY VERSUS PRACTICE

When there appears to be no more reasonable treatment options available, the American Academy of Pediatrics,[24] the Institute of Medicine,[11] professional guidelines,[27] and evolving practice and theory[26] recommend that decisions about end-of-life care (1) be shared among the adolescent patient, family, and physician; (2) be individualized and culturally sensitive; (3) take place when the patient is stable, not in the middle of a medical crisis; and (4) become a routine part of a structured and ongoing process, fully integrated into the health care setting. These goals are ideal, but medical staff have difficulty making the transition from curative to palliative care,[27] and cultural barriers may play a role in preventing some of these discussions.[28]

Working with dying adolescents and their families is different from working with adults because adolescents' preferences are not legally binding. In 1990, Congress passed the Patient Self-Determination Act,[29] which supports the rights of adults (18 years or older) admitted to health care facilities to prepare an advance directive. Current clinical and ethical policy (John Anderson, Ph.D., American Psychological Association, personal communication)[30] and legal discussions[31–33] advocate lowering the legal age for executing an advance directive to 14 years of age. Short of this, adolescent advocates support the importance of involving adolescents and their families in end-of-life deci-sions.[34] Adolescents are beginning to have a voice in their own end-of-life treatment. Research certainly supports this practice, demonstrating that the cognitive capacities required for "informed consent" for medical treatment develop in early adolescence.[35]

OBSTACLES TO RESPECTING THE WISHES OF ADOLESCENTS

Even when the voices of dying adolescents are heard and recorded, adoles-cents' previously expressed wishes are sometimes disregarded by parents and/ or physicians.[36] There is a reluctance to give up hope for recovery by stopping therapies that no longer work,[11] despite adolescents' visible suffering, because their dying is unexpected. Adolescents, like Daniel, may not disclose their preferences to their families in order to protect them by choosing what they think their family wants[37] or to please their doctors and families.[38] This hap-pens even though adolescents do have clear opinions based on their knowledge and experience,[38] as well as from television shows and the media coverage of news events, such as the Terry Schiavo case.

The reluctance to forgo treatment sometimes extends to the interdisci-plinary team of providers, where there may be differences in judgment about whether or not there is any hope to support further medical intervention. Differences in professional judgment between the treatment team who has known the adolescent for years and staff who have only known the adolescent for days may occur.

During the time Daniel was in the ICU, his grandmother stopped visiting him. This distressed the staff because there were decisions that needed to be made and because they felt that his grandmother should be with him, even though he was unconscious. Finally, she agreed to come to a meeting with Daniel's providers. Daniel's grandmother pleaded that she had been through this before with both her daughter and with Daniel and she could not do it again. She expressed the wish to shift the burden of decision making to his physician, Dr. Smith.

Daniel's health care team began acting as a family, taking turns visiting with Daniel, singing him songs, and holding his hand, while he lay unconscious. Differences between the ICU staff and Dr. Smith emerged about continuing medical interventions. In the judgment of the ICU staff, there was still hope of recovery, but Dr. Smith judged further intervention to be futile. He was prepared to shift from an active role to a supportive one. Dr. Smith was also concerned that the grandmother's advance directive for Daniel and Daniel's own expressed Five Wishes®[19] might be misinterpreted. At this point, Dr. Smith requested a consultation with the Ethics Committee.

ETHICS CONSULTATIONS: A HELPFUL RESOURCE

Most hospitals have an ethics committee, an advisory, interdisciplinary group designed to help providers make ethical judgments. They meet regularly to discuss the most difficult cases and to promote good decision making. When appropriate and feasible, the patient and the patient's family are encouraged to be involved and to bring persons who can help support them. Everyone, particularly the patient (when capable) and the family members, is given an opportunity to present their views. In such cases a thoughtful and careful ethical analysis is made, a consensus developed, and a recommendation is given.

During the meeting of the ethics committee, all of the involved staff agreed to continue to provide medical intervention until there was evidence of irreversible organ failure. Daniel continued on dialysis and other life supports. Three days later, Daniel began to experience multiple organ failure. As agreed, medical interventions were then discontinued. Daniel died within a day. Daniel's wish, as expressed in the Five Wishes®, was respected: "If I am close to death, I want to have life-support treatment if my doctor believes it could help, but I want my doctor to stop giving me life-support treatment if it is not helping my health condition or symptoms."

A profound sense of loss and sadness enveloped the health care team with the realization that Daniel's courageous and cheerful presence would no longer be felt in the clinic. In a team meeting that followed, staff members shared recollections of their time with Daniel, honoring his presence in their life.

INDIVIDUALIZED AND CULTURALLY SENSITIVE: AN OXYMORON?

Adding complexity to the process are cultural and family values about the role of adolescents in decision making.[39,40] Cultural patterns may conflict[12] with the tenet of respecting the autonomy of adolescents recommended by numerous position papers from the American Psychological Association[41] to the Society of Adolescent Medicine.[42] In traditional male-dominated families, to give adolescents a say in decision making might be perceived as a threat to, or as disrespectful of, the father's authority. In modern families, to give adolescents a say in decision making is, in contrast, not only respectful of the father, but of all family members. There are also families that believe that planning for death hurries death along, or that involving children in decision making is too burdensome.[40] Nevertheless, open conversations when the adolescent's medical condition is stable may prevent needless suffering.[43,44] Tanya's case illustrates how sometimes efforts to be culturally sensitive may prolong suffering, particularly when patients do not make their wishes known.

Tanya

Tanya was an attractive 20-year-old African American youth who was special to the team because she was the first adolescent born with HIV who had lived long enough to make the transition to the Adolescent Clinic. Tanya worked as an advocate for HIV-positive youth and was highly valued at her job. Consistent with her own and her family's values, she had made no plans for her own death. Tanya's family tended to be disengaged and suspicious of medical providers. By the age of 16, Tanya had been hospitalized five times. She was hospitalized for the last time with renal involvement and AIDS dementia. Tanya's mother and grandmother had predeceased her. While Tanya lay dying, her uncle became the spokesperson for the family. He made the decision to continue life support at all cost. This decision was consistent with attitudes, beliefs, and values among many African American adults.[45] One year later Tanya continued to hold onto life, living in isolation in her hospital room. Her family had stopped visiting. The treatment team continued caring for her by visiting and by consulting with hospice nurses to learn ways to keep her comfortable. One night Tanya became alert momentarily and said to the team nurse who had known her for many years, "Who the hell ever gave my uncle the right to make decisions for me?" She then slipped back into unconsciousness. It was another three months before Tanya died.

Fear of discrimination by hospitals is based on African Americans' historical experience of discrimination by health care institutions.[39,45] Moreover, concerns of genocide may lead African Americans to interpret discussion of DNR orders as euthanasia or an attempt to deny beneficial care.[46] These historically based fears may prevent African Americans from getting the care they would prefer, needlessly prolonging their suffering.

LIVING INTO DYING: END-OF-LIFE CONVERSATIONS—AN ONGOING PROCESS

Adolescence is a time of identity crisis," as described by Erikson,[47] during which teens search for a vocation, a mate, and their own moral code. Having a life-threatening illness is a threat to autonomy and a potential threat to self-determination. The normal family life cycle is also disrupted for the parent(s). Mothers who expected to start a new phase in their life, to pursue their own interests, and to be relieved of the burden of childcare need to put these expectations on hold. This can lead to family conflict or feelings of guilt. Parents who are working may stop to provide care, increasing the threat of bankruptcy.[48,49]

Even in optimal situations where adolescents have made their preferences known and share them with their family, these preferences may change, as a patient is dying, and as the burdens of dying fall on the family.

AJ

AJ was a high school senior whose behaviorally acquired HIV (male who had sex with a male) rapidly progressed to AIDS. His family's belief that AJ's infection was through a blood transfusion was never challenged. AJ's doctor treated his sexually transmitted illnesses and provided education and counseling to end his risky sexual behavior.

At the time of diagnosis AJ had told his family that he wanted everything done to keep him alive. Later, AJ asserted that he did not want to die in the hospital; he preferred to die at home with hospice care. As part of a study, AJ's mother spontaneously stated that her son had told her that he wanted every possible intervention to prolong his life and that was what they were committed to doing.

This discrepancy probably occurred because AJ changed his mind as his disease progressed. He needed to use a wheelchair. He could no longer work or attend school, could no longer control simple bodily functions, and was in chronic pain. His realization that he was dying provoked him to consider other choices, but he had not yet told anyone. He also confided to his psychologist that he and his father had "had a talk." His father had agreed that he would shoot him if things got too bad. With AJ's permission, his psychologist spoke to his nurse practitioner and informed her that AJ no longer wanted "everything" done for him. She scheduled a meeting with the family and AJ, where they reached an agreement about hospice care, and a DNR order was written. AJ discontinued all medical interventions designed to prolong his dying and a hospice nurse began visiting his home.

The absence of an advance directive creates significant problems for emergency department personnel, if the parent or legal guardian is not present at the time of a medical crisis[50]; and for families and health care providers when conflict emerges at the time of medical crisis when patients and surrogates disagree about end-of-life decisions.[36,44,51] In some circumstances, death can be sudden, as may occur with overwhelming opportunistic infections.[52]

Addressing issues about death and dying is anxiety provoking and sad for both health care providers[53] and families.[37,54] Yet in research with adults with HIV/AIDS, those who discuss end-of-life care with their families and health care providers report greater patient satisfaction, an increased sense of control, and a strengthening of their relationships with loved ones.[55-57] A recent study found that no parents who discussed death with their dying child regretted it, whereas 27% of parents who did not discuss death with their child regretted it later.[57] That the majority of parents who did not discuss death with their child did not regret it highlights the importance of individualizing formal programs.

> AJ's mother quit her job so that she could be home with AJ, now that she had the full realization that AJ wanted to die at home and that he was nearing the end of his life. During a period of financial turmoil, and one month after the family meeting, AJ died. His family invited the health care team to AJ's funeral. The service affirmed AJ's life. His family, friends, and health care providers were able to express both their grief for his loss and their gratitude for his life and peaceful death.

ALLOWING A NATURAL DEATH

A movement spearheaded by Children's Hospitals and Clinics of Cleveland strongly urges that the language we use to refer to the order or decision to forgo cardiopulmonary resuscitative measures at a time of an acute cardiac or respiratory arrest be changed from a DNR order to Allowing a Natural Death (AND).[58] Framing the discussion in terms of AND may help families make a decision based on the best interests of the child.[58] This decision is based on the patient/parent assessment that the available treatment(s) no longer benefit the patient.

COPING WITH DEATH AND DYING: A PSYCHOLOGICAL APPROACH

How children understand death and how children cope with their own death is known only through clinical case studies. Bluebond-Langner[37] observed an interaction between the stage of a life-threatening illness and a dying child's self-perception of his or her place in the dying process.

We do not know if, or how often, adolescents are involved in end-of-life decision making, nor do we know if, like adults, their decisions will change as their illness progresses.[59] There is no reason to suspect, however, that young adolescents under stable medical circumstances have less decision-making capacity than those over age 18. The cognitive developmental theories of Piaget[60] indicate that after the age of 12 years, the majority of individuals achieve formal operational reasoning, the ability to use abstract rules. Children ages 14 years and older do not differ from adults in their competence to make informed treatment decisions.[61] There is also no reason to suspect that young adolescents have a less mature understanding of death.[11]

Adults who believe their HIV disease is a punishment for their behavior are less likely to ask for life-prolonging treatments.[62] We do not know if this is true for adolescents, nor do we know if depressed mood influences decision making about end-of-life care, as it does in adults.[63]

Living with HIV is a chronic stressor, which can be understood using transactional stress and coping theory.[64] Unlike earlier theoretical models, this one recognizes that it is not the stressor alone, such as a life-threatening illness, that determines outcomes for an individual. Rather, there are transactions among a range of variables that determine if a person's efforts at coping are effective, contributing to biological survival and psychological well-being.[65]

How a person *perceives* a stressor is consistently identified as a key variable to adaptation.[66] Lance Armstrong, the champion cyclist, illustrates an individual who took his life-threatening illness as a challenge that gave him the energy and focus to become the best cyclist in the world and to beat the odds of his cancer diagnosis.

How a person *copes* with the stressor is another key variable. Research identifies four styles of coping:[67] (1) active, (2) avoidant, (3) distraction-seeking, and (4) support-seeking. Which form of coping is adaptive depends on the circumstances. Armstrong's active coping strategies in choosing his medical team and a very aggressive and painful form of treatment resulted not only in his being alive today, despite a fast-growing tumor, but a source of inspiration to others as well.

However, there are stressors over which a person has no control, such as painful medical procedures. Research consistently suggests that in these cases, a child and parent would be better off using distraction techniques to cope effectively, such as listening to music or imagining oneself in a safe and peaceful place.

Avoidance coping can also be adaptive, if there is no way to control the stress. Recognizing whether or not one can control the stress can be difficult. The serenity prayer speaks to this tension: to have the courage to change the things I can control, to accept the things I cannot control, and to have the wisdom to know the difference.

Research on this theory confirms that giving people choices over those aspects of their lives that they can control enhances their psychological well-being and their adaptation to their illness, even as they approach the end of their life.[66]

COPING WITH DEATH AND DYING: A PHARMACOLOGICAL APPROACH

Tanya first reported, "I just don't want to live anymore," to her primary care team when she was 16 years old after a series of medical hospitalizations. She felt hopeless and had suicidal ideation with a plan to overdose on her antiretroviral medications. She was depressed by her mother's rapid death from AIDS two months before. As Tanya became more depressed, she was fatigued and slept all the time, cried frequently, and was unable to attend school, complaining that her concentration was poor and her memory was worse. She described fears that she was developing AIDS dementia like her mother. Tanya was referred to a psychiatrist who recommended starting antidepressant treatment. She initially refused all antiretroviral treatment while she started the antidepressant stating, "I might as well hurry up and die since I'm going to anyway." After a head magnetic resonance imaging evaluation to reassure Tanya that she was not developing dementia, she agreed to try the antidepressant, but continued to refuse antiretroviral medications that were causing numerous side effects. In a few weeks she responded well to antidepressant treatment and psychotherapy and was able to return to school and work.

Depression is known to influence decision making about end-of-life care.[63,68] Before initiating discussions about end-of-life care with adolescents, it is important to evaluate for depression, bereavement, anxiety, pain, and even unrecognized delirium. Untreated pain can exacerbate depression. Delirium and cognitive decline are poorly recognized in adolescents. Assessment for psychiatric illness is also critical when a request for a DNR is made. In adults, cognitive impairment in patients with advanced AIDS increases the desire for hastened death.[68] Psychiatric illnesses such as depression and anxiety disorders can be identified even in the midst of terminal illnesses, and treatment may alleviate many symptoms and improve quality of life. Tanya's recovery demonstrates that treatment of depression can result in a return to previous functioning.

As the field of palliative care broadens its scope, the question of, "Where does terminal treatment begin?" is underscored by illnesses where recurrent life-threatening episodes occur. Should psychopharmacologic management of children at the end –of life have a different threshold than for children at the beginning of a life-threatening illness that could go on for many years? Psychopharmacologic treatment of depression and anxiety in children and adolescents is a controversial topic.[69] The literature is scant about psychiatric psychopharmacologic management in medically ill children, specifically HIV[70] despite recent data showing that HIV-positive youth have high rates of psychiatric symptoms resulting in psychiatric hospitalization.[71-73] Whether this is due to the virus, disclosure issues, significant psychosocial factors such as poverty and parental death, or some developmental aspect of becoming an adolescent is unknown. Judicious use of psychotropic medications may be able to improve quality of life. Psychopharmacologic management does not replace other comprehensive, interdisciplinary support and treatments, but it may be an appropriate adjunct treatment when symptoms become debilitating.

THE FINAL DAYS OF COMFORT CARE

As Daniel, Tanya, and AJ's examples illustrate, there comes a time when the medical options run out and there is a shift in conversations with the family. "Terminal" pharmacologic treatment has often referred to the last three to six months of care and focused on delivery of "comfort."[74] Symptoms of dying children include fatigue, sedation, pain, and irritability, as well as gastrointestinal symptoms such as nausea, vomiting, or constipation.[75] Psychotropic medications given in this setting such as benzodiazepines for anxiety and opiates for pain can be sedating and induce significant confusion. Strategies exist to manage terminal sedation, while maximizing children's ability to interact.[76]

Pain is common in youth with HIV[77] and is independently associated with increased risk of death.[78] Yet pain management for adolescents is significantly less than that provided to adults.[5] Barriers to adequate treatment of pain include fear of harming children and adolescents with opiates and their side effects, particularly respiratory depression; fears of addiction and abuse or diversion of opiates; ethical and legal concerns about pain relief versus euthanasia; and staff reluctance to ask for assistance from experts in managing pain medications in the terminal setting.[79] Comfort care consultations have resulted in fewer medical procedures and more supportive services to families.[80] Specific treatment guidelines are available to provide adequate pain relief in terminally ill adolescents.[79,80]

COPING WITH DEATH AND DYING: A SPIRITUAL APPROACH

Religious beliefs also influence decisions about advance care planning.[81] Most youth living with HIV described themselves as spiritual or religious.[82] Because the majority of adolescents living with HIV/AIDS in the United States are African American, it is worth noting that African American youth were more likely to report using this coping strategy than youth of other ethnic groups. A patient's belief in a forgiving God versus a punishing God also influences end-of-life decisions.[62]

COPING WITH DEATH AND DYING: EDUCATING THE HEALTH CARE PROVIDERS

The Initiative for Pediatric Palliative Care (IPPC/ ippc@edc.org) has developed a model that includes reflective practice, cultural competence, adopting a collaborative relational stance, and responding to the ethical claim of a child and family. They have developed a curriculum[83] for health care professionals, including a module on adolescents' decision making. These modules provide a base for training professionals to be more comfortable in helping families make difficult choices. An article[84] about care at the end of life also provides useful responses for health care providers to children at various developmental ages.

Boyd Franklin and colleagues'[85] Multisystems HIV/AIDS Model has been a long-standing and valuable tool for practitioners of all health care disciplines. This model offers a conceptual framework to orient care providers to the medical, cultural, psychological, and mental health needs of HIV-infected adolescents and their families. Appropriate psychotherapeutic modalities are described in detail. Hypnotherapeutic techniques for non-pharmacological pain management are also presented. Issues surrounding death and bereavement are addressed with compassion and sensitivity, recognizing that families must cope, not only with the death of the adolescent, but often with the death of both parents.

CONCLUSION

Health care providers need to make explicit the steps in the process of advance care planning to ensure that adolescents' wishes are honored.[86] Research on programs that make these steps explicit may decrease unnecessary suffering and can inform clinical practice,[87] public policy, and law. The *American Heritage Dictionary* defines courage as, "the state or quality of mind or spirit that enables one to face danger, fear, or vicissitudes with self-possession, confidence and resolution,"[88] and AJ and Daniel and their families took this constructive approach, which takes courage, the kind of courage that can be regarded as a normal and healthy response to the challenge of death. Many families and adolescents are ready to act with courage.

REFERENCES

1. CDC. 2005. HIV/AIDS surveillance in adolescents, reported AIDS cases among adolescents 13 to 19 years of age, by sex, 1985–2003, United States. PowerPoint and PDF formats at <http://www.cdc.gov/hiv/graphics.htm>.

2. D'Angelo, L.J., C. Trexler, J. Fletcher, and K. Platky. 2003. Growing up with HIV: The perinatal transmission survivors become teenagers. Annual Meeting of the Society for Adolescent Medicine, Seattle, WA.

3. Brady, M.J., G. Johnson, J.S. Cervia, D.M. Gaughan, and J.M. Oleske for the PACTG 219C Team. 2002. End of life care issues in pediatric HIV/AIDS. Paper presented at AIDS 2002, Barcelona.

4. Nachman, S.A., K. Stanley, R. Yogev, S. Pelton, A. Wiznia, S. Lee, L. Mofenson, et al. 2000. Nucleoside analogs plus ritonavir in stable antiretroviral therapy-experience HIV-infected children. *JAMA* 283(4):492–98.

5. Van Rossum, A.M., P.L Fraaij, and R. de Groot. 2002. Efficacy of highly active antiretroviral therapy in HIV infected children. *Lancet Infect Dis* 2(2):93–102.

6.   Selwyn, P.A., J.L. Goulet, S. Molde, J. Constantino, K.P. Fennie, P. Wetherill, D.M. Gaughan, H. Brett-Smith, C. Kennedy. 2000. HIV as a chronic disease: Implications for long-term care at an AIDS-dedicated skilled nursing facility. *J Urban Health-Bull NY Acad Med* 77(2):187–203.

7.   World Health Organization. 2003. Adherence to long-term therapies. www.who. int/chronic_conditions/adherencereport/en/.

8.   Valdez, H., T.K. Chowdhry, R. Asaad, I.J. Wodley, T. Davis, R. Davidson, N. Beinker, et al. 2001. Changing spectrum of mortality due to HIV: Analysis of 260 deaths during 1995–1999. *Clin Infect Dis* 32(10):1487–93.

9.   CDC. 2003. Late versus early testing of HIV—16 sites, United States, 2000–2003, *MMWR* 52(25):581–86.

10.   Donohoe, M., K.J. Allison, P.A. Garvie, and K.M. Knapp. 2003. Needs and barriers of youth infected with HIV when transitioning from pediatric to adult health care settings. Poster presented at the NIMH Conference on the Role of Families in Preventing & Adapting to HIV/AIDS, Washington, D.C.

11.   Field, M.J., and R.E. Behrman. (Eds.). 2002. *When Children Die: Improving Palliative and End-of-Life Care for Children and Their Families.* Washington, D.C.: Institute of Medicine, National Academy Press.

12.   Field, A., P. Maher, and D. Webb. 2002. Cross cultural research in palliative care. *Soc Work Health Care* 35(1–2):523–43.

13.   American Academy of Pediatrics, Committee on Bioethics and Committee on Hospital Care. 2000. Palliative care for children. *Pediatrics* 106(2 Pt 1):351–57.

14.   Lyon, M.E., M.A. McCabe, K. Patel, and L.J.D' Angelo. 2004. What do adolescents want? An exploratory study regarding end-of-life decision-making. *J Adolesc Health* 35(6):e1-6.

15.   Weithorn, L.A., and S.B. Campbell. 1982. The competency of children and adolescents to make informed treatment decisions. *Child Dev* 53(16):1589–98.

16.   Susman, E., L. Dorn, and J.D. Fletcher. 1992. Participation in biomedical research: The consent process as viewed by children, adolescents, young adults, and physicians. *J Pediatr* 121:547–52.

17.   Lyon, M. Principal Investigator. (2005–2008). R34. From Development to Pilot Study: Family Centered-Advance Care Planning. Funded by the National Institute of Mental Health/National Institutes of Health.

18.   Hickman, S.E., B.J. Hammes, A.H. Moss, and S.W. Tolle. 2005. Hope for the Future: Achieving the Original Intent of Advance Directives, Improving End of Life Care: Why Has It Been So Difficult? *Hastings Center Report Special Report* 35, no. 6.

19.   Five Wishes. Aging with Dignity. www.agingwithdignity.org/fivewishes.html.

20.   Hammes, B.J., and B.L. Rooney. 1998. Death and end-of-life planning in one midwestern community, *Arch Gen Psychiatry* 158: 383–90.

21.   Briggs, L.A., K.T. Kirchhoff, B.J. Hammes, M.K. Song, and E.R. Colvin 2004. Patient-centered advance care planning in special patient populations: A pilot study. *J Prof Nurs* 20:47–58.

22.   National Institutes of Health State-of-the-Science Conference Statement: Improving End-of-Life Care. Dec. 6–8, 2004.

23.   Burdo, T.H., M.Nonnemacher, B.P. Irish, et al. 2004. High-affinity interaction between HIV-1 Vpr and specific sequences that span the C/EBP and adjacent NF-χB sites within the HIV-1 LTR correlate with HIV-1-associated dementia. *DNA Cell Biol* 23(4):261.

24. American Academy of Pediatrics, Committee on Bioethics and Committee on Hospital Care. 2000. Palliative Care for Children. *Pediatrics* 106(2 Pt 1):351–57.

25. Weir, R. F. and C. Peters. 1997. Affirming the decisions adolescents make about life and death. *Hastings Center Report.* November-December:29–39.

26. Larson, D.G., and D.R. Tobin. 2000. End-of-life conversations: Evolving practice and theory. *JAMA* 284(12):1573–78.

27. Henley, L.D. 2002. End of life care in HIV-infected children who died in hospitals. *Developing World Bioeth* 2(1):38–54.

28. Sambamoorthi, U., J. Walkup, E. McSpiritt, L. Warner, N. Castle, and S. Crystal. 2000. Racial differences in end-of-life care for patients with AIDS. *AIDS Public Policy J* 15(3-4):136–48.

29. Patient Self-Determination Act. Nov. 5, 1990. Amendment to Budget Reconciliation Act of 1990.

30. Anderson, John. Director, Office on AIDS. American Psychological Association and Chair, Committee on End of Life Care for Children and Adolescents. janderson@apa.org.

31. Badzek, L., and S. Kanosky, S. 2002. Mature minors and end-of-life decision-making: A new development in their legal right to participation. *J Nurs Law* 8:23–29.

32. Derish, M., and K. Vanden Huevel. 2000. Mature minors should have the right to refuse life-sustaining medical treatment. *J Law Med Ethics* 28:109–24.

33. Doig C., and E. Burgess. 2000. Withholding life-sustaining treatment: Are adolescents competent to make these decisions? *Canadian Medical Association Journal* 162(11):1585–88.

34. McCabe M.A. 1996. Involving children and adolescents in medical decision making: Developmental and clinical considerations. *J Pediatr Psychol* 21(4):505–16.

35. McCabe, M.A., C.H. Rushton, J. Glover, M.G. Murray, S. Leiken. 1996. Implications of the Patient Self-Determination Act: Guidelines for involving adolescents in medial decision-making. *J Adolesc Health* 19:319–24.

36. Rushton, C. H., and M. D. Lynch. 1992. Dealing with directives for critically ill adolescents. *Crit Care Nurse* 12(5):31–37.

37. Bluebond-Langner, M. 1978. *Private Worlds of Dying Children.* Princeton, NJ: Princeton University Press.

38. Hinds, P.S., L. Oakes, W. Furman, A. Quargnenti, M.S. Olson, P. Foppiano, and D. K. Srivastava. 2001. End-of-life decision making by adolescents, parents and healthcare providers in pediatric oncology: Research to evidence-based practice guidelines. *Cancer Nursing* 24(2):122–36.

39. Crawley, L., R. Payne, J. Bolden, T. Payne, P. Washington, S. Williams, Initiative to Improve palliative and End-of-Life Care in the African American Community. 2000. Palliative and end-of-life care in the African American community. *JAMA* 284(19):2518-21.

40. Koenig, B.A., and E. Davies. 2002. Cultural dimensions of care at life's end for children and their families. In Field, M.J., Behrman, R. E. (Eds.), *When Children Die: Improving Palliative and End-of-Life Care for Children and Their Families.* Washington, D.C.: National Academy Press, Appendix D, pp. 509–552.

41. American Psychological Association. 2003. Guidelines on multicultural education, training, research, practice, and organizational change for psychologists. *Am Psychol* 58(5):377-402.

42. Society of Adolescent Medicine. 2004. Confidential health care for adolescents: Position paper of the Society for Adolescent Medicine. *J Adolesc Health* 35(1):1–8.

43. Crawley, L., P.A. Marshall, B.Lo, B.A. Koenigand The End-of-Life Consensus Panel. 2002. Strategies for culturally effective end-of-life care. *Ann Intern Med* 136(9):673–79.

44. Sonnenblick, M., Y. Friedlander, and A. Steinberg. 1993. Dissociation between the wishes of terminally ill parents and decisions by their offspring. *J Am Geriatr Soc* 41: 599–604.

45. Smith, D.B. 2002. *Health Care Divided: Race and Healing a Nation.* Ann Arbor: The University of Michigan Press, pp. 24–27.

46. Emanuel, E. J., D. L. Fairclough, and L. L. Emanuel. 2000. Attitudes and desires related to euthanasia and physician-assisted suicide among terminally ill patients and their caregivers. *JAMA* 284(19):2460–68.

47. Erikson, E. 1963. *Childhood and Society.* 2nd ed. New York: Norton.

48. Himmelstein, D. U., E. Warren, D. Thorne, and S. Woolhandler. 2005. MarketWatch: Illness and injury as contributors to bankruptcy. *Health Aff.*

49. Warren, E., T. A. Sullivan, and M. B. Jacoby. 2000. Medical problems and bankruptcy filings. *Norton's Bankruptcy Adviser,* May 2000. http://ssrn.com/abstract = 224581.

50. Walsh-Kelly, C. M., K. R. Lang, J. Chevako, E. L. Blank, N. Korom, K. Kirk, A. Gray.. 1999. Advance directives in a pediatric emergency department. *Pediatrics* 103 (4 Pt 1):826–30.

51. Terry P. B., M. Vettesse, J. Song, J. Forman, K. Haller, D. J. Miller, R. Stallings, and D. P. Sulmasy. 1999. End-of-life decision-making: When patients and surrogates disagree. *J Clin Ethics* 10:286–93.

52. Wenger, N. S., D. E. Kanouse, R. L. Collins, H. Liu, M. A. Schuster, A. L. Gifford, S. A. Bozzette, and M. F. Shapiro. 2001. End-of-life discussions and preferences among persons with HIV. *JAMA* 285(22):2880–87.

53. Mulhern, R. K., J. J. Crisco, and B. M. Camitta. 1981. Patterns of communication among pediatric patients with leukemia, parents and physicians: Prognostic disagreements and misunderstandings. *J Pediatr* 99:480–83.

54. Bearison, D. 1991. *They Never Want to Tell You.* Cambridge, MA: Harvard University Press.

55. Singer, P. A., D. K. Martin, and M. Kelner. 1999. Quality end-of-life care: Patients' perspectives. *JAMA* 281(2):163–68.

56. Teno, J., J. Fleishman, D. W. Brock, and V. Mor. 1990. The use of formal prior directives among patients with HIV-related diseases. *J Gen Intern Med* 5(6):490–94.

57. Kreicbergs U., U. Valdimarsdottir, E. Onelov, J. I. Henter, and G. Steineck 2004. Talking about death with children who have severe malignant disease. *N Engl J Med* 351(12):1175–86.

58. Children's Hospitals and Clinics. 1999. Children's Hospital of Cleveland.

59. Lockhart, L. K., P. H. Ditto, J. H. Danks, K. M. Coppola, and W. D. Smucker. 2001. The stability of older adults' judgments of fates better and worse than death. *Death Stud* 25(4):299-317.

60. Piaget, J. 1952. *The Origins of Intelligence in Children.* New York: International Universities Press.

61. Weithorn, L. A., and S. B. Campbell. 1982. The competency of children and adolescents to make informed treatment decisions. *Child Dev* 53(6):1589–98.

62. Kaljian, L. C., J. F. Jekel, and G. Friedland. 1998. End-of-life decisions in HIV-positive patients: The role of spiritual beliefs. *AIDS* 12(1):103–107.

63.   Menon, A. S., D. Campbell, P. Ruskin, et al. 2000. Depression, hopelessness, and the desire for life-saving treatments among elderly medically ill veterans. *Am J Geriatr Psychiatry* 8:333–42.

64.   Lazarus, R. S. and S. Folkman. 1984. *Appraisal and Coping.* New York: Springer Publishing Company.

65.   Folkman, S., and S. Greer. 2000. Promoting psychological well-being in the face of serious illness: When theory, research and practice inform each other. *Psychooncology* 9(1):11-19.

66.   Thompson, S. C., A. Sobolew-Shubin, M. E. Galbraith, et al. 1993. Maintaining perceptions of control: Finding perceived control in low-control circumstances. *J Pers Soc Psychol* 64:293–304.

67.   Ayers, T.S., I.N. Sandler, S.G. West, and M.W. Roosa. 1996. A dispositional and situational assessment of children's coping: Testing alternative models of coping. *J Pers* 64:923–58.

68.   Pessin, H., B. Rosenfeld, L. Burton, and W. Breitbart. 2003. The role of cognitive impairment in desire for hastened death: A study of patients with advanced AIDS. *Gen Hosp Psychiatry* 25(3):194–99.

69.   Jellinek, M.S. 2003. Mirror, mirror on the wall: Are we prescribing the right psychotropic medications to the right children using the right treatment plan? *Arch Pediatr Adolesc Med* 157(1):14–16.

70.   Donenberg, G.R., and M. Pao. 2005. Youth and HIV/AIDS: Psychiatry's role in a changing epidemic. *J Am Acad Child Adolesc Psychiatry* 44(8):728–47.

71.   Gaughan, D.M., M.D. Hughes, J.M. Oleske, K. Malee, C.A. Gore, S. Nachman for the Pediatric AIDS Clinical Trials Group 219C Team. 2004. Psychiatric hospitalizations among children and youths with human immunodeficiency virus infection. *Pediatrics* 113(6):544–51.

72.   Pao, M., M. Lyon, L.J. D'Angelo, W.B Schuman, T. Tipnis, and D.A. Mrazek. 2000. Psychiatric diagnoses in adolescents seropositive for the human immunodeficiency virus. *Arch Pediatr Adolesc Med* 154(3):240–44.

73.   Battles, H.B. and L. S. Weiner. 2002. From adolescence through young adulthood: Psychosocial adjustment associated with long-term survival of HIV. *J Adolesc Health* 30(3):161–68.

74.   Himelstein, B.P., J.M. Hilden, A. M. Boldt, and D. Weissman. 2004. Pediatric palliative care. *N Engl J Med* 350(17):1752–62.

75.   Drake, D. F., and D. M. Burnett. 2002. How significant is persistent chest pain in a young HIV-positive patient during acute inpatient rehabilitation? A case report. *Arch Phys Med Rehabil* 83(7):1031–32.

76.   Berde, C., and J. Wolfe. 2003. Pain, anxiety, distress, and suffering: Interrelated, but not interchangeable. *J Pediatr* 142(4):361–63.

77.   Lolekha, R., P. Chanthavanich, K. Limkittikul, K. Luangxay, T. Chotpitayasunodh, and C. J. Newman. 2004. Pain: A common symptom in human immunodeficiency virus-infected Thai children. *Acta Paediatr* 93(7):891–98.

78.   Gaughan, D.M., M.D. Hughes, G.R. Seage 3rd, P.A. Selwyn, V.J. Carey, S.L. Gortmaker, and J.M. Oleske. 2002. The prevalence of pain in pediatric human immunodeficiency virus/acquired immunodeficiency syndrome as reported by participants in the Pediatric Late Outcomes Study (PACTG 219). *Pediatrics* 109(6):1144–52.

79.   Leikin, S., and J.D. Moreno. 1996. Pediatric Ethics Committees, in Cassidy, R. C. and A.R. Fleischman (Eds.) *Pediatric Ethics from Principles to Practice.* New York: Harwood Academic Publishers, pp. 51–66.

80. Galloway, K.S., and M. Yaster. 2000. Pain and symptom control in terminally ill children. *Pediatr Clin North Am* 47(3):711–46.

81. Lyon, M.E., C. Townsend-Akpan, and A. Thompson. 2001. Spirituality and end-of-life care for an adolescent with AIDS. *AIDS Patient Care STDs* 15(11):555–60.

82. Rotheram-Borus, M.J., D.A. Murphy, H.M. Reid, and C.L. Coleman. 1996. Correlates of emotional distress among HIV+ youths: Health status, stress, and personal resources. *Ann Behav Med* 18(1):16–23.

83. Initiative for Pediatric Palliative Care (IPPC). 2003. Pediatric Palliative Care Curricula. Newton, MA: Education Development Center.

84. Hurwitz, C.A., J. Duncan, and J. Wolfe. 2004. Caring for the child with cancer at the close of life. *JAMA* 292(17):2141–49.

85. Boyd-Franklin, N., G.L. Steiner, M.G. Boland. 1995. Children, Families, and HIV/AIDS: Psychosocial and Therapeutic Issues. New York: Guilford Publications.

86. Ditto, P.H. and N.A. Hawkins. 2005. Advance directives and cancer decision making near the end of life. *Health Psychol* 24:563–70.

87. Giban, S., D. Kumar, P.J. de Caprariis, F. Olivieri, and K. Ho. 1996. Pediatric AIDS and advance directives: A three-year prospective study in New York state. *AIDS Patient Care STDs* 10(3):168–70.

88. *The American Heritage® Dictionary of the English Language.* 4th ed. 2000. Boston: Houghton Mifflin Company.

Chapter 14

THE CHILDREN LEFT BEHIND

Audrey Smith Rogers, Ph.D., M.P.H.

Living with Hope

By Travis C.

I am living with hope and hope is living with me.
I am not going to give up because I can see
That I have faith in the past and in the future
But hope is with me
Can't you see
I have beaten the odds
And you may ask why?
There are no certain answers
I know that I love God
I know that God loves me
I know that my mom is still living
With hope and future plans
For a future we can see together
A future without AIDS
But even if this virus lives on
It won't control us
Cause I know we have got hope
In our thoughts and prayers
I know that we have got hope
A message that we will share
With anyone who thinks this disease is over
Or is afraid of HIV

This book has addressed the issues facing HIV-infected American youth, but it has also told stories of a generation of young people faced with difficulties, challenges, and losses that no generation before them has encountered in the United States. American youth have been lost in wars throughout our entire history, but all wars in recent memory have had fewer deaths than those in young people racked up annually in our cities. Other generations of American youth have known severe economic deprivation, particularly in the last century, but none has been exposed to pervasive media consumerism and been offered drug dealing as the easiest and most accessible career path. Many generations of immigrant youth came to America unschooled, but most were pushed through a functional public school system by families that wanted more for them. For most of American history, almost as many young people died from infectious diseases such as typhoid fever, cholera, tuberculosis, and childbirth every year as those who survived. So the morbidity and mortality rates from HIV and the losses they inflict on families have been suffered by families before. But this has not happened in the last 100 years and has not focused so profoundly on one segment of the American population.

For American racial and ethnic minority youth, particularly those living in urban areas, all of these forces coalesce into seemingly overwhelming odds. Yet health care providers and program directors working with many of these youth remain amazed at the resiliency and perseverance that some young people have despite these odds. At the same time, they bemoan the hopelessness and lack of direction in others.

The tragedy in all this is that HIV itself is preventable.

CHANGING DYNAMICS

The individuals who had hemophilia and became infected through a tainted blood supply bore the brunt of considerable stigma and rejection. One can witness Ryan White's story as a prime example.[1] The American public has almost always been warmly supportive of sick children and the efforts of Elizabeth Glazer[2] brought public attention and resources to children born with HIV. But the public could not embrace all the babies born HIV-infected, some of whom were often low birth weight, premature newborns in cocaine withdrawal. These newborns became the "border babies," the infants abandoned in urban hospitals. Good souls adopted some of them; others went into the foster care system. People, in general, have been forgiving of those becoming HIV-infected through no decision of their own, feeling relieved that fate did not deal them such a hand. But their pity did not extend to wanting them as neighbors, co-workers, or friends. No one wanted them attending school with her children. Such paranoia was fueled by reports of health care providers transmitting HIV[3] or functioning knowingly[4]or a young man aware of his infection transmitting HIV to at least 16 young women in upstate New York.[5]

As America moved into the twenty-first century, HIV infections attributable to blood and birth transmissions have virtually disappeared, leaving HIV infection resulting from behaviors presumably dictated by personal choice. And this fact has dramatically changed the dynamic of society's reaction. The overwhelming number of HIV infections today result from personal behaviors: sexual activity or injecting drug use.[6] Many of yesterday's AIDS babies have grown into adolescence and have moved into neighborhood social and sexual networks. They join other adolescents and young adults who are HIV-infected or at risk in communities shredded by drug use, failing institutions, and no viable socioeconomic prospects. They, too, belong to the ranks of youth who, according to much of public sentiment, deliberately make decisions to reject the offered and available American dream of upward social mobility through education, drive, and hard work. Rugged individualism is a core American value. Americans adhere to the belief that everyone can and should be able to pull himself up by his bootstraps. There is, at a minimum in all Americans, a subconscious assignment of blame when one fails to do this; and, at the maximum end, the assignment of blame justifies others in dismantling unearned support systems rather than address abuses introduced by human nature. Individualism is a two-edged sword and blind devotion to it fails to acknowledge debts to others. There is no true "self-made" man. It has been said that the hallmark of privilege is the inability to see it.

THE MARGINALIZATION OF HIV

At this point, American society has been living with HIV for more than 25 years, and the mass hysteria of a rampant epidemic decimating the general population has dissipated. But HIV persists and has moved insidiously from person to person through sexual and injecting drug networks,[7] becoming firmly established in many American cities. Because of these transmission dynamics and the blame they engender, America has been able to effectively sequester HIV infection and AIDS cases "elsewhere" during this past quarter century. "Elsewhere" is the sad intersection of household poverty, single mothers, male unemployment, violence, drugs, school dropouts, and hopelessness. "Elsewhere" and the policies sustaining it became starkly apparent in the aftermath of Hurricane Katrina in New Orleans in 2005 when marginalization by class and race left many incredibly vulnerable. Whether this event will usher in a needed soul-searching is yet unknown. American society has grown coarse and uncivil, fed by ranting ideologues on both sides of the political divide, and informed only by "bumper sticker" debates. One can only hope that the analysis of policy decisions will be informed by wisdom, sincere compassion, and cultural competency. Cultural competency[8] is the result of a true dialogue in which both differences and commonalities are freely discussed, full understanding is achieved, and both groups have been changed.[9] People who believe that they have the absolute and final answers can never enter true dialogue. And without a true dialogue, some of our children will continue to be left behind.

PAST PREVENTION EFFORTS FOR YOUTH

In public health circles there is an often told parable about a town at the base of a treacherous mountain with hairpin turns and steep grades. The town's budget was consumed with an ever-increasing demand for ambulances at the bottom of the mountain to attend to the numerous causalities from traffic accidents occurring above on the mountain. People were so busy attending to the dead and dying that they could not address the simple solution of building guard rails above the carnage.

HIV prevention efforts for young people in America amount to this. There is no sustained comprehensive effort to correct the core problems driving the HIV epidemic among youth. Limited programs targeted at the individual, dyad, or small group can frequently offer short-term success, particularly in measures like reported increases in condom use. Relying on this approach is not justified by such limited results. These short-term outcomes do not translate to measurable differences in the health outcomes of the community's youth. These interventions are based on the assumption that risk behaviors are conscious decisions, the result of rational choices. The focus needs to shift to structural and environmental factors outside the individual that may affect risk behaviors.[10]

Also, a serious problem is how health information has been confused with character formation to the extent that both have been harmed. Health information needs to be evidence-based and factually accurate. It is unconscionable that scientific information should be held hostage to any particular ideology: a society that permits this to happen will pay in increased and avoidable morbidity and death. In the same way, character development is short-changed in such programs. Character development and its base, moral development, cannot be successfully nurtured solely within the context of an isolated short course during adolescence. Rather, it is a process that occurs over the whole span of development and requires an ongoing personal relationship with a committed, engaged, and mature elder. The family is the primary socializing agent for adolescents.[11] So ideally, this process of character development is the responsibility of the family and to the extent that a family is intact, it benefits from community and institutional support to carry out this important function. In the absence of intact families, other systems need to be identified and supported.[12]

NEWER PARADIGMS

American youth need more than short course, small group prevention efforts.[13] Rather, what is required is attention to devising a successful macro-level intervention that can effect structural change while being "bottom-up," sustainable, and effective. This type of intervention need not be a mega-million dollar government program. In his recent book,[5] *The Tipping Point*, author Malcolm Gladwell ingeniously proposes that ideas, products, messages, and behaviors spread just like viruses, and the factors that produce an infectious epidemic operate for social change as well: key people critical for spreading information (vectors); ideas that are compelling, memorable, and capable of spurring action (infectious agent); and the context of the epidemic's setting, that is, the conditions and circumstances of the time and place in which it occurs (susceptibility). Gladwell maintains that this process can be orchestrated for social change. Using that premise, HIV prevention efforts for youth can and should be based on forging relationships with critical key people to fashion a compelling message. The context has already been set in neighborhoods across this nation losing their youth to HIV infection, drugs, and violence. What is needed is community-building and a grass roots conversion to bring the minds and hearts of adults to raising the young.

Movements like this have been successfully developed before: seat belt use, prevention of cigarette smoking, child seat use, bicycle helmet laws, even Mothers Against Drunk Driving (MADD). A few committed persons with drive, organization, and resources have effected structural change through a combination of laws, taxes, and social pressure. However, orchestrating coalition-building and community mobilization to effect structural change for the sake of disease prevention and health promotion when the critical components of organization and resources are missing has proven to be more challenging.[14,15] And sustainability, the sine qua non of success, cannot be achieved in their absence. It appears that the program's primary objective must emerge from the priorities of the community members themselves and not be imposed from without,[15] and that the organization of the basic effort be supported by an expert team responsible for manuals, training, and ad hoc consultation.[16] These two elements are crucial for the life of the effort but typically will only sustain it while funding remains. In the end, sustainability of the effort is inextricably linked to a distributed leadership model through which ownership is transferred and shared. Many lessons were learned from earlier community mobilization efforts[17] and have been incorporated in the design of a current effort, the Connect to Protect® Program, funded by the National Institute of Child Health and Human Development (J. Ellen: personal communication).

In the final analysis, however, none of the infectious scourges of centuries ago were brought under control by appealing to the population to change their behavior. So any public health program that must rely on pronounced behavioral change in a large segment of the population to bring an established epidemic under control is unlikely to succeed even in the short term, without massive attention and resources being brought to bear. Yet even if the political will to do this existed, the plain truth, to paraphrase a common adage, is that a behavioral intervention will work for some of the people all of the time and for all of the people some of the time, but no behavioral intervention will work for all of the people all of the time. HIV, like smallpox and polio before it, will only be effectively controlled when we have a preventive vaccine. And while no one debates the public health mandate to immunize teens before they would be exposed to HIV risk when an effective vaccine is found, it is the road from here to that point that will be the most difficult.

GETTING TO AN HIV VACCINE

Many promising vaccines have been tested only to give disappointing results in the earliest stages of development. Yet each failure is a step ahead in our knowledge and capacity to move the search forward. Within the next decade, it is probable that a large scale trial of a candidate HIV vaccine will take place. This effort will be large and expensive and will require broad support.

The search for a vaccine is complicated by the different HIV serotypes or *clades* and how much cross-reactivity a vaccine mimicking one serotype may have with the virus from another. Specifically, will a vaccine based on the HIV serotype prevalent in America work in Africa? The search is further complicated by our own inherent biologic differences. Each of us carries our family history in our genes. The interplay between our ancestors' immune systems and the environments in which they lived affects how we respond to the infections and exposures we meet in our environment. These reactions can be quite unique. For example, it is accepted that persons with sickle cell disease manifest a resistance to malaria[18]; however, it is death due to malaria that has preferentially selected the survival of the sickle cell mutation. A similar theory exists for HIV, which along with related viruses requires co-receptors like the chemokine receptor, CCR5, in addition to CD4, to gain entry to target cells. Mutant alleles of CCR5 are present at a high frequency in Caucasian populations, thus making HIV infection in them less likely. At the same time, this mutant allele is absent in black populations from Western and Central Africa and Japanese populations.[19] Some have attributed the selection of this mutation to the bubonic plague that decimated Europe in the fourteenth century; others recently proposed that the selective pressures were more likely caused by repeated waves of smallpox.[20] These unique distinctions based on the family history we each carry in our genes are critically important to accommodate in developing a vaccine that will work for all the people who need it. Public health particularly demands that the vaccine offer protection to the racial and ethnic minority populations who are disproportionately bearing the burden of HIV infection. This requires that these populations become active participants in clinical trials to identify an effective vaccine and, for adolescents, that their parents or guardians give permission for them to participate. It was disappointing that the first large-scale trial of an HIV vaccine, AIDSVAX, ended in 2003 with too few African Americans enrolled to state anything definitely about their vaccine response.[21]

A LEGACY OF MISTRUST

It was common practice in the early years of clinical research to experiment on indigent and minority patients being treated in the hospital wards. This experimentation occurred without their consent and often without their knowledge. The practice extended well into the twentieth century and took its worst form in the Tuskegee Syphilis Study in which African American men with syphilis were deliberately left untreated despite the availability of treatment and were, in fact, led to believe that they were being treated. Knowledge of this study coupled with personal experiences with researchers in particular, or health care providers in general, has added to a legacy of mistrust that is severe and pervasive. Many African Americans have little accurate knowledge of research, lack understanding of consent procedures, and distrust researchers.[22] This translates into their shunning of research opportunities resulting in under-representation in clinical trials,[23,24] a situation understood to need remedying[25] because of the dramatic health disparity between American whites and blacks. Vigorous efforts need to be undertaken to dispel this mistrust through providing education about clinical research in laypeople's terms for certain; but more important, minority stakeholders need to be invited as partners in the design and implementation of studies to make participation acceptable and feasible. If people have reservations themselves about joining research studies, how much more so will they react when their own children are involved? One study showed that more than 90% of parents agreed that if a safe and effective vaccine against HIV were available, they would get their child vaccinated, and parent responses did not differ by race.[26] Whether these same parents would permit their adolescents to participate in the early phases of vaccine development after some safety data are available in adults is less clear; however, this is the road before us. Trial data on adolescents will be required as a condition of licensure by the U.S. Food and Drug Administration. Daily, it gets more difficult for minority parents to deny the growing risk their teens face and the impact of AIDS in their neighborhoods. Where will the balance between their perception of risk to their children and the fear of exploitation in research tip? And how can people of good will and pure intention help bridge this critical gap?

A safe and effective HIV vaccine will be an important part of addressing the divide that has left many of these children behind, but it will only be a part. The constellation of social and economic and medical problems that drove the HIV epidemic will no doubt find other devastating outlets in the lives of the children in its path. One need not be mean spirited to walk away from these problems; one needs only to be convinced that one has no solution. Albert Einstein said that the significant problems we face today cannot be solved at the same level of thinking that we were at when we created them. For our children, all our children, let us hope our country can think new thoughts, create new visions, and dream new dreams so that truly, really, we leave no child behind.

NOTE

The views expressed in this chapter are those of the author alone and do not necessarily represent the views of the agency at which she is employed.

REFERENCES

1. White, R., and A. M. Cunningham. 1992. *Ryan White: My Own Story.* Penguin Putnam: New York.

2. Elizabeth Glaser Pediatric AIDS Foundation. http://www.pedaids.org/fs_about_us.html.

3. Cohen, L. A., E. G. Grace, and M. A. Ward. 1992. Changes in public concern about transmission of AIDS from dentist to patient after CDC report. *Clin Prev Dent* 14 (2):6–9.

4. Rogers, A. S., J. W. Froggatt, 3rd, T. Townsend, T. Gordon, A. J. Brown, E. C. Holmes, L. Q. Zhang, and H. Moses, 3rd. 1993. Investigation of potential HIV transmission to the patients of an HIV-infected surgeon. *JAMA* 269 (14):1795–801.

5. Gladwell, M. 2000. *The Tipping Point: How Little Things Can Make a Big Difference.* New York: Little Brown and Company, 20–21.

6. HIV/AIDS among Youth. Centers for Disease Control and Prevention. May 2005.

7. Anderson, R.M., S. Gupta, and W. Ng   . 1990. The significance of sexual partner contact networks for the transmission dynamics of HIV. *J Acquir Immune Defic Syndr* 3 (4):417–29.

8. Cross, T., B. Bazron, K. Dennis, and M. Isaacs. 1989. *Towards a Culturally Competent System of Care,* Volume I. Washington D.C.: Georgetown University Child Development Center, CASSP Technical Assistance Center.

9. Peck, M. S. 1987. *The Different Drum: Community Making and Peace.* New York: Simon and Schuster.

10. Latkin, C. A., and A. R. Knowlton. 2005. Micro-social structural approaches to HIV prevention: A social ecological perspective. *AIDS Care* 17 Suppl 1:S102–13.

11.   National Research Council. 1993. *Losing Generations: Adolescents in High-Risk Setting.* Panel on High Risk Youth. Washington, D.C.: National Academy Press.

12.   Chalk, R., and D. A. Phillips (Ed.). 1996. National Research Council and Institute of Medicine. *Youth Development and Neighborhood Influences: Challenges and Opportunities.* Committee on Youth Development. Washington, D.C.: National Academy Press.

13.   Sikkema, K. J., E. S. Anderson, J. A. Kelly, R. A. Winett, C. Gore-Felton, R. A. Roffman, T. G. Heckman, K. Graves, R. G. Hoffmann, and M. J. Brondino. 2005. Outcomes of a randomized, controlled community-level HIV prevention intervention for adolescents in low-income housing developments. *AIDS* 19 (14):1509–16.

14.   Chervin, D. D., S. Philliber, C. D. Brindis, A. E. Chadwick, M. L. Revels, S. L. Kamin, R. S. Wike, J. S. Kramer, D. Bartelli, C. K. Schmidt, S. A. Peterson, and L. T. Valderrama. 2005. Community capacity building in CDC's Community Coalition Partnership Programs for the Prevention of Teen Pregnancy. *J Adolesc Health* 37 (3 Suppl):S11–19.

15.   Kramer, J. S., S. Philliber, C. D. Brindis, S. L. Kamin, A. E. Chadwick, M. L. Revels, D. D. Chervin, A. Driscoll, D. Bartelli, R. S. Wike, S. A. Peterson, C. K. Schmidt, and L. T. Valderrama. 2005. Coalition models: Lessons learned from the CDC's Community Coalition Partnership Programs for the Prevention of Teen Pregnancy. *J Adolesc Health* 37 (3 Suppl):S20–30.

16.   Kelly, J. A., A. M. Somlai, W. J. DiFranceisco, L. L. Otto-Salaj, T. L. McAuliffe, K. L. Hackl, T. G. Heckman, D. R. Holtgrave, and D. Rompa. 2000. Bridging the gap between the science and service of HIV prevention: Transferring effective research-based HIV prevention interventions to community AIDS service providers. *Am J Public Health* 90 (7):1082–88.

17.   Klerman, L. V., J. S. Santelli, and J. D. Klein. 2005. So what have we learned? The Editors' comments on the coalition approach to teen pregnancy. *J Adolesc Health* 37 (3 Suppl): S115–18.

18.   Friedman, M. J. 1978. Erythrocytic mechanism of sickle cell resistance to malaria. *Proc Natl Acad Sci U S A* 75 (4):1994–97.

19.   Samson, M., F. Libert, B. J. Doranz, J. Rucker, C. Liesnard, C. M. Farber, S. Saragosti, C. Lapoumeroulie, J. Cognaux, C. Forceille, G. Muyldermans, C. Verhofstede, G. Burtonboy, M. Georges, T. Imai, S. Rana, Y. Yi, R. J. Smyth, R. G. Collman, R. W. Doms, G. Vassart, and M. Parmentier. 1996. Resistance to HIV-1 infection in caucasian individuals bearing mutant alleles of the CCR-5 chemokine receptor gene. *Nature* 382 (6593):722–25.

20.   Galvani, A. P., and M. Slatkin. 2003. Evaluating plague and smallpox as historical selective pressures for the CCR5-Delta 32 HIV-resistance allele. *Proc Natl Acad Sci U S A* 100 (25):15276–79.

21.   Understanding the Results of the AIDSVAX Trial. AIDS Vaccine Advocacy Coalition. http://avac.org.phtemp.com/pdf/UnderstandingAIDSVAX.pdf

22.   Freimuth, V. S., S. C. Quinn, S. B. Thomas, G. Cole, E. Zook, and T. Duncan. 2001. African Americans' views on research and the Tuskegee Syphilis Study. *Soc Sci Med* 52 (5):797–808.

23.   Stone, V. E., M. Y. Mauch, K. Steger, S. F. Janas, and D. E. Craven. 1997. Race, gender, drug use, and participation in AIDS clinical trials. Lessons from a municipal hospital cohort. *J Gen Intern Med* 12 (3):150–57.

24.   Sengupta, S., R. P. Strauss, R. DeVellis, S. C. Quinn, B. DeVellis, and W. B. Ware. 2000. Factors affecting African-American participation in AIDS research. *J Acquir Immune Defic Syndr* 24 (3):275–84.

25.   Recommendations of the clinical trials consensus panel. National Medical Association. 2000. *J Natl Med Assoc* 92 (10):464–71.

26.   Zimet, G. D., S. M. Perkins, L. A. Sturm, R. M. Bair, B. E. Juliar, and R. M. Mays. 2005. Predictors of STI vaccine acceptability among parents and their adolescent children. *J Adolesc Health* 37 (3):179–86.

APPENDIX: ADDITIONAL RESOURCES

Susan Keller, M.L.S.

What Is Control Anyway?

By Anita

I cannot control where I live
or who cares for me
I cannot control the virus
inside of me
I cannot bring my mom or dad back
or delete the fact that they are gone
But I can control what I say
what I do and what pills I take
And I can control how I live my life
what goals I set and what friends I keep
I can also decide who I trust
and who I can rely on
during times that are tough
So, while I don't know how long I will live
I can make each day better by what I give
to those I care about and who care about me
and to my body that cries to be free

While looking for resources to include on this list, the authors of the text wanted to make the list comprehensive, but not overwhelming. This list of resources is divided into two main parts. Part I is a guide to evaluating information resources and Part II is an annotated list of (mostly) Internet resources. Part II is further subdivided into:

- General information on HIV/AIDS
- Web sites directed at young people
- Organizations that provide support to families affected by HIV/AIDS
- Resources for educators
- Disability, discrimination, and other legal resources

Of course, there is overlap between these different categories. The Web site addresses were correct as of the date last visited, but the Internet is a fluid place and the addresses may change.

PART I: EVALUATING INFORMATION RESOURCES

Finding information resources about HIV/AIDS on the Internet is easy. For example, a quick search using major search engines returns between 10 and more than 70 million "hits." Unfortunately, not all of this information is credible. To help users decide if an information source is credible, the National Library of Medicine has published a set of guidelines to help users sort out the bad information from the good information. Here are the guidelines:

Healthy Web Surfing

Http://www.nlm.nih.gov/medlineplus/healthywebsurfing.html   (accessed February 24, 2006):

Consider the Source
Use recognized authorities and know who is responsible for the content.

- Look for an "about us" page. Check to see who runs the site: is it a branch of the federal government, a nonprofit institution, a professional organization, a health system, a commercial organization, or an individual?
- There is a big difference between a site that says, "I developed this site after my heart attack," and one that says, "This page on heart attacks was developed by health professionals at the American Heart Association."
- Web sites should have a way to contact the organization or webmaster. If the site provides no contact information, or if you can't easily find out who runs the site, use caution.

Focus on Quality
All Web sites are not created equal. Does the site have an editorial board? Is the information reviewed before it is posted?

- This information is often on the "about us" page, or it may be under the organization's mission statement, or part of the annual report.
- See if the board members are experts in the subject of the site. For example, a site on osteoporosis whose medical advisory board is composed of attorneys and accountants is not medically authoritative.
- Look for a description of the process of selecting or approving information on the site. It is usually in the "about us" section and may be called "editorial policy," or "selection policy," or "review policy."
- Sometimes the site will have information, "about our writers" or "about our authors," instead of an editorial policy. Review this section to find out who has written the information.

Be a Cyberskeptic

Quackery abounds on the Web. Does the site make health claims that seem too good to be true? Does the information use deliberately obscure, "scientific" sounding language? Does it promise quick, dramatic, miraculous results? Is this the only site making these claims?

- Beware of claims that one remedy will cure a variety of illnesses, that it is a "breakthrough," or that it relies on a "secret ingredient."
- Use caution if the site uses a sensational writing style (lots of exclamation points, for example.)
- A health Web site for consumers should use simple language, not technical jargon.
- Get a second opinion! Check more than one site.

Look for the Evidence

Rely on medical research, not opinion. Does the site identify the author? Does it rely on testimonials?

- Look for the author of the information, either an individual or an organization. Good examples are "Written by Jane Smith, R.N.," or "Copyright 2003, American Cancer Society."
- If there are case histories or testimonials on the Web site, look for contact information such as an email address or telephone number. If the testimonials are anonymous or hard to track down ("Jane from California"), use caution.

Check for Currency

Look for the latest information. Is the information current?

- Look for dates on documents. A document on coping with the loss of a loved one doesn't need to be current, but a document on the latest treatment of AIDS needs to be current.
- Click on a few links on the site. If there are a lot of broken links, the site may not be kept up –to date.

Beware of Bias

What is the purpose? Who is providing the funding? Who pays for the site?

- Check to see if the site is supported by public funds, donations, or by commercial advertising.
- Advertisements should be labeled. They should say "Advertisement" or "From our Sponsor."
- Look at a page on the site, and see if it is clear when content is coming from a noncommercial source and when an advertiser provides it. For example, if a page about treatment of depression recommends one drug by name, see if you can tell if the company that manufactures the drug provides that information. If it does, you should consult other sources to see what they say about the same drug.

Protect Your Privacy

Health information should be confidential. Does the site have a privacy policy and tell you what information they collect?

- There should be a link saying "Privacy" or "Privacy Policy." Read the privacy policy to see if your privacy is really being protected. For example, if the site says "We share information with companies that can provide you with useful products," then your information isn't private.
- If there is a registration form, notice what types of questions you must answer before you can view content. If you must provide personal information (such as name, address, date of birth, gender, mother's maiden name, credit card number), you should refer to their privacy policy to see what they can do with your information.

Consult with Your Health Professional

Patient/provider partnerships lead to the best medical decisions.

PART II: ANNOTATED LIST OF RESOURCES

General Information on HIV/AIDS

AIDSInfo, http://aidsinfo.nih.gov/ (accessed February 24, 2006), is a service of the National Institutes of Health. This site contains links to current treatment guidelines, as well as links to clinical trials, new drugs, and other AIDS information.

The Centers for Disease Control and Prevention (CDC) has an enormous amount of information available on HIV/AIDS. One place to start is http://www.cdc.gov/hiv/ (accessed February 24, 2006). This page has links to questions such as, "How can I tell if I'm infected with HIV?" and "Can I get HIV from oral sex?" In addition, the site has links for health care professionals including "Recommendations for the triage of HIV-positive patients in emergencies such as Hurricane Katrina."

Center for HIV Information, http://chi.ucsf.edu/chi?page=home-00-00 (accessed February 24, 2006), is sponsored by the University of California, San Francisco, medical school, and serves as an authoritative source for HIV information for providers and patients. The site has an international as well as local focus. The Center has developed other sites such as Women, Children and HIV, http://womenchildrenhiv.org/, (accessed February 24, 2006).

National AIDS Hotline 1–800–232–4636 (1–800–CDC–INFO)

TTY: 1–888–232–6348

Hours: 24 hours a day, 7 days a week

Email: cdcinfo@cdc.gov

This number takes the caller to a general information recording. The caller is also given the opportunity to speak to a person who can answer questions on AIDS/HIV.

The National AIDS Treatment Advocacy Project (NATAP), http://www.natap.org/ (accessed February 24, 2006). The National AIDS Treatment Advocacy Project is a nonprofit organization based in New York. The organization "provides the latest in HIV and AIDS drug development and treatment information (on topics including protease inhibitors, nucleosides, non-nucleosides, double protease combinations), as well as comprehensive reports and developments from the Fifth Retroviruses and Opportunistic Infections conference, as well as from the ICAR (International Conference on Antiviral Research), ICAAC (Interscience Conference on Antimicrobial Agents and Chemotherapy), IDSA (Infectious Disease Society of America), European and International HIV and AIDS conferences." The site has many links to information about hepatitis, as well as AIDS/HIV.

National Library of Medicine, Special Information Services, HIV/AIDS information, http://sis.nlm.nih.gov/hiv/treatment.html (accessed February 24, 2006). This site contains a variety of links for both patients and health care providers to treatment, clinical trials, prevention, etc.

VA National HIV/AIDS Program, http://www.hiv.va.gov/ (accessed February 24, 2006). According to its homepage, the VA is the nation's largest provider of HIV/AIDS care. The site is easy to read and to navigate. It includes information for both patients and health care providers. The patient page has a section entitled "daily living" with links to sex and sexuality.

Web Sites Directed at Young People

Advocates for Youth, http://www.advocatesforyouth.org/index.htm (accessed February 24, 2006). From the Web site: Advocates for Youth "works both in the United States and in developing countries with a sole focus on adolescent reproductive and sexual health."

The site has a section called: "FAQs for HIV-Positive Youth" with links to topics such as "dating and relationships" and "telling people you are positive."

The Body Positive, http://www.bodypos.org/ (accessed February 24, 2006) is an immense site with links to many AIDS/HIV-related topics. One of the links is to the *Body Positive Magazine.* This magazine has articles written by and about HIV-positive children and adolescents. The magazine index is arranged by topics including, "families and children," "treatment issues," and "dating issues." Linking to the *Body Positive Magazine* will lead to the Web site for The Body. Many of the links found on http://www.positivelife.net/ (accessed February 24, 2006), connect back to the Body Positive site. Positivelife is a Web site sponsored by the Pediatric Clinical AIDS Trials group. It has information useful to those newly diagnosed with HIV, as well as information about living with HIV disease.

Go Ask Alice, Columbia University's Internet Question and Answer Service, http://www.goaskalice.columbia.edu/ (accessed February 24, 2006), provides straightforward answers to many different types of health questions. More than 2,500 answers to questions are available on the site. The site has information divided into categories including alcohol and other drugs, fitness and nutrition, emotional health, general health, sexuality, sexual health, and relationships.

Planned Parenthood (1–800–230–7526) is a long-established organization that provides a variety of reproductive services. The Web site, http://www.plannedparenthood.org/ (accessed February 24, 2006), provides links to clinic locations where anyone can receive care at little or no cost. In addition, the site has health information including topics such as birth control, emergency contraception, teen health, and sexually transmitted diseases. Information is also available in Spanish.

Sex, etc., http://www.sexetc.org (accessed February 24, 2006) is a site that is targeted at teens (and partially written by them as well) and is sponsored by the Network for Family Life Education at Rutgers. The site has a number of sections including "deciding about sex," "guy's health," "girl's health," as well as a bulletin board and forum. The site supports comprehensive sexual education.

The *Teen Care Center,* http://www.teencarecenter.org (accessed February 24, 2006), has an abstinence message throughout. It also has a list of "come-on" and "come-backs" that may be useful for teens looking for support in refusing, or delaying, sexual activity.

Washington State University, http://www.hws.wsu.edu/healthycoug/ Relationships/negotiating.html (accessed February 24, 2006), has a short, easy-to-read list designed to help college-age people negotiate safer sex.

What Udo Organization, http://whatudo.org/ (accessed February 24, 2006), is based at the University of California San Francisco. UCSF Center for HIV Information partners with government agencies, foundations, and international organizations to develop information on HIV care, prevention, and policy and to disseminate this information to care providers, researchers, and policymakers nationally and worldwide. The goal of whatudo.org is to provide straightforward, unbiased, nonjudgmental, accurate, and timely information about HIV/AIDS to young people who are searching for answers on the Web. The site is easy to navigate and is divided into three main categories: "think," "learn," and "do." Visitors to the "learn" page can link to the "Thrive Guide," a handbook for young people living with HIV. Included on the Thrive Guide page is a link to, "Making Meds Work for You," a guide to young people who are thinking about antiretroviral therapy.

Organizations that Provide Support to Families Affected by HIV/AIDS

Children's Hospice International, 901 North Pitt Street, Alexandria, VA 22314, 1–800–242–4453, 1–800–24-CHILD), http://www.chionline.org/ (accessed February 24, 2006). Children's Hospice International provides education, training, and technical assistance to those who care for children with life-threatening conditions and their families. The organization can refer parents/caregivers to local hospices.

Compassionate Friends, Inc., P.O. Box 3696, Oak Brook, IL 60522–3693, Toll-free 877–969–0010, Ph. 630–990–0010, Fax 630–990–0246, http://www.compassionatefriends.org/ (accessed February 24, 2006). Compassionate Friends is a national, nonprofit, self-help support organization that offers friendship, understanding, and hope to bereaved parents, grandparents, and siblings. There is no religious affiliation and there are no membership dues or fees.

The Sibling Connection, http://www.counselingstlouis.net/index.html (accessed August 31, 2005). This site is maintained by a psychotherapist and is designed for siblings who have lost a brother or sister. Coping strategies are included for siblings ranging in age from young child to adult. A booklist is available on the site.

Resources for Use by Educators

The ACT Game: Assertive Communication Training—A Social Skills Training Program for Children in Grades 3–6, http://chipts.ucla.edu/interventions/manuals/intervact.html (accessed February 22, 2006). This program includes six modules: assertiveness, feeling, positive responses to oneself and others, friendship, anger, and criticism and maintenance skills.

Center for HIV Identification, Prevention, and Treatment Services, http://chipts.ucla.edu (accessed February 23, 2006). Based at the University of California, Los Angeles, this center works to promote early detection, effective prevention, and treatment programs for HIV. One of the services provided by the center is an assortment of training manuals (some of these are described below).

Choosing Life: Empowerment, Actions, Results (CLEAR), http://chipts.ucla.edu/interventions/manuals/intervclear.html (accessed February 24, 2006). This intervention has three modules divided into 18 sessions. Some of the session topics covered are: "Creating a vision for the future," "I'm HIV positive," "Attitudes as barriers to future goals," "How do I refuse unprotected sex?" and "Wanting to stay healthy." This program also has three workbooks to accompany the modules.

The National Association of School Psychologists, http://www.nasponline.org (accessed February 23, 2006), has developed a number of guides that can be adapted for use by parents or educators if a student dies including "Death: Dealing with Crisis at School: Practical Suggestions for Educators." http://www.nasponline.org/NEAT/neat_poland.html (accessed February 23, 2006) and Memorial Activities at School: A List of "Do's" and "Don'ts." http://www.nasponline.org/NEAT/memactivities_war.html (accessed February 23, 2006).

The National Association of State Boards of Education, http://www.nasbe.org (accessed February 23, 2006), has developed a sample policy to guide the development of HIV/AIDS policies at the local school level. Although many of the publications on the site require membership in the organization, the document, "Someone at School has AIDS," can be accessed at: http://www.nasbe.org/HealthySchools/Safe_Healthy/sasha.html (accessed February 23, 2006).

School Health Education Clearinghouse, http://www.siecus.org/school/index.html (accessed February 22, 2006), includes a number of resources designed for educators. Facilitators can find the training module, "Culturally Competent HIV Prevention and Sexuality Education," as well as links to sexuality curricula, and a set of guidelines for comprehensive sexuality education.

SIECUS (Sexuality Information and Education Council), http://www.siecus.org/ (accessed February 23, 2006), has a wealth of information on many sexuality topics that will be useful to educators, including the School Health Education Clearinghouse.

Stay Safe! Adolescents Living Safely. AIDS Awareness, Attitudes, and Actions, http://chipts.ucla.edu/interventions/manuals/intervrunawayst1.html (accessed

February 22, 2006). Designed for adults who work with adolescents, this manual includes guidelines for sessions on 20 topics including: "What are my high risk situations?", "Tell me more about sex," and "Dealing with pressures to use drugs/alcohol."

Teens Linked to Care (TLC), http://chipts.ucla.edu/interventions/manuals/intervtlc1.html (accessed February 22, 2006). The three modules of this intervention are divided into 31 sessions. Session topics include: "I'm HIV positive—Attitudes toward living with HIV and exploring future goals," "Should I protect myself or my partner?" and, "How can I have a better quality of life?"

Disability, Discrimination, and other Legal Resources

The ACLU (American Civil Liberties Union), http://www.aclu.org (accessed February 24, 2006), has been active in efforts to protect the civil rights of HIV-positive people. See http://www.aclu.org/HIVAIDS/HIVAIDSlist.cfm?c= 89 (accessed February 24, 2006), for links to information about confidentiality, jobs, and health care.

Americans with Disabilities Act (ADA), http://www.usdoj.gov/crt/ada/adahom1.htm (accessed February 24, 2006). This Department of Justice page has links to many aspects of the ADA. In addition, citizens can use the toll free numbers to call 1–800–514–0301 (voice) or 1–800–514–0383 (TDD) for answers to general and technical questions.

The CDC Business Responds to AIDS/Labor Responds to AIDS, http://hivatwork.org/ (accessed February 24, 2006), has links to resources for employers and employees about HIV/AIDS in the workplace. Sections include HIV/Workplace tools, HIV and the law, and links to other resources.

Family and Medical Leave Act, http://www.dol.gov/esa/regs/statutes/whd/fmla/html (accessed February 24, 2006). The Family and Medical Leave Act of 1993 was designed to ensure that workers could return to work after taking time off for care for a newborn or an ill relative. More detailed information can be found on the Web site.

LawHelp, http://www.lawhelp.org/ (accessed February 24, 2006), is a national organization that works to help low and moderate income people get legal help. Another list of helpful links to legal resources can be found at the National Consumer Law Center, http://www.consumerlaw.org/links/ (accessed February 24, 2006).

National Dissemination Center for Children With Disabilities, http://www.nichcy.org/index.html (accessed September 15, 2005). This site does not mention HIV/AIDS as a specific disability, but it does have links to information about state resources on disability as well as a link to sex education.

Q & A on HIV/AIDS and Discrimination (from the National Association of Social Workers), http://www.naswdc.org/diversity/lgb/hiv_discrimination.

asp (accessed February 24, 2006). This page succinctly describes the rights of HIV-positive individuals and has links to sources that may help those who face discrimination.

United States Department of Education, http://www.ed.gov (accessed February 24, 2006). The United States Department of Education developed a pamphlet in 1991 entitled *Placement of School Children with Acquired Immune Deficiency Syndrome (AIDS).* The pamphlet describes how children are to be served within the public school system. The pamphlet can be found at this Web site: http://www.ed.gov/about/offices/list/ocr/docs/hq53e9.html (accessed February 22, 2006).

INDEX

ABOUT THE EDITORS AND CONTRIBUTORS

PAMELA J. BACHANAS, Ph.D., is a behavioral scientist in the Global AIDS Program (GAP) at the Centers for Disease Control and Prevention (CDC). She is the Team Leader of the Behavior Change Communications Team in the HIV Prevention Branch of GAP. Before joining the CDC, Dr. Bachanas was an Associate Professor in the Departments of Psychiatry and Behavioral Sciences and Pediatrics at Emory University School of Medicine and the Director of Pediatric Mental Health Services in the Grady Pediatric/Adolescent Infectious Disease Program and the Adolescent Primary Care Clinic in Atlanta. She is an experienced pediatric psychologist who has worked with children, adolescents, and families with HIV and other chronic and terminal illnesses. Dr. Bachanas is a certified trainer for the American Psychological Association's HIV Office for Psychologist Education in pediatric/adolescent HIV/AIDS, and she is a trainer for the National Institute of Health's Pediatric AIDS Clinical Trials Group sites in South Africa. Dr. Bachanas has also served as a faculty mentor for the Elizabeth Glaser Pediatric AIDS Foundation for student intern award recipients. In addition, she has been the Principal Investigator on several studies assessing the psychological and neuropsychological functioning of children, adolescents, and caregivers with HIV/AIDS and prevention of HIV and STDs in at-risk youth.

LATOYA C. CONNER, Ph.D., is a Licensed Psychologist and an Assistant Professor of Pediatrics and Psychiatry in the Division of Adolescent and Young Adult Medicine at Children's National Medical Center, The George

Washington University Medical Center in Washington, D.C. Dr. Conner received her Ph.D. in counseling psychology from Columbia University, Teachers College. She completed her internship in clinical and community psychology at Yale University School of Medicine, The Consultation Center. Dr. Conner's research focuses on medication adherence, risk-reduction behaviors, quality of life and substance use among adolescents living with HIV/ AIDS, and elimination of health disparities and social inequalities that place youth at increased risk of mental, physical, and economic health challenges. Recently, the American Psychological Association's HIV Office for Psychology Education (HOPE) selected Dr. Conner to be a HOPE Trainer. She is dedicated to educating other psychologists and health care practitioners about culturally congruent, effective, and ethical ways to deliver services to diverse individuals and communities who are living with HIV/AIDS.

RICHARD A. CROSBY, Ph.D., is an Associate Professor in the Department of Health Behavior in the College of Public Health at the University of Kentucky. Crosby received his B.A. degree (1981) from the University of Kentucky in school health education and his M.A. (1984) in health education from Central Michigan University. His Ph.D. (1998) is in health behavior and is from Indiana University. He was formerly an Assistant Professor at the Rollins School of Public Health, and previous to that appointment he was a Fellow of the Association of Teachers of Preventive Medicine. He currently teaches graduate courses in public health and research methods. Crosby's research interests include development and application of behavioral theory to health promotion, particularly in adolescent and young adult populations. He is primarily involved in health promotion practice and research that contributes to reducing the incidence of sexually transmitted diseases, particularly infection with human immunodeficiency virus. Also affiliated with the Rural Center for AIDS and STD Prevention, Crosby has published numerous journal articles that report empirical findings relevant to the sexual risk behaviors of adolescents and adults.

LAWRENCE J. D'ANGELO, M.D., M.P.H., is chief of the Division of Adolescent and Young Adult Medicine at Children's National Medical Center, Washington, D.C. His academic affiliation is with The George Washington University School of Medicine and Health Sciences, where he holds the rank of tenured Professor of Pediatrics, Medicine and Health Care Sciences, and at the George Washington University School of Public Health and Health Services, where he is a Professor of Prevention and Community Health and Epidemiology. A graduate of Harvard College, Duke University Medical School, and the Harvard University School of Public Health, Dr. D'Angelo trained in internal medicine at Georgetown University Hospital. He completed a medical chief residency at the Veterans' Administration Hospital in Washington, then joined the U.S. Public Health Service and was stationed as an Epidemic Intelligence Service officer at the Centers for Disease Control and Prevention in Atlanta, Georgia. Dr. D'Angelo returned to Washington, D.C. to help found the Division of General Medicine at Georgetown University in 1979 and in 1982 accepted the position of Chairman of the Department of Adolescent and Young Adult Medicine at Children's. The author of more than 100 articles and book chapters, Dr. D'Angelo has a particular area of interest in a wide variety of acute and chronic diseases in adolescents and young adults. His special area of interest has been the clinical and epidemiologic aspects of HIV infection in teenagers. Special research findings from his work have included a documented increase in the annual seroprevalence of HIV infection in adolescents from 1987 until 1993, and a clear link between drug use and sexually transmitted diseases in this region. In addition, Dr. D'Angelo is interested in the participation of HIV-infected adolescents in AIDS clinical trials. In 1991, as a Visiting Scientist at the National Institute of Allergy and Infectious Diseases' Division of AIDS, Dr. D'Angelo worked to incorporate adolescents into the clinical trials network. He is the recipient of a special NIAID award recognizing these efforts. Dr. D'Angelo was also the first chair of the Adolescent Scientific Committee of the AIDS Clinical Trials Group (ACTG) of the National Institutes of Health and has also chaired two protocol teams for the first two adolescent-specific protocols being conducted in the ACTG research.

RALPH J. DiCLEMENTE, Ph.D., is the Charles Howard Candler Professor of Public Health and Associate Director, Emory Center for AIDS Research. He holds concurrent appointments as Professor in the School of Medicine, in the Department of Pediatrics, in the Division of Infectious Diseases, Epidemiology, and Immunology, and the Department of Psychiatry. He was recently, Chair, Department of Behavioral Sciences and Health Education at the Rollins School of Public Health, Emory University. Dr. DiClemente was trained as a Health Psychologist at the University of California San Francisco where he received his Ph.D. (1984) after completing a Sc.M. (1978) in Behavioral Sciences at the Harvard School of Public Health and his B.A. (1973) at the City University of New York (CCNY). His research interests include developing decision-making models of adolescents' risk and protective behaviors. He has a particular interest in the development and evaluation of theory-driven HIV/STD prevention programs for adolescents and young adult women. He has published numerous books and journal articles in the fields of adolescent health and HIV/STD prevention. He currently teaches a course on Adolescent Health and serves on numerous editorial boards and national prevention organizations.

ELIZABETH FREIDIN is a Research Assistant for the "Parent/Preado-lescent Training for HIV Prevention—Competing Continuation," coding qualitative data, performing quantitative data entry, cleaning data files, and performing preliminary data analyses in order to examine the quality and specificity of parent-child conversations about HIV. She received her B.A. in Psychology from Columbia University. Prior to joining the Hunter College Center for Community and Urban Health, she worked as a behavioral thera-pist for autistic children.

CHRISTOPHER GODFREY, M.A., Ph.D., Clinical Psychology, Long Island University, is the Director of Project Management and Operations at the Hunter College Center for Community and Urban Health. He is the Co-Investigator for "HIV Prevention Case Management Initiative—Program Evaluation (PCM)," an Investigator for "Adolescent Risk—Social Settings and Prevention Issues," and the Project Director for "Parent/Preadolescent Training for HIV Prevention—Competing Continuation." He has extensive experience developing and evaluating community health interventions for life-threatening illnesses, such as HIV infection, AIDS and end-stage renal disease. Mr. Godfrey is well-versed in qualitative and multivariate quantitative data analytic techniques, such as structural equation modeling and non-numeri-cal, unstructured data indexing and searching. His content expertise includes HIV prevention in clinical and community-oriented settings, peer interven-tion strategies in HIV prevention, and communication between chronically ill individuals and their families and communities. He has taught HIV prevention counseling with gay and bisexual men, Introduction to Psychology, Psychologi-cal Testing and Measurement, and Computers and Social Science.

ROBERT KAPLAN, Ph.D., English, The Graduate Center of the City Uni-versity of New York (CUNY), is the Director of Writing and Communica-tions at the Hunter College Center for Community and Urban Health. He is responsible for editing the Center's grant applications, publications, presenta-tions, curricula, manuals, abstracts, project reports and materials, and any other significant internal or external Center documents, as needed. He conducts workshops on writing concept papers, abstracts, literature reviews, and other types of writing and research used in public health. Prior to joining the Cen-ter in 2003, Mr. Kaplan worked in the Hunter College Urban Public Health program, assisting faculty to develop writing-based public health curricula and helping undergraduate and graduate students to develop the critical writing, reading, and thinking skills needed by public health professionals.

SUSAN KELLER, M.T. (ASCP), M.L.S., has been a medical librarian at Children's National Medical Center in Washington, D.C. since 2002. Before returning to graduate school, she worked as a medical technologist in several hospital laboratories. She also has worked as a community organizer for an organization dedicated to social justice. Ms. Keller enjoys working as a medical librarian and believes that making health information accessible is one way of helping people make health-promoting decisions.

LINDA J. KOENIG, PH.D. is a senior behavioral scientist in the Division of HIV/AIDS Prevention (DHAP) at the Centers for Disease Control and Prevention (CDC). She received her Ph.D. in clinical psychology from Northwestern University in Evanston, Illinois, and completed a National Institute of Mental Health postdoctoral fellowship at Stanford University in Palo Alto, California. Before joining the CDC as Chief of the Social and Behavioral Studies Section in the DHAP Epidemiology Branch and then serving as Assistant Chief for Behavioral Science in the Mother-Child Transmission & Pediatric/Adolescent Studies Section, Dr. Koenig held academic appointments at Kennesaw State University in Kennesaw, Georgia, and Emory University in Atlanta, Georgia, where she also served as director of clinical training. She has received service commendations for her work on the CDC Violence and Reproductive Health Working Group, and the Anthrax Efficacy, Adverse Events and Adherence Team, for which she received the Secretary's Award for Distinguished Service. Her research addresses the psychosocial aspects of HIV/AIDS among women, children, and adolescents, including violence and abuse, risk behavior, and medication adherence.

BEATRICE J. KRAUSS, Ph.D. is the Executive Director of the Hunter College Center for Community and Urban Health (formerly the Center on AIDS, Drugs and Community Health), the Director of Administration and Coordination, and the Director of Collaborations and External Relations. She oversees more than 15 research, demonstration, and evaluation projects, and is also Professor of Community Health Education in the Hunter College Urban Public Health program. In 1989, Dr. Krauss became a researcher at Memorial Sloan-Kettering Cancer Center, concentrating on psychosocial adjustment to illness, adjustment to HIV in women and gay men, and HIV risk reduction. In 1993, she joined the National Development and Research Institutes (NDRI), becoming the Deputy Director of both the Institute for AIDS Research and the Center for Drug Use and HIV Research. Dr. Krauss has been involved with nearly 30 privately, city, state, nationally or internationally funded HIV-related research projects; she has published and presented extensively on HIV prevention and on adjustment to HIV in highly affected communities, as well as on methodological issues in field research and on the dissemination of research-supported interventions. Dr. Krauss has participated in NIH reviews, chairing several special emphasis panels. In 1998, she received the Kurt Lewin

Award from the Division of Social Issues of the New York State Psychological Association for her contribution in the area of HIV/AIDS. She has been appointed a Fellow of the American Psychological Association and its Health Psychology Division, effective 2006. Her highly regarded NIMH-funded Parent/Preadolescent Training for HIV Prevention (PATH) has been replicated in Mexico City under World AIDS Foundation funding, in Miami under NIMH funding, and in Mumbai under both World AIDS Foundation and NIMH funding.

MARGUERITA LIGHTFOOT, Ph.D., conducts research within the Department of Psychiatry at the University of California, Los Angeles. Her research specialization is in the areas of adolescents, intervention, and prevention. Dr. Lightfoot is particularly interested in using new technologies, such as computers, to engage youth in health promotion. She is currently designing and testing computer-based and Web-based interventions. She has delivered, developed, and tested interventions with ethnically diverse populations including low-income populations, youth and adults living with HIV, runaway and homeless youth, and youth on probation and in alternative education settings. She has conducted HIV prevention research both domestically and internationally with youth in Uganda. Dr. Lightfoot is also interested in bringing research to practice. She has been involved in several projects aimed at translating and developing efficacious interventions into approachable, user-friendly programs that can be implemented by service providers. In addition, she has also worked as a mental health clinician serving those infected and affected by HIV. She has provided individual, group, and family therapy at mental health sites in underserved, impoverished areas of Los Angeles.

MAUREEN E. LYON, Ph.D., A.B.P.P., is a licensed Clinical Psychologist and Associate Research Professor in Pediatrics at George Washington University Medical Center within the Division of Adolescent and Young Adult Medicine at Children's National Medical Center in Washington, D.C. Dr. Lyon holds a Diplomate in Health Psychology from the American Board of Professional Psychology, and she is a member of the National Register of Health Service Providers in Psychology. Dr. Lyon is also a member of the American Psychological Association (APA) and former Chair of the Committee on Psychology and AIDS. She has been trained in the APA's HOPE program to provide training to other mental health professionals treating adolescents and adults with HIV/AIDS. She has also been trained to conducts workshops for professionals on Ethical Issues & HIV/AIDS. Dr. Lyon's research interests and efforts focus on the study of adolescents living with HIV and their families, as well as supporting individuals with other life-threatening illnesses. Dr. Lyon has published work in peer-reviewed journals on HIV/ AIDS and a range of other subjects.

Dr. Lyon has a private practice in Alexandria, Virginia, with a specialty in working with adults with eating disorders and other health-related conditions, as well as a general practice treating depression, anxiety, and relationship problems. She also enjoys testing children for entry into private schools. Dr. Lyon's theoretical orientation is Interpersonal/Psychodynamic and Cognitive/Behavioral, depending on the presenting problem. She conducts community workshops to increase stress management, to increase adherence to medication regimens, and to decrease pain through such techniques as hypnosis, deep muscle relaxation, and meditation. Dr. Lyon is a certified yoga instructor.

JOANNE O'DAY, M.A., Forensic Psychology, John Jay College of Criminal Justice, is the Field Operations Coordinator and the Project Director for "Adolescent HIV Risk-Social Settings and Prevention Issues" at the Hunter College Center for Community and Urban Health. Ms. O'Day has experience facilitating health education groups, groups for substance users and focus groups, both in the community and in jails, and is bilingual English/Spanish. She is a New York State certified Alcohol and Substance Abuse Counselor and has written treatment sessions for a manual-based cognitive-behavioral treatment curriculum used with substance-using populations. She has special expertise in field-site management, developing interventions and questionnaires that use language and concepts appropriate to clients, and implementing scientific protocols in field settings. She has conducted oral history interviews with substance-using populations, and has extensive experience facilitating groups, including for women who have been victims of domestic violence, for men who have been charged with domestic abuse, and for substance-using populations in community, treatment and jail settings, as well as health education groups both in community and jail settings.

MARYLAND PAO, M.D., works at the National Institutes of Health as Deputy Clinical Director in the Office of the Clinical Director in the Intramural Research Program (IRP) at the National Institute of Mental Health (NIMH). Dr. Pao serves as Chair of the NIMH IRP Institutional Review Board and is a Staff Physician on the Psychiatry Consultation Liaison Service in the Clinical Center. A native of Bethesda, she attended Wellesley College before completing a BA/MD program at Johns Hopkins University School of Medicine. She completed Pediatric and Psychiatric Residency training, as well as a Child and Adolescent Psychiatry Fellowship at Johns Hopkins Hospital. Before returning to the Bethesda area, Dr. Pao directed the Pediatric Consultation Liaison Service in the Children's Center of Johns Hopkins Hospital. She also served as the Director of Pediatric Consultation Liaison and Emergency

Psychiatric Services at Children's National Medical Center in Washington, D.C. for many years. She is board certified in Pediatrics, General Psychiatry, and Child and Adolescent Psychiatry. She is a Clinical Assistant Professor of Pediatrics and Psychiatry at George Washington University and at the Johns Hopkins University School of Medicine. Dr. Pao's clinical research interests are in the complex interactions between somatic and psychiatric illnesses in children and adolescents. She has been especially interested in how children cope and adapt to chronic illness, the prevalence of psychiatric disorders in adolescents with HIV, and understanding the neurobiology and treatment of pain in children.

WILLO PEQUEGNAT, Ph.D., is Associate Director of International Prevention Research, Center for Mental Health Research on AIDS at the National Institute of Mental Health (NIMH), National Institutes of Health (NIH). As the Senior Prevention Scientist, Dr. Pequegnat has primary responsibility for a wide range of national and international projects and provides intellectual leadership in research, with expertise in behavioral preventive interventions, neuropsychological assessment, stress and coping, mental and physical functioning, and quality of life. Her research involves multilevel social organization and complex relationships: couples, families, communities, societal (media, policy), technological (Internet, Web, etc.) in national and international settings. She is working on the issue of social instability, such as consequences of war, terrorism, migration, and female and drug trafficking on HIV/STD transmission. She developed a research program on the role of families in preventing and adapting to HIV/AIDS and chairs the only national annual international research conference on families and HIV/AIDS. She co-edited the book on this program of research entitled, Working with Families in the Era of AIDS, Community Psychology and AIDS, and From Child Sexual Abuse to Adult Sexual Risk. Dr. Pequegnat initiated and is co-editor of How to Write a Successful Research Grant Application: A Guide for Social and Behavioral Scientists. She plans and implements workshops, conferences, and national and international symposia on HIV/STD, and represents NIMH on science policy-making committees and workgroups in the Public Health System on a broad range of HIV/STD issues. She received her Ph.D. in Clinical Psychology from the State University of New York at Stony Brook in 1988.

LIGIA PERALTA, M.D., FAAP, is Associate Professor of Pediatrics and Epidemiology, Chief Division of Adolescent and Young Adult Medicine and Director of the Adolescent HIV Program at the University of Maryland School of Medicine. With more than 16 years of experience in adolescent health and HIV care, Dr. Peralta is responsible for developing, supervising, evaluating, and managing HIV prevention and education programs, clinical services, and research initiatives for adolescents including those at risk for HIV. Dr. Peralta developed the "One Stop Shopping" model of service for adolescents and young adults which includes anonymous, confidential, and free HIV testing and counseling; advanced GYN examination including colposcopy, sexual and substance abuse counseling, and treatment; pharmacy; dental care; and legal services. Dr. Peralta's areas of research include HIV-testing technologies and HIV-disease progression and spectrum of disease, including AIDS fatigue and wasting in adolescents, sexually transmitted infections, and expanding nontraditional ways of delivering care to special youth populations and health disparities. She is a successful investigator and is currently the Principal Investigator of the Baltimore Unit of the Adolescent Medicine Trials Network for HIV/AIDS Interventions (ATN). ATN is a national collaborative clinical trials network established by the National Institute of Child Health and Human Development (NICHD) to conduct clinical trials and related research both independently and in collaboration with existing research. She is the National Representative of the Society of Adolescent Medicine to the American Medical Association. She has spearheaded the National HIV Agenda in her native country, the Dominican Republic. Dr. Peralta serves on the National Pediatric and Family HIV Resource Center Working Group on Antiretroviral Therapy and Medical Management of HIV-Infected Children and has been the recipient of numerous awards including the 2000 Latinos of Distinction Award conferred by the Food and Drug Administration and the White House.

AUDREY SMITH ROGERS, Ph.D., M.P.H., holds degrees in nursing from the University of Maryland, and clinical pharmacy, public health, and epidemiology degrees from the University of North Carolina at Chapel Hill. She held postdoctoral fellowships at the University of North Carolina and later at the Johns Hopkins University School of Medicine where she remained on staff, later serving as Chief of AIDS Epidemiology for the Maryland State Department of Health and Mental Hygiene. She joined the National Institute of Child Health and Human Development at the National Institutes of Health (NIH) as the Science Officer for the Adolescent Medicine HIV/AIDS Research Network (1994–2001) and the Adolescent Medicine Trials Network for HIV/AIDS Interventions (2001–2006). Dr. Rogers has been active in the Society for Adolescent Medicine, particularly in the development of guidelines for adolescent participation in and the ethical conduct of research. She has served as a consultant to the World Health Organization on adolescent HIV care issues particularly related to their participation in HIV preventive vaccine trials. Dr. Rogers has received the 1996 Ryan White Youth Service Award from Metro Teen AIDS in Washington D.C., the 2002 Secretary's Award for Distinguished Service from the Department of Health and Human Services awarded to the branch, and the 2002 National Institutes of Health Director's Award for her work in adolescent HIV infection.

HANS SPIEGEL, M.D., Ph.D., is Assistant Professor of Pediatrics, Microbiology and Tropical Medicine at George Washington University and the director of Special Immunology Service, Division of Pediatric Infectious Diseases at Children's National Medical Center in Washington, D.C. The program provides comprehensive care for children and adolescents with human immunodeficiency virus (HIV) infection. He is the Principal Investigator in the Washington D.C. Consortium Pediatric AIDS Clinical Trials Unit. He is the recipient of the Elizabeth Glaser Pediatric AIDS Foundation scholarship award.

HEATHER D. TEVENDALE, Ph.D., conducts research within the Department of Psychiatry at the University of California, Los Angeles. She completed her doctorate in clinical psychology at the University of Missouri-Columbia. Her current research focuses on designing and testing preventive interventions for high-risk youth, with a particular focus on reducing behaviors that place young people at risk for HIV. Her research also seeks to identify individual intervention targets that, if modified, could reduce risk for multiple negative outcomes. She is currently developing an intervention for runaway and homeless youth intended to both improve mental health outcomes and reduce sexual and substance use behaviors that increase risk for HIV. Also, Dr. Tevendale has engaged in planning and delivery of community mental health and prevention services, particularly in rural areas.

LORI WIENER, Ph.D., A.B.P.P., has been working in the field of HIV/AIDS since 1982, when the disease was known as gay related immune deficiency (GRID). Originally from New York, Dr. Wiener accepted a position at the National Institutes of Health in 1986 to help the Chief of the Pediatric Branch of the National Cancer Institute incorporate pediatric HIV disease into the existing pediatric oncology program. More than 600 HIV-infected children and their families have been cared for at the HIV/AIDS Malignancy Branch of the National Cancer Institute. Dr. Wiener has published numerous book chapters and research studies examining parental needs and coping, children's coping, and interventions designed to meet their needs. She also brings with her a wealth of information about the inner worlds of medically challenged children, some of which have been published in a book entitled *Be a Friend* (Albert Whitman and Company, 1994), a workbook for children living with life-threatening diseases called *This Is My World* (Child Welfare League of America, 1998), and in *An Alphabet about Families Living with HIV/AIDS,* published in 1998. Dr. Wiener uses many forms of creative writing and art work as part of her therapeutic interventions with children, adolescents, and young adults.

ARNITA M. WILSON is a Youth Advocate for Youth Connections at Children's National Medical Center in Washington, D.C. She provides HIV counseling and testing to at-risk youth. She also provides outreach to the community to identify new HIV-positive youth, as well as providing intensive case management services to newly diagnosed youth. She also works tirelessly to reengage HIV-positive youth lost to follow-up care. Ms. Wilson started as a peer educator at Children's, and she has been working in health care-related fields since then. She has an optician's license. Ms. Wilson plans to graduate this fall with a Bachelor's degree in Education.

LAUREN V. WOOD, M.D., received her M.D. degree from Duke University School of Medicine and completed dual residency training in internal medicine and pediatrics at Baylor College of Medicine Affiliated Hospitals in Houston, Texas, before coming to NIH to receive subspecialty training in allergy and immunology at the National Institute of Allergy and Infectious Diseases. Her research, while in the laboratory of Dr. Anthony Fauci, focused on investigating cellular and humoral immune responses in HIV infection. Dr. Wood obtained her board certification in pediatrics, internal medicine, and allergy and immunology, and in 1992 she joined the Pediatric HIV Working Group of the National Cancer Institute (NCI). There she conducted clinical trials of novel antiretroviral and immune-based therapies for HIV infection as a senior staff member in the pediatric HIV clinical research program. Dr. Wood is currently a Senior Clinical Investigator in the Vaccine Branch, NCI, where she continues to conduct studies of vaccines for both cancer and HIV infection.